Little Aston Golf Club
1908 - 2008

Little Aston Golf Club
1908 - 2008

David & Patricia Davies

Grant Books, Worcestershire 2010

First published 2010

ISBN 978-0-907186-74-8

*Published for Little Aston Golf Club
in a limited edition of
500 copies*

Typeset in 11 on 13 point New Baskerville
and printed in Great Britain by
Hughes & Company
Kempsey, Worcestershire, England

Published by
Grant Books
The Coach House, Cutnall Green
Droitwich, Worcestershire WR9 0PQ
www.grantbooks.co.uk

Contents

January 2008

Mr J. Cooke
Captain
Little Aston Golf Club
Roman Road
Streetly
Sutton Coldfield
B74 3AN

Dear Captain

On behalf of the members of The Royal and Ancient Golf Club, I send you our warmest congratulations on your Centenary.

The Little Aston Club is by common consent one of the finest courses in the United Kingdom and your Members have, for decades, never hesitated to place it at the disposal of the R&A for its International Matches and Championships. Only recently the Club has hosted Regional Qualifying for the Open, and we are delighted to be holding the Boys Championship in 2008 – which attracts young competitors from more than twenty nations around the world.

The R&A has another cause to be grateful to Little Aston – some of your members have served our Club in various capacities, and notably of course John Beharrell, as Captain, and David Pepper who has been Chairman of both the Rules and Championship Committees and is currently serving as Chairman of our General Committee.

We would hope that this excellent relationship between our respective Clubs will continue to flourish into the next century and beyond.

In conclusion we trust that your Members both present and future will enjoy their golf and the friendships made and renewed during your celebrations.

With all good wishes for your continued success.

Yours sincerely

DAVID HARRISON
Captain

Telephone +44 (0)1334 460000 · Fax +44 (0)1334 460001
www.randa.org · www.theroyalandancientgolfclub.org
Secretary - Peter Dawson

Congratulations from The Professional Golfers' Association

It is a great honour to be able to write these few words of congratulations from The Professional Golfers' Association to Little Aston Golf Club on achieving its Centenary year. From its inception the club has always had a strong relationship with professional golf. It was one of the Association's founding fathers, Harry Vardon, who laid out the original course in 1908 which was only seven years after the formation of the PGA itself.

The club and course quickly established a reputation as one of the finest in the land and after hosting the English Amateur Championship in 1927, staged its first professional event in 1937. The champion on that occasion was Sam King with Henry Cotton in runner up position. Following the interruption of the war years a strong bond between the PGA and Little Aston continued with the staging of the Dunlop Masters on five occasions as well as the Daks, the Penfold and the Martini tournaments. With all these leading events of the day being staged at the club all the great Ryder Cup players of the era played and enjoyed the fine course and even Abe Mitchell and Percy Alliss, who were members of our inaugural Ryder Cup team in 1927, played a memorable exhibition match.

One cannot speak of the Ryder Cup and Little Aston without recognising Charlie Ward whose name is synonymous with the club. I am sure that his influence is indelibly stamped on the club's first one hundred years.

In closing I wish Little Aston Golf Club outstanding success as it celebrates its centenary year and looks forward to its next 100 years of great golf played in the true spirit of the game.

Sandy Jones
Chief Executive

THE PROFESSIONAL GOLFERS' ASSOCIATION

NATIONAL HEADQUARTERS, CENTENARY HOUSE, THE BELFRY,
SUTTON COLDFIELD, WEST MIDLANDS B76 9PT
TELEPHONE 01675 470333, FACSIMILE 01675 477888

The Professional Golfers' Association Limited. Company limited by guarantee. Registered in England N° 1861161

21 February 2008

J G Cooke Esq
Captain
Little Aston Golf Club Limited
Roman Road
STREETLY
B74 3AN

Dear Mr. Cooke

On behalf of the Executive Council of the Ladies' Golf Union, it gives me great pleasure to congratulate Little Aston Golf Club on reaching its 100th anniversary.

The Ladies' Golf Union is indebted to the Committee and members of Little Aston for the club's support over the years and looks forward, after a period of absence, to returning to your excellent course for the Seniors' Home Internationals in September 2008.

Our two organisations have had a longstanding relationship, which the Executive Council trusts will continue well into your second century.

A Centenary Year is always cause for celebration, and all at the Ladies Golf Union wish the officials and members of Little Aston a very happy year, and a successful and enjoyable golfing season.

Kind regards

Yours sincerely

Joan Neville

Joan Neville
President Ladies' Golf Union

The Scores · St. Andrews · Fife · KY16 9AT · Tel: 01334 475811 · Fax: 01334 472818 · www.lgu.org · Email info@lgu.org

President: **Elizabeth Earnshaw**, OBE

INVESTOR IN PEOPLE

Driving women's golf

English Women's Golf Association
11 Highfield Road, Edgbaston
Birmingham B15 3EB

Tel: 0121 456 2088
Fax: 0121 452 5978
Email: office@englishwomensgolf.org
Web: www.englishwomensgolf.org

/ljw

26 February 2008

Little Aston Golf Club
Roman Road
Streetly
Birmingham
B74 3AN

Dear Members

On behalf of the Management and Operational Board of the English Women's Golf Association I would like to congratulate Little Aston Golf Club on reaching its centenary in 2008.

Over the years your golf club has hosted several English Championships:

English Stroke Play	1996 and 2006
English Close Amateur	1998
Seniors' Stroke Play	2005

Little Aston Golf Club has always been the perfect host and you as members have always made our Association welcome and given assistance.

I hope your centenary celebrations are successful and are enjoyed by all the members of this great golf club.

Yours sincerely

Jim Robinson
Chief Executive

PETER ALLISS - GOLF LIMITED

Little Aston will always hold a very special place in my heart. The number one reason, of course, is that it was here that I won my first full professional golf tournament; the year 1954, the event The Daks. I had played the course a couple of times before that with the legendary Charlie Ward, the home professional. How much I enjoyed the 'feel' of the clubhouse and that magnificent putting green, which seemed to cover at least an acre of ground, where you putted between banks of the most beautiful blooming heather. Usually standing at one corner, chipping and practising his putting, was the mighty Charlie Ward, Britain's finest professional in the post-war years.

I was just twenty-two years of age and was befriended by one of the senior members by the name of Foster Ward, no relation to Charlie, who took me under his wing and was a great source of inspiration. Also, he had a lovely home within a short walking distance of the course and he kept a very good table!

The golf itself was quite spectacular. There are two points I remember very clearly. It was before the leaders went out last and I was drawn to play with Bernard Hunt. We were off first and we completed the final two rounds in under four hours. Now I can assure you that, even in those days of quick, quick golf, two rounds in three hours and fifty-eight minutes caused quite a stir! But it certainly occurred.

Also, I had a long wait by the side of the 18th green, looking down the fairway to see the formidable figure of the great South African, Bobby Locke, easing his way up the fairway requiring a four to tie. He played his second shot to the right, looking for that familiar curve in towards the hole but, no, it caught a branch, dropped down, he pitched up and missed the putt and Peter Alliss was the Daks Champion of 1954. I can remember the delight in accepting the cheque for £400 and climbing into my Morris Minor convertible, which my father had sold me at quite an advantageous price, the windows down, singing at the top of my voice as I left the clubhouse, driving between those magnificent banks of rhododendrons.

I've returned many times since and I have always been enchanted by the condition of the course, the peace and tranquillity of the area, considering you're only a handful of miles from the centre of Britain's second largest city and long before the term 'millionaires' golf' was bandied about, they were playing just that at Little Aston.

A very special Club, with a fascinating collection of members, many of whom have added their own particular mark to the Club and its reputation. Long may you prosper.

Acknowledgements

THIS BOOK would never have happened without great commitment and endeavour. Whilst many members have helped in various ways, for which thanks are conveyed, it is to David Moseley, chairman of the Research Committee, together with his team of researchers Peter and Janet Denham, Hugh Cave, David McAllister, Tony Holroyde and John Owen, that enormous gratitude and appreciation must be recorded. They have committed themselves to hours of work and imagination from start to finish.

Grateful thanks are also extended to the author, Patricia Davies, for all her hard work and the manner in which she took on the role following the sad death of her husband, Dai. Thanks also to Michael Blair for his help with the writing, particularly on the course, the Borastons and the Centenary celebrations.

In Bob Grant the Club has had the most experienced publisher of golf books and he has given much advice and guidance in bringing everything together for which thanks are extended.

Centenary President

Foreword

WHEN IN 1908 Charles Arnold called a meeting to set about the formation of a new golf club and course at Little Aston he cannot have possibly imagined the story and success that lay ahead for this great Club. In the 100 years since then Little Aston Golf Club has matured into one of the most resoundingly successful clubs based upon a wonderful golf course, excellent golf and warm fellowship amongst all its members.

This immensely readable history records the highs and the lows, the amateur and professional championships, and the fantastic characters that have moulded the Club into what it is today. Patricia Davies tells the story with humour and style and I hope this history will provide readers with much enjoyment.

Little Aston is well placed to continue and retain its reputation as the pre-eminent golf club in the Midlands and one of the best in the United Kingdom. If future generations can emulate the initiative, dedication and foresight of Charles Arnold, Wilfrid Bigwood, Norman Russell and those early influential officers of the Club mentioned in Chapter Three, into a second century then I am sure that when it comes to write a history of the second 100 years the reputation of Little Aston will be the equal of any golf club in the country.

It has been an enormous honour and pleasure to have been captain during the centenary year and to stand alongside all those fine captains that have preceded me in this office.

Jeremy Cooke

Centenary Captain

Chapter One

In the Beginning

CHARLES ARNOLD, a Birmingham solicitor who played at Sutton Coldfield, was the man who called the meeting at the Grand Hotel in Birmingham on 15th May 1908 and in effect started Little Aston Golf Club. His trump card was that he already had an agreement with Arthur Greatrex, another member of the Sutton Coldfield club, to take up an option to lease 141 or so acres of land by Little Aston Hall. Greatrex, a Walsall leather merchant, was a keen golfer and had been prescient enough to buy nearly 335 acres in October 1907 when Joseph Bennett Clarke, another solicitor, who had bought the Hall in January that year, was selling off most of his 1500 acres for development and farming. Greatrex bought another 55 acres in March 1908 and this is where the clubhouse was built and the 1st, 2nd, 17th and 18th holes were laid out.

Sutton Coldfield Golf Club, established in 1889, had reached its limit of 300 members by 1907 and the fear of municipalisation cannot be overstated. The Edgbaston course at Warley Park was municipalised and the golfers of Sutton Coldfield, playing over publicly owned land in Sutton Park, faced the loss of their independence. This was more than likely the catalyst that hastened the formation of Little Aston Golf Club. On 14th January 1908, one of the Birmingham newspapers ran the following news item under the heading Sutton and Municipalisation:

The advocates of the scheme for municipalising the golf links in Sutton Park are not letting the grass grow under their feet. During the last week a petition has been circulated and freely signed for presentation to the Town Council. The memorial sets forth:-

1. That it is desirable in the public interest that the golf links in Sutton Park should be municipalised.
2. That such links are greatly in demand, not only in Sutton Coldfield itself, but in the Birmingham district.
3. That within this area there is a vast number of golfers and others who would gladly avail themselves of a course so established.

Original clubhouse in the snow, circa 1911

4. That the experience of many towns where golf links have been provided in close proximity to large cities proves conclusively that such provision is a profitable public investment and also brings in its train a large amount of business to local tradesmen.
5. That we the ratepayers and inhabitants of Sutton Coldfield are entitled to have extended to us, at least, the same facilities which a private club (Streetly) now enjoys.
6. That such provision would be in accordance with the conditions of Bishop Vesey's gift to the township.
7. That in view of these and other circumstances, we humbly pray that you, in your corporate capacity, will take such steps and measures as may be deemed necessary to give effect to this our petition.

Sutton escaped municipalisation. On 4th April 1908, the *Walsall Observer & South Staffs Chronicle* reported that the park and estates committee of the Sutton Coldfield Town Council had decided that they were "unable to recommend any municipalisation of the present golf links" on grounds of cost but that year the Council did introduce a new bye-law prohibiting the playing of any game in the park on a Sunday.

It was no wonder that men of independent mind and means set about looking for somewhere more secure to play and they did not have far to look. There had been a manor house at Little Aston as far back as 1333 but the hall was rebuilt in 1730 and has since undergone numerous further embellishments, extensions, conversions, changes of ownership and use and a reduction in the size of an estate that once covered thousands of acres. Little Aston Golf Club owes its existence to one of these sales and the foresight of Greatrex and Arnold in particular, but it owes its reputation in large part to its location and centuries of work on a dense mass of woodland.

In *Gone Are the Days*, his fascinating book about Little Aston and the surrounding area, published in 1986, Ted Hiscock wrote that:

A game of golf at Little Aston takes the player through one of the finest and most spectacular of English countrysides. It is due to the careful landscaping of Humphry Minchin and William Tennant who each planted and planned this beautiful parkland around their home of Little Aston Hall some 200 years ago.

Minchin started his work in 1765 and was followed by a succession of Tennants, who charged architect James Wyatt and a landscapist called Eames to create "a little paradise amidst the surrounding desert".

Hiscock also revealed that although Clarke, shrewd, hard-working and philanthropic, split up the estate, he ensured that the only digging done would be of foundations, along with the ploughing of the odd furrow and the excavating of a bunker or two, by buying the mineral rights to the property:

[He] purchased all coal, mineral and brick mining rights from the Midlands Mining and Finance Syndicate Limited who had commenced exploratory mines on the south west corner of the estate close to the Midland Railway line in Roundabout Wood. The Mining Syndicate had taken a long lease in 1897 giving them the right to work the minerals under the estate and it was estimated that considerable quantities of coal were below the surface. Even whilst the transactions over Little Aston Hall were ensuing, other wealthy prospectors from the Black Country made very handsome offers for the mineral rights but, fortunately, unsuccessfully.

Mining was out and golf, shortly, would be in.

We think that golf was first played at Little Aston Hall in the early 1890s when the Hall was let to Dr. Frederick John Gray to accommodate his Home for the Cure of Inebriety. As one of our wits remarked, nothing much has changed. In the *Golfers Annual* of 1907 there is an entry for Little Aston Golf Club "instituted March 13th 1895. The course of 9 holes varying from 120 to 440 yards (par 35) is a mile and a half from Streetly Station". Gray was described as a "Medical Licensee and Member of the British Medical Temperance Association, and Society for The Study and Cure for Inebriety, London" and he and his son Frederick John Swithin Gray ran the Old Park Hall Retreat, for men, and the Daisy Bank Retreat, for women, near Walsall.

Old Park Hall boasted a host of facilities including "a Lake well stocked with fish, on which is a boat; there are Lawns for Cricket, Tennis and Bowls, Quoits and Golf can be played, and a Carpenter's Shop. The walks for exercise are over a mile in extent". Such activities could also be accommodated at Little Aston Hall and the records show that the Grays were

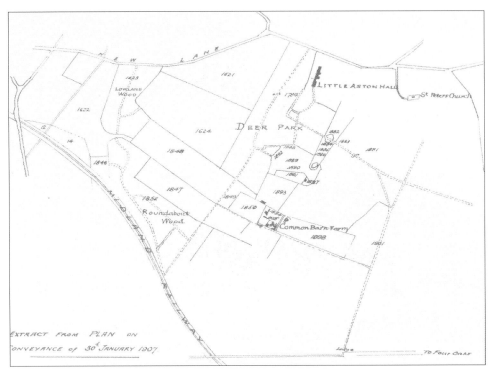

Plan from the sale of Little Aston Hall and Estate to Joseph Clarke, 1907

The Deer Park

keen golfers. In *The Midland Golfer* of May 1912, H.W. Pooler recalled that Ward End, later The Castle Bromwich Golf Club and then Maxstoke Park, played their first ever club match on 16th April 1898, at Little Aston, against Little Aston Hall, not, Pooler stressed, the Little Aston Club of present date, who won handily. A year later on 21st April 1899, Little Aston Hall proved kinder hosts and Ward End won three of four foursomes matches.

Golf had been thriving in the Midlands for some time. In 1882, Sutton Corporation granted permission to Robert Ward to play golf in the park for an annual fee of 20s., Whittington Heath was founded in 1886, Coventry in 1887, Kenilworth and Sutton Coldfield in 1889 and numerous clubs in the 1890s including South Staffordshire, Leek, Harborne, Handsworth, Sandwell Park, initially called West Bromwich, and Edgbaston. In *The Birmingham Golfer* of August 1911, J. Albert Spittle recalled that golf had been played in Birmingham, albeit on a small scale, as early as 1868:

The 'links', if they could be so called, were situated in Aston Park from Albert Road, there being no Frederick Road then, and Trinity Road, on the side where Bevington Road was afterwards made. I am under the impression that my father was instrumental in obtaining permission from the Birmingham Corporation, the owners of Aston Park, for the game to be played there. The game was played by a Government official, a Mr. J.M.G. Tennant, a Scotchman, who had been transferred to the Tower, Bagot Street, then in possession of the Government, and it was there that my father was introduced to him.

Naturally, coming from a golfing district, Musselburgh, where Mr. Tennant was a well-known player, he was anxious to play his national game here and coming to live in the Aston district, the Park was fixed upon as the most convenient spot to play. The players were few, and a kindly interest was taken in the play by a fair number of spectators, who were surprised as to what could be done with so small a gutta percha ball. Of course, no one could come up to Mr. Tennant's standard of play, his chief rivals being a Mr. Cooper, also a Scotchman, who was a Birmingham manufacturer, and Mr. Alfred Rodway, senior, the then curator of Aston Hall, both of whom he used to beat easily ... Great was the regret when he left the district, and golf seemed to go with him.

It was the development of the national rail network that helped golf to thrive by making courses accessible. The stationmaster was on the Christmas Box list for years and there was a pony and trap to run the members up to the Club. The railway line from Walsall to Birmingham via Streetly and Castle Bromwich, which was completed by 1879, enabled housing to be developed at Streetly. The line from Birmingham to Sutton Coldfield, completed in 1862 and extended to Lichfield in 1882, did likewise for Sutton and Four Oaks. In addition, the line through Shrewsbury and Welshpool to the central Wales coast gave Midlanders access to the courses at Aberdovey and Harlech, Royal St David's, founded in 1892 and 1894 respectively. Then came bikes and cars: in the 1890s bicycle manufacturers raised £30 million on the stock exchange but by 1910 34,000 cars a year were being built in the UK and by 1925 the total was nearer 200,000.

GOLF ILLUSTRATED 68 July 9th, 1926

People Who Really Matter in Golf.

No. 4.—The Station "Cabby"—the fellow who conveys you to the golf club in his own good time. He is a leading light in the local branch of the Society for the Prevention of Hustle and Bustle!

In 1895 The Midland Counties Championship, which was renamed The Midland Golf Competition in 1899, was held at Sutton Coldfield, Streetly, and thirteen teams of three entered but not Little Aston Hall. The Stafford Club won The Daily Gazette Challenge Cup with a total of 299 and only five players broke 100. Little Aston (Hall) first appeared in 1898, at Kings Norton, represented by F.J.S. Gray (92), J.L. Turner (96) and L. Roper (118), total 306. In 1899, at Sutton Coldfield, a team of Grays scored 292 - F.J.S. (90), E.S. (95), C.O. (107). Then, in 1912, at Leamington & County, B. Lorrimer (86), T. Pollock (89) and W.J.W. Bourne (90), representing the new Little Aston Golf Club, finished 22nd (out of 29) with a total of 265, twenty shots behind Castle Bromwich, the winners.

In the first issue of *The Midland Golfer* in March 1912, James Coventry, the honorary secretary of the Midland Counties Competition, recalled that first championship in 1895:

The wave of golf was then sweeping over the district and the meeting was promoted at the right time to direct it into a proper channel. The promoters were ambitious, and they were enthusiastic, and … for a couple of years the now defunct Stafford Club was in danger of becoming famous. In 1895 they were 'champions' with a score for their three players of 299, and in the following year they chopped 33 strokes off this total …

It was in 1896 that Edward Swynfen Parker-Jervis, who had bought Little Aston Hall and Estate in 1840, died and his family lost control of the property. There is no mention of a golf course in the family records and Roger Parker-Jervis, ESP-J's great grandson, said:

I don't think it could be held that ESP-J laid out the original golf course for his sons! If that had happened I think my father would have known about it because he was brought up at Footherly Hall near Shenstone and, prior to 1896, his father and uncles often shot over the Little Aston estate.

A few years later, it was noted in a family memoir that: "Part of the Park with other land was made into a golf course which has since become well known …"

Chapter Two

The First Year

A<small>T A MEETING</small> held at the Grand Hotel Birmingham on Friday the 15 day of May 1908:

Present: C.F. Arnold in the Chair, G. Fowler, J.E. Pritchard, J. Sheldon, E.H. Tanner, A.E. Cheatle, A.E. Horton, W. Bellamy, W. Briscoe, S. Powis, F.C. Hardy, T. Vaughton, A.R. Walker, T. Warmington, F. Winder, H.S. Player, F. Sampson.

Resolved: That in the opinion of this meeting it is desirable to form a Golf Club to be carried out by the registration of a Limited Company and to take over the option obtained by C.F. Arnold of land at Little Aston contained in an Agreement made between A.W. Greatrex of the one part and C.F. Arnold of the other part.

Resolved: That the name of the Company to be formed be The Little Aston Golf Club Limited.

Resolved: That Messrs: J.A. Fletcher, T. Pollock, A.E. Horton, F.H. Winder, H.T. Buckland, J. Sheldon, F.E. Barker and C.F. Arnold be elected a Committee with power for them to add to their number to carry out all the necessary matters connected with the Club.

The Victorians were formidable achievers, digging, building and manufacturing with verve and confidence. Birmingham was the manufacturing hub of the Empire so the founders of Little Aston were not men to dilly or dally and in just over a year the clubhouse was built, the links, as the course was referred to at that time, laid out and membership increased to 139 plus one junior. The first members were experienced, enthusiastic golfers well acquainted with how to run a club. Seventy-nine of the first one hundred members were already members of Sutton Coldfield Golf Club but the most crucial, in that he was the catalyst, the person who started it all off, was Charles Frederick Arnold, a man of drive and foresight, born in Kings Norton in 1854. He was a solicitor in Arnold & Son, later Arnold Son & Rose, at 3 Waterloo Street, Birmingham, which is where the Club was registered until the clubhouse was built. In 1908 he lived at The Red House, Hartopp Road, Four Oaks but by 1924 he had moved to Wentworth Cottage,

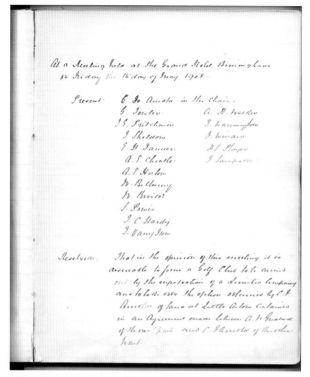

Hand-written minutes of the meeting at the Grand Hotel, 1908

Wentworth Road, Four Oaks, where he stayed until he died in 1941 at the age of eighty-seven.

In 1906 Arnold leased part of his garden at The Red House to Four Oaks Tennis Club and sold them the freehold in 1920. They are still there and we are still here, so the local sporting fraternity owes Charles Arnold a great deal as the *Birmingham Post* acknowledged in its obituary:

It was with much reluctance in recent times that he broke the routine of a lifetime by not attending at his office. A monocle imparted severity to a countenance that masked human sympathies; and in the area of Four Oaks where he resided for many years, he was regarded as a personality. He was an enthusiastic golfer and was chiefly responsible for establishing the club at Little Aston.

His two sons, Oliver and William, were also founder members. William resigned in 1911 and Oliver, who won the bogey competition under handicap at the Spring Meeting of 1911, was killed during the war.

Arnold senior was elected honorary secretary at the first committee meeting on 20th May 1908, held at Sandycroft, Streetly, the home of A.E. Horton. He, Arnold, J. Sheldon, F.H. Winder, F. Barker and A.J. [sic] Fletcher were present:

Resolved that: all Gentlemen to whom circulars were originally sent be elected members without ballot provided their application be sent in writing before the 15 of June.

Resolved that C.F. Arnold be elected Sec pro tem.

Resolved that Pollock, Fletcher, Winder, Sheldon be a committee to lay out the links & report to the Committee before finally deciding the same & have power to employ any necessary assistance.

Resolved Buckland, Horton & Barker & the Hon Sec be a committee for building the Golf Club House.

Resolved that F.E. Barker be elected Treasurer.

The committee was diligent and month by month, meeting by meeting, minute by minute got things done. On 28th May, Arnold produced the first draft of the Memorandum and Articles of Association, which was agreed, with minor alterations. He also produced the draft lease of the links and Mr. Barker was added to the committee for the laying out of the links. The next meeting was on 18th June at 3 Waterloo Street, where most subsequent meetings were held until the clubhouse was ready. Mr. John Ernest Pritchard was elected auditor after Mr. Walter L. Lewis had declined; Mr. Haywood Farmer was to be the architect and design the clubhouse in consultation with the house committee; Harry Vardon, the leading player of the day, as dominant on the course as Jack Nicklaus or Tiger Woods, was to be called in to "advise on laying out the links at a fee of ten guineas and expenses"; the purchase of a motor mower was also sanctioned; and there were to be two members, chosen by the honorary secretary who would draft the necessary deed, to act as trustees for the debenture holders.

By the following month the company had been registered and it was decided that entrance fees only were to be called up and subscriptions deferred. Two thousand pounds was to be raised by means of debentures of £10 each at four per cent, secured on the whole present and future assets of the company and issued from time to time at the discretion of the treasurer.

Foden was engaged as groundsman at a wage of 25s. per week and by 27th July Vardon had "visited the grounds and reported favourably thereon and laid down a course". Such was his fame that *The Gazette and Express* had asked, and were granted, permission to accompany him on his visit. Work on the course was to begin at once, with "such variation as the greens committee consider desirable" and Mr. Winder was to ensure that the men employed on the links were insured.

On 20th August, the honorary secretary reported that the lease had been sealed and exchanged. The house committee, which considered that "a comfortable house is essential", decided that Mr. Farmer's first design for the clubhouse was too expensive and asked him to amend it and "reduce the size of the rooms and rearrange certain matters". Plan No. 2 was the result and was recommended "subject to the price being within means of the Club". The estimate was £1,350 and included 170 double lockers and all fittings but not the laying on of water. It was estimated that to bring it 610 yards from Rosemary Hill Road would be about £130 and then there would be the laying from Roman Road to the clubhouse. Furnishing would cost not less than £200 to £250 and the total cost of £1,600 would not include any fencing.

A decision was delayed until the honorary secretary looked into acquiring some extra land and at the end of September it was resolved that he obtain "an option on lease for 99 years of an acre of land on the corner of the

The clubhouse as originally constructed, circa 1911

Birmingham Wood at a price not exceeding 1d. per square yard". In October, the Club took up the option, "Mr. Greatrex the Ground Landlord approved the plans of the Club House" and the builder Mr. W. Watson's estimate of £1,440 was accepted. It transpired that Mr. Watson underestimated by £67. 9s. 6d. but his bid was still the lowest of six and by November the contract had been signed.

It was also decided that the total raised by debentures be increased from £2,000 to £2,500 and 165 debentures were issued at once and sealed.

In the following months the search began for a house steward "at wages not exceeding £75 per year"; £170 10s. 0d. was paid to the South Staffordshire Water Company; a fire hydrant was erected; Messrs. Milligan, Barker and the honorary secretary were charged with drawing up a draft of rules for the Club; and there were discussions with the City of Birmingham Gas Department about extending the main to the clubhouse.

At a General Meeting of the Club held on 11th March 1909 at Queens College, Birmingham, the committee's work met with approval and they were given "the best thanks" for the work they had done. By April, the house steward and his wife had been appointed; it was decided to advertise for a professional; and not to open the links for play at Easter. In May, Mr. Barker reported that the house furnishings would amount to £300. 0s. 0d.; the draft rules were altered and approved in the meantime; the Gas Department was given the go-ahead; and the builder said that the house would be completed no later than 15th June.

Things moved on apace. It was proposed that the professional be a teacher, club maker and player and that a greenkeeper, not being the professional, be employed, but an amendment proposing that a "professional be appointed who shall supervise the course and the

The cash register

men" was carried; Messrs. Fletcher, Horton and Barker were elected as the house committee; it was decided to leave "the Bogey of the Course, the stroke holes and providing of Caddies to the Greens Committee"; not to fence the part of the land fronting Roman Road; and "the time of opening the Club & closing be from six o'clock in the morning to seven o'clock at night".

In June 1909 a cash register was purchased for £13. 0s. 0d. (it is still around); it was resolved that "the office of the Company be removed to the Club House" where the committee held their first meeting on Saturday 12th; and the first cards were printed.

On 19th June, there was a General Meeting of the Club and the bye-laws were gone through and passed, with certain alterations. But in July fifteen members called for a Special General Meeting to change Article 23A of the Articles of Association to read "At the first and every subsequent Annual General Meeting of the Club the Officers and Members of the Committee shall retire and shall be eligible for re election". The requisition was signed by John Wylie, Henry S. Player, Guy F. Clarke, L.A. Evans, F.H. Winder, Frank Edge, Noel Clarke, Jas. Fyshe, W. Derry, E.E. Lamb, Gerald Fowler, Arthur W. Heaton, George Heaton, Frederick Sampson and A.W. Vaughan and at the S.G.M. on 24th July 1909 the motion, proposed by Wylie and seconded by Player, was carried.

The first Annual General Meeting in the clubhouse, on 14th August 1909, ran smoothly. Mr. Edward Ansell was elected president, Mr. C.W. Milligan was captain, Mr. C.F. Arnold, honorary secretary, Mr. F.E. Barker, honorary treasurer, Mr. J.E. Pritchard, honorary auditor and the committee was re-elected en bloc and accorded a vote of thanks.

Little Aston was up and running.

Chapter Three

The Early Members

THERE WAS A bit of a hiatus when Arnold tendered his resignation in April 1910 but the committee asked him to reconsider and he served until August 1918, steering the Club through the difficulties of World War I. He became president of the Club in 1922 on the death of Walter Wilkinson and in 1927 was made an Honorary Life Member in recognition of his services.

Arthur Whitehouse Greatrex was not at the meeting at the Grand Hotel but he and his sons William and Gilbert were founder members. His daughters, Evelyn, Marguerite, known as Daisy, and Nancy, were also golfers and played at Sutton Coldfield Ladies Golf Club. The Greatrexes were leather manufacturers and curriers in Walsall, major suppliers of coach, saddle, bridle and harness leather. Greatrex senior moved from Moss Close, an ornate Gothic house in Mellish Road, Walsall, to The Retreat in Little Aston Park after buying 389 acres of the estate and securing plots for himself and all his children. He died in 1926 and his debentures, worth £2,000, were transferred to his sons.

Gilbert Greatrex was match secretary from 1923-1924 and was appointed honorary house steward in 1924. He was captain from 1932 -1934, president from 1954-1956 and elected an Honorary Member in 1965. He presented the Club with a horse in the summer of 1932 and was the last of the founder members to die, in February 1980. His son Christopher was a member for a few years and his brother William remained a member until his death in the late 1950s. William's wife Irene, nee Precey, was captain of Sutton Coldfield Ladies from 1927 -1930 and captain of Aston Wood Ladies Golf Club, about which more in due course, from 1926-1938.

Frank Ernest Barker, who was chairman and joint managing director of Barker Bros., Silversmiths Ltd., played a major role in the early administration of the Club, being the first honorary treasurer and serving on the sub-committees for the laying out of the course and the building of the clubhouse. He also presented one of the first trophies, The Club Challenge Cup, to be played for at the Spring Meeting, a thirty-six hole medal, best aggregate gross score. In 1913, when he gave up being treasurer, the Annual General Meeting:

resolved that the best thanks of the Club be given to Mr. F.E. Barker for the great ability and courtesy with which he has performed the duties of Hon Treasurer since the formation of the Club and to express their regret at his resignation of the office … [and he] be requested to have his photograph large size taken that the same be framed and hung in the Club House.

Barker stood in as treasurer again from 1917-1921, was captain from 1922-1923 and president from 1923-1925. In 1927 he, Wilfrid Bigwood and G. Douglas Smith formed the sub-committee that looked after the arrangements for the English Amateur Championship, the first national event to be played at the Club. Barker died in 1941.

J.A. Fletcher was one of the signatories of the Memorandum of Association on 22nd June 1908. He was thirty-two, lived at The Cottage, Aldridge, near Walsall, listed his occupation as secretary – his father had a currying (leather not spices) business – and had a handicap of 9 as a member of Sutton Coldfield. He was the first named committee member elected at the inaugural meeting, served on the committee "for the laying out the links" and was then appointed to the green committee, which, apart from two years, he chaired until 1930. His judgement was so respected that hc was also one of those elected to engage the first house steward and chaired the house committee from 1909-1910. By September 1911 he had reduced his handicap to 2 and in 1934 he was elected a Life Member.

Plus players

Frank Scarf, referred to as Frederick in the *Birmingham Post*, was an excellent golfer, a left-hander who at one time boasted a handicap of plus 3. He was the principal of Bromford Iron Company of West Bromwich and joined the Club in 1911 shortly after Frank Carr. They had quite an influence on the development of the course, being devotees of Harry Colt, who was then working wonders with courses in the Midlands and was to transform Little Aston's bunkering. From 1900-1903 Scarf was captain of Sandwell Park, a course that owed so much to Colt's remodelling that it is considered a Colt course. Scarf once lopped four strokes off the amateur record there with a startling 68, when his driving was excellent and his putting uncanny. At Little Aston, in the medal on 6th October 1923, despite a 7 at the 3rd, he had a score of 75, which constituted a new course record.

Scarf, a reformed cricketer, was one of the best Midland golfers and the ever diligent editor of *The Birmingham Golfer* wrote:

Members of the Greatrex family at Spring Hill, Jesson Road, Walsall, circa 1905.
Arthur Whitehouse Greatrex is seated on the steps

I don't suppose that there is a more "holy terror" playing golf in the Midlands today than Mr. F. Scarf, the left-handed crack of the Sandwell Park Club. If he will allow me to say so, he never looks half as good as he really is. Watch him off the tee, and he just seems to hit a reasonably good ball down the middle of the course, then plays a second on to the green, and if he does not hole out in three, leaves the ball so near to the hole that his opponent will give him the putt; or, if it is a medal round, he can afford to knock it in with the back of his putter …

"There is always trouble," he told me, "in getting left-hand clubs. So few are stocked that you never get a reasonable pick of them. You can send a favourite one to be copied and it may come back something like the original, or it may come back a monstrosity. But then, what can you expect. It must be awfully hard for a right-handed club maker to make a left-handed club. My saving clause was the rubber-cored ball; now a club lasts a really long time, and so I am not bothered so much, but in the old gutty days when wooden heads wouldn't last, the poor left-hander had a terrible time of it …

Scarf played for Little Aston regularly, sat on several committees, was captain from 1920-1922 and president from 1936 until his death in 1944. He was president of the Staffordshire Union of Golf Clubs from its inception in 1923 until 1939 and he and Wilfrid Bigwood played a huge part in building the Club's reputation throughout the golfing world between the world wars and establishing Little Aston as a place to test the best.

Carr, a plus man who played for England in 1911, played most of his golf at Handsworth but his expertise was much respected and he was appointed to the Little Aston green committee soon after he joined. In 1911 he had lunch with *The Birmingham Golfer* and made clear his passion for the game:

During lunch Mr. Carr drew all sorts of diagrams on the table cloth, showing his idea of course architecture, and his hieroglyphics would undoubtedly puzzle the next man who sat at that table, but he showed me his conception of a good hole and how to make it so ...

He was born in September 1881, at Moseley, played his first game at Kings Norton in 1894 then moved to live in Grimsby. "In 1900," Carr recounted, "business brought me to Birmingham and I joined the Handsworth Club. I played Mr. C.A. Palmer a friendly game in which he gave me a lot of strokes, and as I had just come back from Machrihannish [sic] I was in good form and the game ended on the 13th green. For this I was put on the 4 mark."

Carr was a great man for practical jokes and he was more than happy to undertake a wager, once betting that he could hole out Handsworth in under eighty strokes in less than eighty minutes. It was no contest. Carr went round in 76 in fifty-six

Frank Scarf

minutes and that included a 7 at the 10th. He did not survive the war, dying of his wounds in a Turkish prisoner of war camp in Gaza, Palestine, in 1917. The Midland Counties Amateur Championship is still played for the Frank Carr Memorial Trophy.

Carr's nephew Stanley Lunt joined Little Aston in 1919 with a handicap of 16; by 1921 he was down to 4, by 1923 scratch and by 1926 plus 2; he won the English Amateur Championship in 1934, although he was no longer a member then, having resigned in 1930. A modest and likeable man, he also broke the Little Aston course record, with a round of 69, in the Midland Counties Tournament in 1933. Stanley's son Michael was a Walker Cup player who won the Amateur Championship in 1963, and was runner-up the following year, losing to Gordon Clark at the 39th, and the English in 1966. He was also a captain of the Royal and Ancient Golf Club but sadly died in 2007 during his year of office.

Sir Hallewell Rogers was a man of some influence, being Lord Mayor of Birmingham in 1902 and 1903 and M.P. for Moseley briefly, from 1918-1921. His obituary painted a picture of a progressive, energetic man:

Born at Hampstead in 1864, he came to Birmingham at the age of seventeen to begin his commercial training. Five years later he bought the business of Howes and Burley, carriage lamp manufacturers, in Bishop Street, and subsequently the brush businesses of William James and Co. and John Lea. Later on he became chairman of Thomas Carlyle (Limited), Aston, Messrs. Chamberlain, King and Jones; and Harris and Sheldon (Limited). But the success which attended his efforts as a business man was best seen in his long association with the Birmingham Small Arms Company, of which he became chairman … It was during his chairmanship that the B.S.A. acquired the Daimler Company, of which Sir Hallewell Rogers became deputy-chairman …

The most important event in the years he presided over the Council was the opening in 1904 of the Elan Valley Waterworks – one of the greatest schemes embarked upon by any municipality. In the carrying to a successful issue of this great engineering feat by which Birmingham's water supply was assured Alderman Rogers took a leading part, and when the late King Edward performed the opening ceremony opportunity was taken to confer the well-deserved honour of knighthood upon the city's chief magistrate.

On the Gas Committee, whose chairman he became in 1901, Sir Hallewell rendered services equally valuable, and under him the department made rapid progress. During his term of office, which lasted until 1919, the city saw the introduction of high-pressure gas and its use for many industrial processes … Sir Hallewell touched the life of Birmingham at many points, and by his ability and genial disposition commanded the respect and affection of a large section of the community …

Sir Hallewell also managed to fit in a bit of golf and had the distinction of being the winner of the first head-to-head contest in representative golf at Little Aston, a result that stands securely in the annals of the Club. In May 1912, in a match between his Council and Birmingham University, Alderman Sir Hallewell, as his rank would insist, was first out in the singles and beat Sir Oliver Lodge. In ten of the other fifteen singles matches it was City Council nil and while Sir Hallewell outplayed Sir Oliver again in the afternoon foursomes, the University won by sixteen points to eight overall, the two titled gentlemen having entertained everyone to lunch. Little Aston was now on its way to becoming a venue.

Sir Hallewell, whose son was killed during the war, was president of the Club from 1914-1921 and his help proved invaluable. In August 1915, for instance, with a dramatic drop in income and the implementation of Colt's bunkering scheme still to pay for, Charles Heaton, the captain, and the committee found themselves needing £350 and Sir Hallewell offered to pay £100 if the other members raised the balance. They all pitched in.

In 1925, Thomas Ansell offered to present a cup for the winter and summer competitions to replace the Sir Hallewell Rogers Cup which had become the possession of Stanley Lunt who had won it three times. Sir Hallewell, who had also been influential in the wider world of golf as president of the Midland Counties Golf Association, resigned from the Club in 1930 and it was unanimously decided to elect him an Honorary Member. He died in 1931 at the age of sixty-seven.

Edward Ansell, who was the first president, was chairman of Ansells Brewery, which had been founded by his father. He lived at Moor Hall and was famous for his social and philanthropic work. He died in 1929 and the Post described him as a "delightful personality – as genial in temperament as he was generous in disposition".

The Milligan Bowls presented by the Club's first captain

C.W. (Colin) Milligan was the first captain, holding office from 1908-1911 and, appropriately enough, was one of the first winners on the newly opened course as the minutes of 9th July 1909 recorded:

The Hon. Sec. reported that the first monthly medal had been won, the Senior by Mr. C. W. Milligan (the Captain) with a score of 86 less 6 net 80 and Mr. Briscoe, the Junior with a score of 94 less 13 net 81.

Milligan was also a member of Edgbaston and was chairman of the Birmingham Stock Exchange for eighteen years. He died in 1947 at the age of sixty-one. His son Wyndham Milligan was an actor. Milligan was succeeded by Thomas Pollock senior, who was a committee member for many years and a colourful character with the sort of background that would have appealed to P.G. Wodehouse. He was born in Russia of Scottish parents in 1862 and worked as an engineer on the Trans-Siberian Railway as well as on the design and introduction of the tubular steel bicycle, which he raced with success in Nizhny Novgorod in 1893. His great grandson Fergus still has the cup, inscribed in Russian.

Towards the turn of the century Thomas took over the Accles premises in the Black Country, naming his firm Accles and Pollock. In 1913, the company was granted a patent for the first tubular steel golf shaft but it was not until 1929 that the R&A sanctioned their use in place of hickory. Some clubs pre-empted the governing body and allowed the use of steel shafts in club competitions much earlier but in 1919 Little Aston, with Thomas Pollock senior on the committee, played by the book: "The question of steel shafted golf clubs having been considered it was resolved that the use of the same be not allowed in competition such use being at present prohibited by the St Andrews ruling."

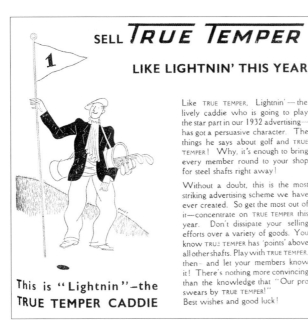

SELL *TRUE TEMPER*

LIKE LIGHTNIN' THIS YEAR

Like TRUE TEMPER. Lightnin'—the lively caddie who is going to play the star part in our 1932 advertising—has got a persuasive character. The things he says about golf and TRUE TEMPER! Why, it's enough to bring every member round to your shop for steel shafts right away!

Without a doubt, this is the most striking advertising scheme we have ever created. So get the most out of it—concentrate on TRUE TEMPER this year. Don't dissipate your selling efforts over a variety of goods. You know TRUE TEMPER has 'points' above all other shafts. Play with TRUE TEMPER, then—and let your members know it! There's nothing more convincing than the knowledge that "Our pro swears by TRUE TEMPER!"

Best wishes and good luck!

This is "Lightnin'"—the
TRUE TEMPER CADDIE

True Temper shafts and Apollo stemmed from Accles and Pollock but the Black Country and Birmingham are no longer the manufacturing force they were and the shafts are made elsewhere now.

Thomas Pollock junior, his brother Willie, Willie's son Robert and Dennis, Fergus's father, were all members.

The Rev. (Herbert) H.S. Pelham was the Club's first scratch player when he joined in July 1909 from Sutton Cold-field. He played many times for Oxford University but never got a Blue. He was head of the Birmingham Street Children's Union, an association of seventy youth clubs, and was also on a committee of Midland golfers investigating the employment of boys as caddies and their future welfare. Pelham was a member for only two years before joining Kings Norton but he played in many Club matches and competitions and it was largely through his good offices that, in February 1914, Oxford University brought a team to the course to play a side of Birmingham golfers, captained by Mr. F.A. (Frank) Woolley, of Kings Norton.

The Midland Golfer noted that very few Oxford undergraduates played golf in those days. The team was made up by professors who might have added dignity to the team but not a great deal of golfing acumen and they lost fourteen points to five, losing eight of the ten singles. The great secret that Oxford, apparently, had not discovered was that tee shots had to be properly placed. Still, the match was rated as one of the most enjoyable to have been played in the Midlands. It was specially enjoyable for Frank Carr, representing Birmingham, who won his singles 8 and 7 and his foursomes 6 and 4. The course was highly praised for being "in excellent condition, the greens being particularly good for the time of year".

Then, in August, came the stark intervention of the Great War and most of the staff and many of the members joined up. Oliver Arnold, Frank Carr, E. Hallewell Rogers and H.G. Neville did not return.

Some sporting members

Willie Pollock, pipe ever present

M.K. (Maurice) Foster, one of the famous sporting Fosters of Worcestershire, joined in 1931. He and his six brothers all played cricket for Worcestershire and one, R.E., played for England; his three sisters played hockey for Worcestershire and one played golf for England. In the 1920s he kept Worcestershire from disintegrating with his efforts as captain and leading batsman, in four successive seasons he scored more than 1300 runs, and made his final appearance for the county in 1938, at the age of forty-seven. Maurice was a scratch golfer who represented the Club on many occasions and won a lot of trophies, not least with his wife Betty in the mixed foursomes. He was a talented and loveable man and died, aged fifty-one, in 1940 after catching a chill on duty as a superintendent of the Special Constabulary during one of the air raids on Coventry.

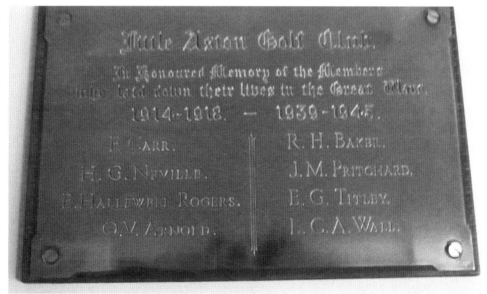

Mrs. Isobel Milne (the first lady to qualify as a doctor from Aberdeen University) and her two sons, Mearns and Gordon, photographed in the daffodil field in 1936. The daffodils had been planted by Harry Scribbans to commemorate one of Mrs. Ada Scribban's birthdays. The field had remained attached to the Hall until it was purchased by the Club from Esso in 1964, when the walled garden and lake were also repurchased. Dr. V.E. Milne was captain at the time of the acquisition and later became president. He played football as an amateur for both Aberdeen and Aston Villa and attended both the Villa players and Scribbans family professionally

In 1932, he started the Public Schools Midland Golf Meeting, which was to be his lasting golfing legacy. It is a foursomes competition which has grown to become the largest society meeting of the year at the Club, with up to 130 people playing two rounds, despite some of them being inclined to linger over lunch. They play for the M.K. Foster Cup and Richard Pepper is the member who has been organising the event for nearly half a century now.

Roger Bayliss, who played much of his golf at South Staffordshire and played for England in 1929, 1933 and 1934, joined the Club in 1932 and deserves a mention not least for his unusual, probably unique, sporting switch. He gave up golf to concentrate on figure skating and resigned in 1937. He skated in an exhibition in front of Adolf Hitler and competed in the English Ice Skating Championship several times. He rejoined the Club after the war and played regularly for the Midlands and Staffordshire. He won the

20

Staffordshire title in 1955 and 1956, having first won it in 1933, and was a member of the team that won the County Championship in 1956.

And, finally, two footballing golfers: Chris Buckley, a scratch handicapper, became a member in 1934. He had joined Aston Villa as a centre half in 1906 and played 143 games for them before moving to Arsenal. He was the younger brother of Major Frank Buckley, the legendary manager of Wolverhampton Wanderers, and was elected to Villa's board in 1936, serving as chairman from 1955-1965, at the time of writing the only former player to be chairman.

Dr. Victor E. Milne played for Aberdeen and Villa as an amateur and was Little Aston's captain from 1963-1965 and Club president from 1968-1970. His son Gordon was captain from 1991-1993 and president from 2002-2004.

Distinctions

31st May 1947: E.B. Handley, honorary gardener, elected to Life Membership.

12th July 1947: H.H. Sherwood, honorary treasurer, R. Marsh Evans, honorary auditor and Holland W. Hobbiss, honorary architect, all having served for twenty-five years, elected to Life Membership.

The bearded Arthur Greatrex

21

No. 1716, May 16, 1934] THE TATLER

GOLF CLUBS AND GOLFERS

LITTLE ASTON GOLF CLUB—By "MEL"

Some twenty-four years ago the Little Aston Golf Club was formed by a few members of the Streetley Golf Club, and Mr. Colin Milligan was made the first captain. The course itself is an excellent test of golf and is not only one of the best but also one of the prettiest courses in the Midlands. The membership is not a large one—only some 150—but it is full of well-known people in Birmingham and district. Mr. Wilfred Bigwood, among his many activities, finds time to carry out the duties of hon. sec., and the club is very fortunate in having his services. Martin J. Lewis—known to all as "Mark"—has been the professional since the club started and is a very popular man in Midland golf

Chapter Four

The Raison d'être

THE CLUB having been formed, the next priority was a course and Little Aston went straight to the top, to Harry Vardon. The name, then as now, was the thing.

Vardon, who gave his name to the grip that he adopted with such success, was born in Grouville, Jersey, in 1870 and discovered golf when the Royal Jersey club was established in 1878. He won the Open Championship six times, in 1896, 1898, 1899, 1903, 1911 and 1914 and won the US Open in 1900. He, J.H. (John Henry) Taylor and James Braid were known as the Great Triumvirate, with Sandy Herd not far behind. Andrew Kirkcaldy, a gifted contemporary, said that if twenty of the best professionals were asked to write down their top four players, they would put down "Vardon, Taylor, Braid and Herd. If these four were asked to name the greatest among them, all save Vardon would put a cross against his name".

Vardon wrote in 1905 that a course should be set up to challenge the scratch player and not the handicap man:

A course that is laid out for the latter very often inflicts severe punishment on the scratch player, and it is surely hard that the man who has spent many years in the most patient and painstaking practice should be deliberately treated in this manner when the comparative novice is allowed to go scot free... The straight driver is not the man to be punished. It is the player who slices and pulls and has obviously little command over his club and the ball, and who has taken no pains to master the intricate technique of the drive, for whose careless shots traps should be laid. As often as not the bunker in the centre of the course lets off the ball with a bad slice or pull on it.

Vardon insisted that the handicap man would, eventually, greatly improve his game if he had to exert his strength and his capabilities in order to carry those hazards that were a threat from the tee. Between 130 and 145 yards was his recommended distance from the tee to the first centrally placed bunker. There were, however, no Vardons at Little Aston and some fifty per cent of the members, it seems, had difficulty reaching the fairways. Nowadays, courses are all straining for more length, with new clubs, new balls and new muscles pointing even great places like St Andrews and Augusta National, in terms of length, towards antiquity if not downright obsolescence so it is fascinating to discover that Little Aston, in its infancy, was considered by some to be, in one important respect, too long.

Golf club members, then as now, were capable of taking the art of complaining to choral levels and Charles Arnold was fully aware of the gathering crescendo on the subject. In July 1909, he seconded Mr. Winder's motion that the carry from all the tees be reduced. Not more than 100 yards was the resolution and it was carried when C.W. Milligan, in the chair, exercised his casting vote in favour. The course had only just been opened!

Golf clubs have a tendency to alter their courses according to the frequency with which they change their green committees and early records suggest that Little Aston's corps of enlightened visionaries was as numerous and as vociferous as any other club's. Within two years of the opening of the course, Harry Colt, a decent amateur player whose reputation as a designer is now on a par with Vardon's as a player, had been invited along to take a look at the course.

To be fair to Vardon, golf equipment was moving far beyond traditional conceptions and the rubber cored Haskell ball changed everyone's thoughts on how long golf holes ought to be. Patented in 1898 and produced by the Goodrich Rubber Company in Akron, Ohio, the new ball flew at least twenty yards further than the gutty. In 1901, Walter Travis won the US Amateur Championship with a Haskell and the following year, at the Open at Hoylake, Vardon had personal experience of its efficacy when he played with the old ball and finished one shot behind Herd, who was using a Haskell.

Golf course architecture was in its infancy and technology notwithstanding Colt's way of thinking was markedly different from Vardon's, although they did collaborate, for example, on the design of Sandy Lodge in 1910, as he made clear with this exposition of his philosophy:

Some few years ago it was a very common idea that the first-class player was the only person to be considered when the course was laid out. Considering how few they are in number, it often strikes one how extraordinarily successful they were in getting their own way ... It is by no means impossible to give a weak player every opportunity of enjoying the game within his powers, and at the same time to provide a test of golf for Harry Vardon or James Braid at his very best. To do this the designer of a course should start off on his work in a sympathetic frame of mind for the weak, and at the same time be as severe as he likes with the first-class player. The more frequently he stamps on the mediocre shot of the latter, so much the better, so long as he does not become vindictive ... There must always be a certain amount of conflict between the various classes of players. In the one case the ripe veteran must be occasionally sacrificed, and told that when the ground is soft and the wind in his teeth he must carry 300 yards or so in two shots or play short; and on the other hand, the committee may occasionally have no pity for the slashing young player of twenty or so and provide him with a pitfall when he hits an extra long one under rather abnormal conditions. We have to accept this if we are to have interesting approach play for the vast majority of players under normal conditions.

Colt's work at Sandwell Park made a huge impression and as his reputation grew *The Midland Golfer* kept its readers abreast of his activities:

Mr. Colt does not do things by halves. He is not a tinkerer, and he is not the man to bring in if you only want to spend a hundred pounds. The policy of [a] progressive golf club to-day is to pay for the best advice, and then follow it out in its entirety …

Round Birmingham we have, are still getting, and are about to get, a very plethora of 'Colt courses'. Mr. H.S. Colt seems to be with us every other week, and candidly speaking, this is all for the best, for in another year or so the Midlands will be able to boast the possession of a very fine lot of courses, finer, with the exception of the London area, and where there is sea-shore to help, than will be found in any other district in the country.

Sandwell Park and Little Aston hold to-day [December 1913] pride of place round Birmingham, while Copt Heath and Moseley promise to come into the very front rank before another year is out. These four courses have been practically finished, but there are many more in the making. Robin Hood, a club which has taken over the old Olton course, Castle Bromwich, Brand Hall, and Blackwell will be completed Colt courses in a few months time, and this great course architect has given advice to Kings Norton and to Olton, while I hear that there is a strong feeling in favour of the same action being taken by the Ladbrook Park Club … the better our courses, the better our standard of golf will become, because you cannot play a good course badly and do well on it, while you may play an indifferent course badly, and do indifferently well on it.

At Little Aston a trawl through the records reveals a Club more or less obsessed with the course and its care. Hours of time, agonies of theorising and acres of memoranda went into the decisions on preferred species of grass seeds and general conditioning, for example. Colt was to make three visits with reconstructions in mind and two other eminent designers, Fred Hawtree and Charles Lawrie, were also on site in the first fifty years as perfection was pursued.

None of this came cheap and, in 1911, the year of Colt's first visit and the year that the Club bought a mowing machine, a group of members proposed that the annual subscription be increased by one guinea, a rise of thirty three and a third per cent, and the entrance fee by two. It was passed, not least because of the need to finance Colt's proposed scheme of new bunkers. The diagonal hazards at the 4th, 6th, 7th, 14th, 15th and 18th were more than likely part of Colt's bunkering scheme, as were the plateau greens at the 5th and 17th. Originally, the green at the 5th was sited in an artificial punch bowl surrounded by a grass bank with a bunker in front and Colt altered it to a flat hole with a plateau green surrounded by bunkers. In 1980, the narrow front of the green was removed and the front bunker reinstated against the new front to the green. This is probably the green that was sometimes referred to as "the wren's nest".

The semi-plateau green at the 1st was constructed following Colt's second visit and those at the 6th and 11th were built immediately after World War II. Colt believed that "the vast majority of links needed plateau greens and 'hummocky' ground badly" and he was very fond of diagonal hazards and doglegs. Vardon was more of a man for straight lines and placed his bunkers down both sides of the course.

There is no copy of Colt's report from his first visit to the course in the late summer of 1911 but at a committee meeting on 25th November "the Greens Committee was authorised to deal with four holes in such a manner as they think best under the scheme explained by them at this meeting" – the go-ahead for Colt's bunkering scheme.

In December, Mr. Barker reported that he had paid Colt's fee. In 1913, Mr. Keay was thanked for a donation of £10 "for a bunker" and, in November, Mr. Fletcher reported that there was still plenty of work to carry out, notably "Finish bunker on 4th hole; some hillocks near bunkers to the right at 3rd hole; a pot bunker on left at 7th hole; small extension of bunkers on 8th close to the green; 16th and 17th holes still to be bunkered".

A few weeks earlier the Midland professionals had failed to distinguish themselves during their Autumn Meeting and it was reported that the course "proved a big stumbling block" although there was nothing but praise for it:

The course itself was playing beautifully, and it has been improved in the last year or so out of all recognition. Although there is still a little more work to be done – and what course is there where there is not always just a bit more wanting doing? – it is today beautifully bunkered, and the holes are of such a good length that you have to be going well to do anything like a score. The new 5th green is certainly a huge improvement, and that hole is now as good a 'one shotter' as there is to be found in the Midlands. But for all its bunkers, and despite the fact that the holes were cut on some of the greens in by no means the easiest of places, the play of our professionals was distinctly disappointing. I fancy the players unconsciously let the course beat them, rather than they attempted to beat the course. The difficulties of Little Aston had been freely discussed beforehand, and the majority of the competitors seemed frightened of it.

G.V. Tuck was the winner, the best of an apparently bad lot.

At the beginning of 1914 there was no hint of the carnage to come as *The Midland Golfer* looked forward with optimism:

This year our big meeting will be of more than ordinary interest, because it is sure to be held on a course that will call for the very best golf. We shall be playing either at Sandwell Park or at Little Aston, and whichever of these two is selected, there can be no doubt as to the merit of winning upon it. Both courses have gone through a big transformation during the last two years. They have been made longer, and the quality of the golf required of them has been put on a higher level. They are the two pioneer courses round Birmingham. There may be other fine courses in the making, but these two courses are made, and we who have played upon them know that they call for championship golf.

World War I

Colt's bunkering scheme had been completed by the outbreak of war in August but priorities had to be drastically amended. At least the course was not taken over, unlike Whittington whose members were given courtesy of Little Aston, as were officers of various regiments. The officers based at Whittington Barracks were made temporary members in 1914 at a subscription of two guineas for six months and in 1917 presented the Club with a cup.

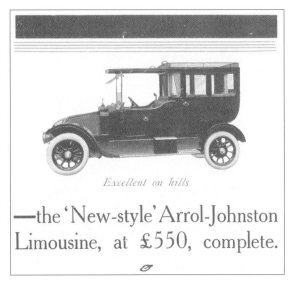

Excellent on hills

—the 'New-style' Arrol-Johnston Limousine, at £550, complete.

The First City Battalion did use the course for manoeuvres and at various stages it was mooted that the clubhouse should become a convalescent home or an annexe to Longfield Hospital, which was based at a large house in Park Drive but nothing materialised, although wounded soldiers at Longfield were given permission to walk over the course. Money was tight and in February 1916, instead of buying blackout blinds, it was decided to close the clubhouse one hour after sunset. This edict followed the bombing of Walsall, apparently mistaken for Liverpool by an errant Zeppelin.

In 1917, Arnold was instructed to advertise the course for grazing and ask Winterton & Son, auctioneers and valuers, to advise on how best to use the links in aid of the war effort. Their report confirmed, if anything, that the terrain was perfect for golf:

The land is moor turf, not profitable for local sheep or cattle, only for hill sheep. The fences are very bad and it is almost impossible to get labour to repair them. We understand that last year you shut up the land for mowing and that the crop off one hundred acres realised £80. We do not think you could use the land for a better purpose and we think you are best serving the national interest by mowing it for hay. We have considered ploughing but the sub-soil is sand and gravel and there is very little depth of soil. It would require a heavy dressing of manure, which at the present time is unobtainable.

The lengthily titled War Agriculture Executive Committee for the County of Stafford issued an order to graze the land and it was let to Mr. Robert Brown for cattle and sheep grazing at £35 per annum, the Club taking no responsibility for the fences, until his rights were terminated in 1919.

Maintaining a golf course was hard physical work and towards the end of the war members were being asked to volunteer to work on the course to aid a greenstaff reduced to "the two Hills and a boy". It was not until the 1920s that the mowing machine started the demise of men with scythes and it was not until 1927 that Little Aston acquired one of Ransomes' newfangled triple mowers, albeit still horse-drawn.

Arthur Greatrex, about to drive

View from the back of the 17th green, 1927

Chapter Five

The Course Between
the Wars and Beyond

A LL DIFFICULTIES considered, the course survived the war relatively unscathed and its reputation as a severe test proved undiminished. In March 1920, the Midland professionals were back, to play in their first post-war foursomes tournament and it was reckoned that hardly anyone there had struck a ball alternately with a partner since February 1914 when G.V. Tuck and A. Ham won the event at Stourbridge. Tuck, of South Staffordshire, won again, this time with L. Holland, Church Brampton, beating Ham, of North Shore, and George Cawsey, of Harborne, at the 37th. The course had worn well too: "The lies, even off the fairway, are so good that the punishment for deviating from the straight path is not too severe … the fairways and greens were perfect …".

In September that year, at the Midland Counties Meeting, the team event, eighteen holes, three players per side, each score to count, was won by Stourbridge with an aggregate of 259, the highest score since Cannock Chase's winning tally of 262 at Sandwell Park in 1902. Stourbridge were the only team with three scores under 90. Little Aston were third, on 263: Frank Scarf, 81, W.R. James, 90, S.L. Fillingham, 92. Carl Bretherton of Handsworth was the only player under 80 and his 79 equalled the recently fixed scratch score for the course.

The Birmingham Post enthused about the course if not the golf:

The weather could not in any way be blamed for the epidemic of high scoring. It was a perfect day for golf, cold, with a fairish breeze; but that is all in the game and adds to the interest. The course, too, was in perfect condition and the meeting served to demonstrate how excellent a test Little Aston is … It must be confessed that it is probably the most difficult course on which the competition has been played. It is a glorious course in a glorious situation, but it is a course for, shall we say, scratch men. It makes one in turn confident and perplexed; it may be, as some asserted after a nerve-racking experience of some of the bunkers, that justice is not always tempered with mercy. That is a matter of opinion, but the high scores suggested that either the players found the course very difficult, or they suffered from a severe attack of 'scoritis' …

			MEDAL CARD.					Senior.

LITTLE ASTON GOLF CLUB.

PLAYER _F. Scarf_   DATE _Oct 6th 23_

Holes	Length Yards	Bogey	Score	Holes	Length Yards	Bogey		Score
1	365	5	4	10	428	5		4
2	406	5	5	11	293	4		5
3	493	5	7	12	466	5		4
4	308	4	4	13	144	3		2
5	157	3	3	14	275	4		4
6	408	5	4	15	520	5½		5
7	357	5	4	16	335	4½		4
8	358	4	5	17	339	4		3
9	175	3	3	18	380	5		5
	3027	39	Total out 39	Out	3180 / 3027	40 / 39	Total In ..	36
							„ Out ..	39
				Total	6207	79	Gross Score	75
							Handicap..	+1
SCORER _G. Douglas Smith_							Net Score .	76

Scarf's course record card of 75, 1923

In late 1921, the Midland amateurs beat Cheshire twelve points to five, avenging a defeat at Delamere in July. In the top singles, Bretherton beat G. Tweedale on the 17th, where the Cheshire man failed to negotiate a stymie, but they played the 18th and were both round in 76, which equalled the amateur record of Ben Lorrimer, a Little Aston member. The *Post* waxed lyrical about the setting "It was a glorious October day, and players and spectators alike enjoyed their visit to this fine course, which in its magnificent setting is at present a perfect wonderland of autumn beauty."

Stymie: a situation in matchplay golf in which an opponent's ball on the green blocked the line to the hole. The stymied player had to play round his opponent's ball or, if skilled enough, chip over it. A stymie did not apply if the balls were less than six inches apart and at one time cards measured six inches unfolded, on the diagonal, so the distance was easy to check. The stymie was a legitimate tactic if controversial and it was always unpopular in the United States ... In 1930, the year he won the grand slam, Bobby Jones beat Cyril Tolley in the fourth round of the Amateur at St Andrews when Tolley accidentally laid himself an impossible stymie at the 19th; in 1951, in the final of the English Championship G.P. Roberts won at the 39th when he laid a stymie that H. Bennett could not negotiate. The R&A and the USGA abolished the stymie later that year. Norman Russell was one of those to regret its passing.   *With thanks to the Shell International Encyclopaedia of Golf*

Aerial view of the course, circa 1940

In 1923, the Midland professionals soundly thrashed the Midland amateurs twenty-eight points to five in a match reported with a certain amount of jollity:

Twenty-four of the amateur golfing stars of the Midlands went out to Little Aston to take their annual dose of medicine from twenty-four of the Midland professionals. They swallowed it nobly, without batting an eyelid, losing the foursomes (in the morning) by ten matches to two, and the singles (in the afternoon) by eighteen matches to three, three matches being halved. At times the downpour was so great that shots were frequently hastily played in order that the player might once more seek refuge beneath his gingham.

Considering the weather, the golf was exceptionally good, and some really wonderful scores were registered. The first nine holes at Little Aston demand that the player shall keep absolutely dead straight and, though greater latitude is allowed by the majority of the second nine, the course is a severe test on any day and under any conditions, however favourable.

The Club also hosted what was to become the Midland Open Championship, sponsored by the *Birmingham Gazette*. It featured the top twenty-five professionals from the News of the World qualifying rounds and first fifteen in the Midland Amateur Championship. A.R. Wheildon, professional at Moseley, won with two wonderful rounds of 75 and 73, a new course record, three shots ahead of Len Holland of Northampton. The consistent Bretherton was leading amateur with rounds of 77 and 81. The first eight professionals shared prizes amounting to nearly £100 and the three leading amateurs received gold medals.

In 1925, there was an England trial in which the North and Midlands beat the South sixteen points to thirteen and Bernard Darwin, who was selected for the South but did not play, was more impressed with the course than with a lot of the golf. He wrote in *The Times*:

Little Aston is a good testing course where good golf will have its reward. One feels inclined to write of it in the American language as 'well trapped', for there is something of American thoroughness in the bunkers that punish the inaccurate approacher. It was a pity that the wind was blowing behind the players at the down-hill holes, so that some of the approaches were difficult to the point of luckiness, but that was the fortune of war. The greens were excellent, and more delightful turf on which to walk it would be hard to imagine.

This really was a seal of approval and the Club was anxious to build on the success. Colt was called back for a further visit, providing that his charges were not excessive, and he was very complimentary. In a letter dated 21st December 1925 he wrote:

Dear Mr. Fletcher,

I enjoyed seeing your course after an interval of more than 10 years, very much indeed. The fairways are really wonderful and I thought that the golf looked very interesting and entertaining. There are such a number of good holes and there is not very much to be suggested. You have, of course, only three one shot holes which is rather considered now-a-days to be a small allowance, and each one of these holes is an odd number, so that in a foursome, the short holes are not distributed between the partners. On the other hand you have several drive and pitch holes, and I have attached three of them, as I think that the approach shots are not nearly difficult enough having regard to the distance. This applies particularly to the 4th and the 14th.

I enclose a copy of the notes which were taken by me on going round the course, and I quite agreed with the suggestions regarding the 1st hole and 11th hole. I also enclose a rough sketch plan for the 1st green and one showing my ideas for the 11th hole. I think that with these to assist you, you will be able to carry out what I have in mind.

It would be a very good thing to get the work done on the very best lines, and I can recommend the firm of Messrs. Franks, Harris Bros., Guildford. They have done a very large amount of work under my supervision. If you desire me to do so I should be pleased to supervise the work, but you may not think that this is absolutely necessary.

Yours sincerely, H.S. Colt.

The famous architect came again two years later by which time Gilbert Greatrex had offered to sell the fields at the back of what is now the 11th tee. Colt drew up a plan using all the additional land but the sub-committee appointed to consider the suggestions advised against them, presumably on the grounds of cost. It was just two years since the Club had bought the 136 acres of land on which the course and clubhouse were and had issued new debentures to cover the cost. In the end, in July 1929, the Club bought eight and a half acres, about an eighth of the land on offer, from Greatrex and eventually, in 1945, this was used to change the 10th and 11th holes.

Scribbans, the walled garden, daffs and other matters

The land in the links lease was bought from A.W. Greatrex in 1925, along with an additional nine acres which included the five acre walled garden but not the daffodil field adjoining it. In 1926, to alleviate the cost of building the ladies' extension, of which more in another chapter, the garden was sold to Harry Scribbans, who had bought Little Aston Hall in 1925. Scribbans had started working life as a baker's boy and ended up making a fortune from slab cake, which he sold to the troops "by the mile". When he died in 1935, he left £2.5 million, a vast amount considering that he spent lavishly on the Hall, inside and out, and his hospitality was legendary. One year, in honour of his wife Ada's birthday, he planted a million daffodils and Little Aston members enjoy them still every spring.

In May 1925, the secretary wrote to Scribbans saying that if he wanted to become a member of the Club, he would be put up for election once he had filled in the necessary form. In July, Scribbans asked if he could purchase the walled garden, which was where the practice ground is now, and the pool beside the 17th. The deal was done by the end of March 1926 and included a right of way for Scribbans along the bank of the pool and the right for members to retrieve their balls from the wood to the left of the 17th fairway. The total cost was £2,000 and later, in July 1927, a piece of land behind the 18th tee, fronting the pool and old drive, was exchanged for a narrow strip of land running the length of the 18th hole.

In 1938, the orchard was converted into a practice ground and the adjoining cottage, which was eventually demolished in the 1960s, continued to be occupied by Ernie Jones, one of the Club's long-serving greenkeeping brothers, who had first rented it in 1928, at a fee of 10s. a week.

No dogs

Interestingly, it was Jones's chickens that led to the dearth of dogs at Little Aston. In 1932, the greenkeeper's prize chickens were being decimated by dogs owned by H.D. James, who lived at Stonehouse nearby and Jones was so upset that the honorary secretary was instructed to pursue compensation on his behalf. The claim was successful and members were reminded of Club Rule 32(e) "No dog shall be allowed on the Links or premises of the Club." Earlier in that somewhat freewheeling decade there had been another flurry over birds when K.W.C. Dobson was reprimanded for shooting pheasants on the course. He had to apologise to Scribbans, whose pheasants they were, and the upshot was that no member was allowed to bring firearms onto the course.

In 1964, the walled garden was bought back by the Club along with the lake and daffodil field and, in 1975, it was decided to abolish the remaining walls of the garden and extend the practice ground.

Trees

It used to be said that Little Aston was defined by its bunkers but now its trees have come into their own and added another dimension to playing the course. There was an extensive tree planting scheme after World War II, part of the post-war reconstruction scheme for course and clubhouse devised by the forward-looking wartime committee under the captaincy of George Beharrell. Ronald Godfrey Horton, the chairman of green from 1942-1944, and Roland Antrobus, a member who was an expert in arboriculture, inspected the trees on the course in 1943 and their recommendations formed the basis for the new planting. Horton and F. Bernard Clark, chairman of green from 1944-1949, were mainly responsible for the work and they, Beharrell and Alfred Clifford Warmington, known as Alfie or Warmie, donated £150 towards it.

Looking after the trees is an ongoing process as storms, old age and disease take their inevitable toll. In the 1970s when Dutch elm disease ravaged the country, the magnificent elm that stood on the left of the 15th fairway, more or less in line with the 5th green, failed to come into leaf and had to be felled. Charles Lawrie, the architect who was called in to re-design the hole, called it a "great sadness" and a "tragic loss". He suggested putting in two small plantations and the two-tier green. The work was done in-house under the guidance of Alan Boraston, whose mastery of shaping with little more than a spade and a shovel was legendary.

Water

Let it never be said that Little Aston would be influenced by the fad for such modern American imperatives as water holes but there was an area to the left of the green on the long 12th, boggy, nondescript scrub land scattered with willows, that lent itself to the idea of a proper little lake and, in 1962, plans were made for its improvement. The work was twice put in abeyance but in 1966, under the direction of Tom McMillan jun., the lake was established, helping the drainage and enhancing the hole. It is by general consensus one of the categorical improvements to the course.

Water in the right places is vital for a course and as early as 1924 concerns had been aired about the difficulties of getting the greens properly freshened. A water cart was the first answer and four years later the firm of Veal & Cole were paid £6. 15s. for laying on water midway between the practice putting green and the 18th green. To have laid on water for all the greens would have cost approximately £400 and after swallowing this expensive piece of information, the Club decided to set the matter aside until the accountants had presented the complete balance sheet for the year. Decision deferred, it said in the minutes. Not indefinitely, however.

By 1930, there was a new acknowledgement of the water question. It was now an imperative and Mr. J.E. Willcox, the Club's 100th member, elected in July 1908, was asked to report on the practical possibility of building a pumping station which would cater for the entire course. Could water be stored or would it be supplied by the South Staffordshire Water Works Company? Or could it be privately obtained from the pool belonging to Scribbans? He was in the United States, so again the matter was put in abeyance. An engineer pondered the problem, the heads of all and sundry were put together and the whole issue grew in prominence. Scribbans came home but the year came and went, so did the whole of 1931 and, in 1932, there was a stark entry in the minutes "Water on the Course: it was definitely decided to abandon this project for the time being" .

No sooner had the project been "abandoned" than a sub-committee had been formed to make further investigations. The debate had been reinvigorated and the green committee made a formal recommendation for the "laying of water on the course". Mr. J. Wylie was the president but his amendment that the matter be deferred yet again was defeated on a division.

It was put to the members that the trustees for the debenture stockholders be authorised to release £967. 14s. 6d. towards the cost of installing a water system on every green. This was carried. Six hundred feet of hose were purchased, a fountain was erected near the 12th and 13th, meters were installed and an agreement was signed with South Staffs Water. Finally, in May 1933, the job was completed and the records state that "great benefit had been derived therefrom", with thanks to Wilfrid Bigwood for suggesting the scheme and to Willcox for services rendered.

The water question was far from done and dusted, however, because in July 1934 South Staffs Water dropped a bombshell: because of a prolonged drought, drastic steps would have to be taken to curtail the use of water by golf clubs, on pain of severe penalty. No one had warned the Club of this eventuality; indeed, South Staffs had said that such a contingency had never arisen in the past and in their opinion it never would. Now the Club was forced to consider a borehole and another protracted headache ensued.

What would be the site of the bore? What would it cost? The outcome was that there was no borehole and the next mention in the minutes of the water problem was four years later.

Periodically it was raised again and in 1971 we hear that "the new water tank has now been fitted out and is expected to be an unqualified success". In 1991, it was finally accepted that the original watering system had seen better days and a new automatic system was installed to take care of both greens and tees. Cost: £75,000.

And in October 2006, praise be, "it was agreed to proceed with the installation of a borehole producing 4400 gallons of water per day". Cost: £6,250.

A bit about bogey

In *The Historical Dictionary of Golfing Terms* Peter Davies notes:

bogey, originating as the standard of play of a good amateur, was always a little more lenient than the slightly older par, which became the standard for professionals and for championship-level amateurs. Many courses assigned both par and bogey; for most holes they were the same figure, but for a few holes bogey was one stroke higher than par. Professionals and low-handicap amateurs, especially in the United States, thus came to regard a bogey score as a failure to achieve par, while many amateurs, especially in Britain, preferred to keep bogey as an attainable standard of good play.

Now the universal meaning is one over par.

To begin with there was no uniform system of handicapping and clubs did their own thing. Little Aston's first cards were printed in June 1909 after the committee decided "to leave the Bogey of the Course, the stroke holes and the providing of Caddies to the Greens Committee". Vardon's original course probably had a bogey of 80.

In November 1911, holes 1, 8, 15 and 18 were reduced by a stroke, with the bogey reduced to 76 and all handicaps raised by two.

In March 1920, the Midland Golf Competition proposed sending a committee to all Midland courses to "arrange a scratch score for each with a view to arriving at a uniform basis for handicaps". The Club agreed, with the caveat that "they cannot pledge themselves beforehand to accept such recommendations". The MGC recommended that Little Aston's scratch score should be 79, an increase of three strokes, and the greens committee concurred. The 1st hole was increased from 4 to 5, the 15th from 5 to 5½, the 16th from 4 to 4½ and the 18th from 4 to 5. By this time, Colt had probably added 200 yards to Vardon's layout.

In 1921, there was communication with the R&A "concerning the bogey of the course" and in October 1923 it was reduced to 78, eliminating the halves at the 15th and 16th.

His Royal Highness The Prince of Wales at Little Aston

By 1927 the terminology was starting to change as a minute of 15th February indicated:

Score of the Course. It was resolved that as from the 15th January, the bogey for the first hole will be 4 instead of 5, and the standard scratch of the course will be 77.

And there was this on 18th February 1933:

Standard Scratch Scores and Par of Course. It was resolved to defer consideration of this matter until it was imperative to do so.

That happened in July when the SSS came down to 75, reducing the 7th and 8th by a stroke. Colt had added another 200 yards by this time.

In November 1975, just before the introduction of the English Golf Union's latest Standard Scratch and Handicapping Scheme, the Staffordshire Union of Golf Clubs set out the criteria:

The total yardage of each course is again the basis of the standard scratch score but the county union can take into consideration:
a) the terrain and general layout of the course.
b) normal ground conditions – is run average, above average or below average?
c) sizes of greens and whether watered or un-watered.
d) hazards – are greens well guarded or open?
e) width of fairways, the effect of trees and nature of rough.
f) nearness of 'out of bounds' to fairways and greens.
g) is the course exposed and subject to high winds for most of the year? Is it sheltered from the full effects of adverse weather?

Little Aston's committee expressed themselves happy with that, providing the SSS remained at 72 and was not reduced.

The 10th hole under construction, circa 1950

The 10th hole after completion, looking down the fairway, circa 1950

The 16th hole from the tee showing the former groundsman's cottage, foreground left, circa 1950

Chapter Six

Evolution of a Hole: the 17th

ALL COURSES are in a constant state of flux, not least because grass grows and trees sometimes fall over; it is the nature of the beast. If the course had been left exactly as Vardon laid it out, it would be a museum piece, a curiosity, not a living, breathing, properly playable golf course. Little Aston evolved as people worked on it and played it; it has been a long, thoughtful labour of love with changes and adaptations introduced carefully over time and very few revolutions.

Take the 17th as an example. There is even a suggestion that it may have been a par 3 because the tee started off in a completely different place but that is generally dismissed as unlikely. What is certain is that the hole, which underwent its first major reconstruction at the end of 1913 as a result of recommendations by Colt, earned its reputation as a rather fearsome par 4. Prior to the English Amateur in 1927, Bernard Darwin wrote:

There is a 17th hole which should in the course of the English Championship see some comedies that will be tragedies for the players. The green is extremely narrow, and is an island set in a sandy sea. The length of the second shot should be no more than a short mashie shot, but I can imagine the most eminent people making, under pressure, the saddest mess of it. The last hole possesses a cross bunker, and a cross bunker always has a nasty look to the agitated eye; still, by comparison with the 17th it is innocuous …

Earlier, in the county finals, he wrote:

Surrey took a strong lead with a team consisting of one American, two Scotsmen, and an Irishman. Short of the proverbial stroke of apoplexy nothing could prevent them winning, but Major Hezlet [the Irishman] infused some interest into the proceedings by a rather apoplectic eight at the 17th, going over the green with his second, then back into a bunker, and so on to the bitter end …"

It is not as formidable as the Road Hole at St Andrews but it preyed on many a player's mind well enough even before its 21st century transformation. Tom Scott, writing about the course in *Golf Illustrated* in 1947 said:

There are many attractive holes, too many to describe here, but one I like particularly is the 17th, a 358-yard hole that has blighted many hopes of a good score. The green is on a platform and the pitch must be dead accurate for the green is not large and there are bunkers right, left and front. It is a four hole and if a player can keep out of the wood situated on the right of the fairway and put his second on the green, he richly deserves his four. A good many players, I fancy, will be perfectly satisfied to have a five recorded on their card.

Frank Pennink, English Amateur champion in 1937 and 1938, golfing correspondent for the *Sunday Express*, chose his favourite thirty courses for a book published in 1952 and included Little Aston. He wrote:

The show hole of Little Aston is the seventeeth: trees on the right, out of bounds on the left, a plateau green in a frame of bunkers, and a lake on the left of it, all contribute to make this a splendid drive and pitch hole. The last is 384 yards long and has a cross-bunker guarding its green: being uphill it often needs two woods to get up, and it makes a good finish. The course measures 6,681 yards, quite a distance where there is little run in spring and autumn when the S.S.S. of 73 applies.

The 17th was one of Charlie Ward's favourite holes, being singled out for particular praise in his notes in the booklet that was the forerunner of the modern Strokesaver:

We now come to the most beautiful hole on the course. The trees on the right make a really testing drive for the long hitter. Having produced the ideal drive we have to play a very high pitch with a No.7 or 8 iron to a plateau green surrounded with bunkers with a lake on the left to trap a hook: this is a difficult second shot for the short driver, who has to play a long iron shot to this most tricky green. A hard four.

It had become a hole that demanded a well-placed shot from the tee and a perfectly weighted second, a classic par 4 in other words and no less a personage than Tony Jacklin included it in his top eighteen holes in the country, helicoptering in to play it as he did his nominated round in one day with the film cameras in tow. Admittedly, Jacklin had particularly fond memories of the 17th because, as the new Open champion, he pitched straight into the hole for an eagle 2 during the Dunlop Masters in 1969, generating perhaps the biggest roar ever heard at Little Aston. He used a 9-iron.

That shot added much to the lore and legend of the 17th, so why change a hole that could enhance the name of a man who won the Open Championship and the US Open Championship? Why change a hole that was this famous and this good?

Well, to have one of your best holes reduced to a drive and a flick by the best players is galling to say the least and Little Aston, like so many classic courses that were once considered long, was in grave danger of being overtaken by the events that have always overtaken golf courses: better equipment and conditioning, both of the best players and courses. Sizeism

The Evolution

The 17th hole from the tee showing the original three beech trees on the right, circa 1980

Looking at the original green, circa 1990

The new 17th green as it was in 2007

reared its ugly head and it is a fact that having stretched the course by 400 yards in its first twenty years, following Colt's visits, it took another eighty years to find the further 400 yards which are deemed, by modern standards, to be imperative.

To say that there has been a great deal of food for thought is to put it mildly, starting even before a contestant in the English Amateur Championship of 1927 had put six 3s on his card by the 12th hole. A number of spectacular scores were subsequently recorded and as Little Aston came to be regarded as the premier course in the region, questions were quietly asked about its continuing suitability to host big events. It was no longer a prospective venue for professional tournaments but its reputation as a host for prestigious amateur events was jealously guarded.

Donald Steel, a distinguished architect who was an accomplished player and writer, was called in to make an extensive report in 1992, which reflected the general concern. Steel was particularly critical of the bunkers, contending that most of them were now in the wrong place, with the longer hitters blithely unaffected by hazards that were once designed to make them think. Some new bunkers were added, some modified and a few filled in but Steel's more radical suggestions were rejected. The special sub-committee studying the report concluded that "the bunkers at Little Aston are a great

42

visual feature much remembered by visitors and that their wholesale removal would destroy the character of the course, even allowing that most are now in the wrong place".

Some people feel that an opportunity was lost here, that if the emphasis had been on the course's lack of length, the Club might have made the purchase of more land a priority over refurbishment of the clubhouse. In September 1992, the Club was given the chance to buy fifty-five acres of land to the left of the 4th and 8th holes, the same land that Greatrex had offered to sell in 1927, but they were eventually sold to another party in 1996. Hindsight, of course, wins every major.

Steel was called in again, in 2000, to review the course and in February 2005 he was back again "to make recommendations for the 17th hole" and "to consider new back tees on the 2nd, 3rd, 8th, 9th, 13th, 16th and 18th …". His preferred option for the 17th was the most dramatic: to move the green to the other side of the lake into the daffodil field. This was rejected as impractical, not least because an old oak tree on the site of the new green proved sacrosanct and too expensive, and it was decided to move the green into the lake instead. New tees could then be built for the 2nd and 18th and they would be safer places altogether, easing congestion and reducing the danger of being hit by errant approaches to the 17th.

It was a profound change and, to a degree, contentious and not under-taken without much agonising but the committee took the plunge and the work started towards the end of 2006, not helped by some filthy weather. A temporary green was installed so that the 17th was, indeed, played as a long par 3.

The first task had been to drain the lake, the contents were pumped into Foster's Lake, and all traffic, excavators, dumper trucks and the like, passed through where the water used to be. Aggregates of old tyres measuring two by two by one metres and weighing two tons apiece were hauled around a periphery of wire-encased granite blocks, thirty-eight of them, of a total weight of between eighty and ninety tons. The drains were laid in gravel, the Soil Technology Research Institute made their recommendations and on 10th June 2007, the day of the members' invitation, the new green was in play. It was, generally, well received but was still regarded as merely experimental. It had to be made more difficult still and further work was carried out, with more alterations to the shoreline of the lake and a new bunker installed requiring a carry of 278 yards off the tee. For those sceptics who feared that the 17th was being lengthened for length's sake, the answer is that the new hole is only sixteen yards longer than the old one. And it is widely regarded as being even more pleasing than it was before. There is now a view across the lake that was not previously available.

Fond are the memories of the old 17th. It was a great hole, the members say. And it still is, they say again.

The original cost estimate for all the course development work was £55,000, which included £5,000 irrecoverable VAT. This allowed for a big input from the greenstaff but the committee decided that John Greasley Limited, who rebuilt and contoured all the greens at Royal Birkdale, offered such a competitive price to help build the new tees and turf the 17th fairway that it made sense to make use of their expertise to complete the work more quickly. In November 2006, the final revised figure of £83,600 was inclusive of all construction work, professional fees, planning costs, contingency and irrecoverable VAT. The expense was eased by a grant of £10,000 from the R&A, who had long prized Little Aston as a venue. In the end, the architects were Mackenzie and Ebert.

The committee was ever mindful of the "responsibility to ensure a good quality legacy for future generations of members" and Geoff Wyatt, the honorary green steward, worked tirelessly to ensure the success of the project. The sums all seemed to add up and proved well within the Club's financial capabilities. At the end of the financial year, with the 17th green paid for, the closing bank balance was £95,000. Visitors continued to relish a day out at one of the best maintained and most enjoyable courses in the country and the normal annual income raised, a fraction under £260,000, played a vital part in keeping subscriptions reasonable despite the small membership.

Neil Andrews mused in *LA News* that his captaincy would probably be remembered for the 17th green and could not resist a fraternal dig: "At least that is a little better than my brother Keith who, despite considerable opposition from the then hon sec, only managed to get a toilet built between the 7th and 14th holes when he was captain in 1994!"

Unquestionably, however, both schemes were completed to the relief of all.

The Putting Green

Practice putting greens, conventionally, are laid as a general replication of the greens on the course. Conventionally, they are the rehearsal stage for the round of golf that is to come. In the conventional sense, therefore, Little Aston does not have a practice green, which surprises and sometimes disturbs a number of golfers.

What Little Aston does have is an area of ground that was laid for either the aesthete or, depending on your point of view, those golfers who like a quirk in their lives. Heather on the green? Flowers? That is what you get here on ground that undulates and turns sharp corners.

Peter Alliss, for one, has never forgotten it:

They had the most wonderful putting green. It was not your usual, it had flower beds and banks of heather running all through it. It must have been the best part of half an acre in size. I remember watching Charlie Ward chipping and putting there for hours on end.

Charlie loved the putting green and was always getting the hosepipe out and watering it when he had got nothing else to do. It was such a big part of his life that after he died in December 1976 his ashes were scattered there. In a moving ceremony, David Moseley said: "Charlie, we are immensely proud of all you achieved when carrying the flag for our Club and this putting green will henceforth be even more special in the hearts of those who knew you so well".

So, how did this unique testing ground come about? As early as 1913 Mr. Wyndham Brodie – he and Thomas Ansell were the garden committee – suggested laying out a putting green but the answer was no and it was not until 1925 that a sub-committee considered the matter with a view to "improving the front of the Club House". In 1927, when the annual subscription was nine guineas, five members, Frank Barker, Gilbert Greatrex, Thomas Ansell, Charles Heaton and John Wylie, put five guineas each towards laying down a putting green. Rhododendrons were removed and two elm trees and later a beech tree, with the elms being sold for £6. 10s. 0d and the beech for £2. 10s. 0d.

E.B. Handley became the honorary gardener and was elected a Life Member in 1947. His green-fingered successors included John Cooke and John Beharrell, who is now the keeper of this particular green, supplying the plants and looking after them with great pride and devotion. He is one of the champions of the layout because he is sure that golfers enjoy its uniqueness: "They love the vision from the clubhouse and the terrace and it is pretty special, isn't it? A lot of wagers have been taken on how to get around it and a great deal of fun has been had."

Often the first thing people think of when you mention Little Aston is "that wonderful putting green" but be warned, there is a lot of work to it and John said:

We've had one or two clubs come to have a look and I've tended to steer them away. They watch the Masters on television and think, 'Oh we must plant some shrubs' and before you know where you are the weeds are coming out of the top and there's no greenkeeper wants to do gardening, the two don't go together. The putting green needs constant attention and unless it's well looked after it's no good at all.

There are people who do not particularly like the green, claiming that you cannot really practise your putting properly on it, although there is a flat area, if you look carefully enough, and even John conceded:

I think if you want to hone a beautiful stroke you probably wouldn't do it there but it's been there since 1927, with very few changes. In latter years I've given it a facelift and tried to make sure it's well maintained and looked after. And in the spring it is beautiful.

Chapter Seven

Bigwood and Jinks

AFTER WORLD WAR I, A.H. Lewis and H.P. Bell put in short stints as honorary secretary but Wilfrid Bigwood, who joined the Club in 1921, and took on the post in 1923 at the age of thirty-five, was a formidable character and set the standards for the stability, consistency and secure sense of self that were to prove the hallmarks of the Club.

Bigwood, the fourth son of Alderman E.J. Bigwood of Barnt Green, was educated at Bromsgrove School and then spent some time travelling in Australia, New Zealand, Canada and the United States. On the outbreak of the war he joined the New Zealand Expeditionary Force and served in Egypt and Gallipoli. He transferred to the Worcestershire Regiment and served with the 10th Battalion in Flanders during the battle of the Somme, winning the Military Cross in 1916. In his book, *The Worcestershire Regiment in the Great War*, Captain H. Fitz M. Stacke recounted the action:

Soon after dark on September 15th 2/Lieut. Bigwood and a small covering party climbed out of the trench, carrying a 'Bangalore torpedo' – a length of metal piping closed at both ends and filled with explosive …

One minute before 10 pm the British artillery suddenly opened a heavy fire. 2/Lieut. Bigwood fired the 'torpedo', which blasted a wide gap through the German wire. The raiding party advanced, crawling at first. Then, as the guns lifted their fire, the attackers sprang to their feet and dashed forward through the gap made by the explosion … The enemy opened fire at point blank range; but with a quick rush the raiders leapt the ditch, scrambled up the parapet and closed with bomb and bayonet.

A fierce little fight followed … and some twenty of the enemy were killed or captured. Just as he decided to order retirement 2/Lieut. Bigwood was wounded and his ankle broken; but he refused to leave the trench until he had collected his men …

Bigwood was right at the centre of some of the biggest moments in the history of the Club, most notably the biggest of all, in 1925, when the lease of the links was nearing its end and Arthur Greatrex agreed to sell. Bigwood and Frank Edge, the Club's honorary solicitor, were entrusted with the negotiations and bought the land for £10,360, roughly equivalent to £2

Wilfrid Bigwood, honorary secretary 1923-1944   *Horace Jinks, honorary secretary 1944-1948*

million now, using the Average Earnings Index. The Club was a tenant no longer.

In 1927, Little Aston hosted the third English Amateur Championship with great success and in the ensuing years the number of green fees and visiting societies increased. The Institute of Brewers Golfing Society was one of the first, not least because Bigwood was chairman of the Allied Brewers Traders Association. His brother, Guy, who became president of the English Golf Union, was honorary secretary of Blackwell for several years and the annual match between the two clubs is one of the oldest and most convivial on the fixture list.

Bigwood was elected an Honorary Life Member in 1927 at the same time as Charles Arnold. A man of many commitments, Bigwood was a partner in Sedgwick Collins, insurance brokers in Birmingham, and by 1930 even he conceded that he needed help with the running of the Club. Horace Jinks, universally known as Jinky, Bigwood's right-hand man at Sedgwick Collins, was pressed into service. At a committee meeting on 12th April 1930 he was appointed secretary of the Club, starting officially on 1st July at a salary of £120 per annum. His role was to provide "all clerical assistance to the Hon. Treasurer and Hon. Secretary, who will continue to act officially in their respective appointments".

Jinky, a doer par excellence, was a character in his own right, full of bounce and bonhomie and he became honorary secretary in 1944 when Bigwood became president. The pair had served as joint honorary secretaries since 1940 and Jinky had waived his secretarial fee in 1939 when World War II started. He was described as the "Prince of Golf Club Secretaries" in *Golf Illustrated* and in 1937 had been presented with a gold watch in appreciation of services rendered during the Daily Mail competition.

The Bigwood-Jinks era provided a model for the continuity that characterised the Club and added to its clout. Bigwood was a big man in every sense and a pillar of the community. To name just a few of the positions he held, he was a director of the Birmingham Syphon Company, an alderman of Warwickshire County Council, County Commander of Warwickshire Special Constabulary, chairman of Sutton Coldfield Magistrates and Mayor of Sutton Coldfield. As mayor he was automatically president of Sutton Coldfield Golf Club and featured in the club's Mel cartoons. He was not a man to be trifled with, as Henry Cotton, one of the world's best golfers and an Open champion, discovered one year. The only Cotton more formidable than Henry was his wife, Toots, a tiny Argentine with a glare that would melt glaciers. The Cottons, accustomed to getting their own way, went out to play at Little Aston on the Sunday preceding the Daily Mail event, despite the fact that women were not allowed on the premises, and Bigwood duly had them thrown off the golf course. He also threatened to withdraw the use of the course and let the tournament go elsewhere unless he received a personal apology from Cotton. He did.

World War II

The course remained open throughout the war and the membership level was maintained: between September 1939 and December 1944 there were forty-three resignations and fifty-eight elections. The annual subscription of nine guineas remained the same as in 1925 but in August 1940, at a Special General Meeting attended by more than sixty members, the entrance fee of twelve guineas was dropped for the duration of the war. At the same meeting, members declined to allow ladies to play on Saturday mornings or Sunday afternoons subject to restrictions and the number of permit holders dropped from eighty-nine in January 1940 to thirty-two in August 1942. Yes, women had become a fixture at Little Aston and there is a whole chapter on how it happened.

Visitors were few and far between and rationing, particularly of petrol and food, began to take its toll. All members who were still playing were encouraged to take up debentures. It was suggested that a wider distribution should be made of debenture stock and that members who had no holding should be canvassed to take up stock in £5 multiples with a limit of £250. This led to seven debenture holdings amounting to £5,010 being spread among forty-three members, with a reduced rate of interest of four per cent.

Although money was short and it was an uphill struggle to hold things together, standards had to be maintained. In October 1942, Mrs. Finnemore, one of the permit holders, wrote offering a donation to Club funds and was rebuffed, albeit gently. She was thanked for her kind offer and informed that the Club was in a good position but would be delighted to take advantage of her offer "if we get into difficulties later".

Very little escaped the vagaries of war. Early on, the ladies' drying room was equipped as a first aid post; the ladies' lounge was used one morning a week as a local sewing and knitting centre for the provision of war casualty equipment; the local Red Cross Association held classes in the Club, including lectures on gas emergency; in 1940 trenches were dug across the 6th and 10th fairways to prevent enemy troops from landing, and not filled in until 1944; and two hundred sheep munched their way happily across the course, helping trim the fairways without having to use too much precious fuel. There were lambing pens to the left of the 4th and 8th holes and there was a local rule allowing free drops in the bunkers, where the sheep liked to shelter. The sheep grazed rent free at first but after consultation with local clubs Walmley, Blackwell, Walsall and Moor Hall, the Club charged the farmer a rent of £50 a year, later raised to £75.

Even with the sheep course maintenance was a struggle. At the start of the war there were six green staff and by 1941 the only one left was Ernest Jones, who had fought in World War I and was a member of the local Home Guard. John Harper, who lived in Barnes Farm on the left of the 3rd fairway, and Gilbert Greatrex worked with Jones and Mart Lewis, the professional, to keep the course in some sort of shape.

In 1942 there was a big outlay on twenty dozen bottles of port at £12 a dozen. To put that in context, luncheons cost 3s. 6d. with sweets, sixpence less without. It was not an easy time. To encourage the sale of more meals the house committee suggested cutting down on the size of portions in the hope that this would mean being able to apply for more rations because more meals were being served. In the absence of increased rations the house committee decided that no visitor should be served unless they had applied at least a day in advance and non-playing members were designated non-eating members.

Perhaps most important of all, in 1942, the Regional Commissioner visited with a view to taking over the clubhouse for the housing of 100 men for civil defence purposes. There was an emergency meeting, Wilfrid Bigwood held more meetings and negotiated expertly and it was agreed that no further steps would be taken without further consultation, except in the event of an invasion.

That same year the Americans arrived and their officers were granted permission to use the course and facilities. In 1945, the honorary secretary wrote to the commanding officers of the U.S. forces based at Sutton Coldfield and Whittington to say how much the Club had enjoyed their visits and hoping they would call in if they ever returned to England. In appreciation the officers of the 10th U.S. Replacement Depot presented the America Cup which has been played for since 1946. Lieutenant Colonel Greenwood, V.C., D.S.O., M.C., and officers of the 13th Pioneer Corps, who played matches against the Club during the war, presented the Pioneer Cup, which goes to the winners of the men's fourball medal competition.

As early as 1943, the committee started looking ahead to post-war reconstruction of the course and improvements to the clubhouse, and F. Bernard Clark, aided by Mart Lewis and Holland W. Hobbiss, the Club's long-serving honorary architect, drew up some plans. After a committee meeting in September 1944 members received a letter stating that the proposals had been completed and were posted up in the clubhouse. Fifty pounds were allocated to buying young trees, plus an annual allowance for looking after them until they could be planted. There was, for the Club, to be life after war after all.

In 1947 Jinky, an ebullient, extrovert presence, presided over the introduction of the Ladies' section, no doubt a test even of his bonhomie and diplomatic skills, but in October 1948 the members were shocked and saddened when he died of a heart attack. The choice of successor proved inspired. John Cooke, the captain, called an emergency meeting and within four days Norman Herbert Russell, a member since 1934 but a committee member of less than a year's standing, took over and held the breach to such good effect that his intended interregnum developed into a reign of Victorian and Elizabethan longevity. Norman, a chartered accountant, was thirty-two at the time, still a bachelor – he made the wise decision to marry Betty Butler in 1953 – and well aware of how things were done at Little Aston. He was so devoted to the task and so adept that he remained in post for fifty-one years and virtually merits a book on his own.

Wilfrid Bigwood, who died suddenly in 1950 at the age of sixty-two on holiday in Germany, helped Norman settle in and Bigwood's son Peter played a full part in the life of the Club after the war. Prior to the war he had lessons from Mart Lewis using hickory clubs and became a handy golfer, losing to Joe Carr, who went on to become a legend in Ireland, spiritual home of all legends, in the fourth round of the Boys Championship at Carnoustie in 1939. Peter saw active service in North Africa and Italy and when he came home became a chartered surveyor and a low single figure golfer. He was a clubbable man, a great friend of Norman Russell and liked nothing better than discussing matters of the day at the bar, when he was not at the races, another passion. Not that he was always successful. He once owned a horse called Edward Bigshot; in its first race at Chepstow it came to grief at the first

LITTLE ASTON GOLF CLUB

VISITORS FEES

AS FROM JANUARY 1st, 1947

	WITHOUT MEMBER		WITH MEMBER	
	All Day	Single Round	All Day	Single Round
SATURDAYS, SUNDAYS and BANK HOLIDAYS	20/-	20/-	10/-	10/-
WEEK DAYS	10/-	5/-	5/-	2/6

It is requested that Visitors use only the White Tee Markers except when playing in Organized Competitions, when Red Tee Markers may be used.

H. W. JINKS,
Hon. Secretary.

fence; in its second race at Cheltenham it fell at the second; and at Plumpton it was pulled up six from home; its name was changed to Grimleys Son. Peter was captain from 1973-1975 and president in 1983, during the seventy-fifth anniversary celebrations.

Bill Jinks, son of Jinky, also became president, in 1992. There's that continuity again.

The '49 Rumpus

A rumour without a leg to stand on will get around some other way (John Tudor)

The A.G.M. of 1949 was rather more uproarious than most and it remains one of the few disharmonious notes in a Club renowned for its smooth running. Norman Russell and Arthur Gregory both refer to it as though it were something exceptional but contested elections were not uncommon in the early years, although the last one had taken place in 1930 and does not appear to have been in the least acrimonious.

Fifty-seven members attended the meeting of 19th November 1949, with the Club's president and honorary solicitor Frank Edge in the chair. At first, candidates for committee put up by members were not permitted but after much legal argument were finally accepted and put to the vote along with the committee's nominees. On the first count it was found that there were more ballot papers than members present and on the second count one of the committee's nominees was defeated and one of the non-committee candidates elected. This was J.C. Allday, who had been proposed by E.A.

Lieutenant Colonel South, founder of the Boys Championship in 1921

Denham and seconded by T. South. Alan Denham joined the Club in September 1945; in 1932, playing out of Streetly, he won the Little Aston Spring Cup. Lieutenant Colonel Tom South O.B.E. had been the founder of the British Boys Championship.

The minutes recorded: Mr. J.C. Allday elected. Mr. A. Morley and Mr. W.G. Streather not elected.

The brouhaha caused a few ructions and after numerous discussions it was decided to hold an Extraordinary General Meeting on 26th August 1950 at which Article 5 was altered to read:

No member other than a retiring member shall be eligible for election to the Committee unless a letter of nomination signed by two members has been delivered to the Club not less than twenty-eight days before such meeting.

In 1956 the Articles were further altered so that one retiring member would not be eligible for re-election.

On the day of the E.G.M. the resignations from the Ladies' section included Mrs. J.C. Allday and in September it was noted that "Mr. J.C. Allday wished to resign from the Committee"; Tom South resigned in November. In June 1951 Allday, who had moved to the Bridgnorth area, became a country member and in March 1952 he resigned altogether.

There is no doubt that Little Aston Golf Club was constituted as a members' club, a company limited by guarantee, which ensures that no one person, or group of persons, other than a majority of members entitled to vote at general meetings, can gain control. For practical purposes clubs constituted in this way bestow wide powers to their committees to run the club's affairs. However, to retain a measure of membership control certain provisions are usually made within the club's articles, such as: the facility for a defined number of members to requisition a general meeting; an obligation on the club committee to give effect to any resolution passed at a general meeting; a clause setting out the requirements for member nominations for office and committee. Little Aston's early members directly influenced the Club's affairs by requisitioning E.G.M.s, for example, one to change the rules, another to instigate "necessary improvements in the course" and one, in 1920, to discuss the question of ladies playing on the course. Frank Edge was a signatory to the first two.

In 1949, part of the problem was that there was no provision or time limit for submitting resolutions to the A.G.M. in the new rule book, revised after the formation of the Ladies' section in 1945 but not printed until December 1948, nor in the Articles of Association, an oversight that undoubtedly led to all the toing and froing.

When Norman Russell mentioned the incident in his speech at the dinner to celebrate his forty years as honorary secretary, his memory was selective – "the Committee won easily" – but there can be little doubt that the experience made him determined to keep politicking to a minimum. For the next forty-nine years every A.G.M. was done and dusted inside thirty minutes.

Tom South letter to *Golf Monthly,* published May 1949

Frederick Guthrie Tait, who was only thirty when he died leading a charge of the Black Watch at Koodoosberg Drift in 1900, won the Amateur Championship twice and was twice equal third in the Open, in 1896 and 1897:

> Little Aston Hall
> Little Aston
> Warwickshire
>
> Sir Guy Campbell's article and the communications you publish from America by players who were in contact with Freddie Tait, and that the Boer War started on a Sunday in a place called Dundee, I was in the battle where Freddie was killed and I saw his body laid out for burial at a farm near Reit River Drift. We had been fighting away on the right under the command of General Wavell, whom I imagine must have been the father of the present General of that name. It is forty-nine years ago, and I can see poor Freddie laid out with a few of his comrades as though it were last week. I can remember every incident of that day. But here is another sequel about that grim and bitter battle and its tragic losses. In 1932 the Boys' Amateur Championship Committee were being entertained to dinner at the Royal Lytham and St Annes Club where the championship was held that year and there was a fine picture of Freddie Tait on the wall when after some talk about Freddie and the fateful battle, one of the ex-captains, I forget his name at the moment, said, "What an extraordinary coincidence. I got there the day after he was buried and took a photograph of his grave." He then left the table and brought the snap for us all to see.
>
> These coincidences do happen so often in life!
>
> T. South, Lieut.-Colonel.
> (Boys' Amateur Championship Committee)

Chapter Eight

Norman Russell: Last of a Line

F OR FIFTY-ONE years it was Norman Russell who ensured that Little Aston ran smoothly. Very much the benevolent dictator of legend in public, with a fierce, sometimes gruff manner, he was, his admirers insist, a soft-hearted man of consensus. His modus operandi was more collegiate than dictatorial, although his stern demeanour disguised his democratic soul. His philosophy, espoused in an avuncular interview for Swedish television in 1993, was simple "You get on with everybody if you can; it's no good getting too serious; keep everybody friendly and happy. Just all together. We have so few members, we've always been a happy club."

John Beharrell summed Norman up thus:

He was an amazing man. Very kind, very good-natured, with a heart of gold. He loved Little Aston, had a lovely wife, they never had children and she never played golf. He enjoyed his golf, had a lot of friends, was a good businessman, a good chartered accountant and just put a lot into life.

The stories about Norman are legion and legendary but one of the best insights into his character, and into the character of the Club, is provided by the speech he gave at the dinner held at the Belfry to celebrate his fortieth anniversary as honorary secretary. It is quite brilliant, even delivered only on the page.

Norman Russell's speech

There have been all kinds of rumours as to how I came to be appointed the Honorary Secretary of this club but I will tell you what happened.

Monday 24th October 1948 was I suppose a turning point in my life for on that day a very sad thing happened. Our previous Secretary – Jinky – came down to make the early morning tea and had a heart attack and died. It was very sad for us all at Little Aston because he was a wonderful person. I can see him now with his shock of white hair, playing every Saturday, after a good lunch often with Austin Morley. They sometimes would play a full round then repair to the bar and Jinky would climb into his car, a red Morris Oxford, you know one of those with a straight radiator with a thermometer on top. I would think it always showed maximum heat with Jinky breathing on it through the windscreen. Officially he was our secretary from 1941 to 1948 but I know that Peter Bigwood would not mind me saying that he did most of the work whilst Wilfrid Bigwood was Honorary Secretary from 1923 to 1941. Wilfrid and Jinky were a marvellous pair at Sedgwick Collins – the insurance brokers. We have only had eight Secretaries since 1908 and we cannot thank Jinky enough.

At the time of Jinky's death John Cooke was Captain and he called a meeting for the Thursday evening and asked me whether I would help them out and take over the position and that I could have the same remuneration as Jinky. I agreed and during the next week collected the books from Sedgwicks.

I must say I do not know why they chose me because I had no qualification for the position. In fact I was not as qualified as Peter Bigwood who during the war was asked by his Colonel to take over as Adjutant as he seemed to have had the necessary qualifications for the position. He drank, played bridge and annoyed the Padre! Excellent credentials I should have thought: no wonder we won the war with such men as those about.

I looked through the books and knowing the generosity of the club flew straight to the Petty Cash Box to see what my remuneration was to be; to my great delight I would get twenty pounds at Christmas! John Cooke did tell me some years after that he was sure Jinky's remuneration had been increased. I told him I had not found the Minutes but the bad news is that only last month I did come across the Minute showing the increase from twenty pounds to one hundred and twenty pounds so again the bad news is that the club owes me four thousand pounds but would suggest we forget it!

During my early days I cannot thank John Cooke enough for all the help and encouragement he gave me. He was the person I always turned to when in doubt and he has been a magnificent friend to me. I also received marvellous advice from Wilfrid Bigwood to whom I owe a debt of gratitude – I don't think – because the previous year he had persuaded me to take over as Secretary of the Midland Section of the ABTR [Allied Brewers Traders' Association], a really teetotal lot. How I got home after some of the

Committee Meetings I shall never know. In fact on one occasion I did finish upside down in my Ford Zephyr. I took a bend too fast and just rolled over. The engine was still running when upside down – enough of that …

As I have said on many occasions I could not have done my job without the understanding and consideration of the marvellous members who we have had at the Club throughout the years. They have put up with the many imperfections in the way I have carried out my duties. Do you know we have only had one acrimonious General Meeting throughout the forty years and that was early on when a certain few wished to challenge a recommendation of the Committee. I remember the meeting well – a certain member turned up with several legal books under his arm ready for the fray but the President who was Frank Edge was ready for him. Frank was a well known Birmingham Solicitor, a huge man and was the only man I know who must have ordered his butler to break a boiled egg over the lapel of his jacket before leaving home because it was always so well stained!! A few legal skirmishes took place with the legal books being brought into play. A ballot was called for and on the first count there were more ballot papers than attendees at the meeting. A new ballot was taken, the Committee won easily and all has been quiet ever since. Of course the opposition is much better organised these days as we have a Shadow President, Captain, Secretary and other officers – all positions being taken by our good friend Barrie Andrews who keeps us all on our toes. I am glad to say that he has now turned his attention to Oswestry Golf Club on a free transfer!

We have had some wonderful characters in this Club and I am glad we still have six pre war members who many of us will remember well. The six are John Cooke, Peter Bigwood, David James, Mick Franks, Tom McMillan and myself.

There was a clutch of members who hunted together, Wilfrid Bigwood, Fox Crossland, Billie Bowater and Ben Lorrimer and the stories of those four are legion. Ben Lorrimer was a man who if anyone had the impertinence to drive into his four would pick up the ball and hit it back. Under what rule you played it I do not know, but he was not having any of that sort of thing at this Club.

Then there was the regular eight ball plus caddies on a Sunday comprising Trevor Heaton, Warmie, Bill Pollock, John Cooke, Peter Bigwood, Dick Fisher etc, etc … a fearsome eight' They nearly always played an eight ball one pound a hole Accumulator.

Bill Pollock was another, with his pipe of mixes, golden ram and gold block and his tankard with two in a can and always late on the tee after lunch on Saturdays because of having to back his horses. Always telling us of his good bets. Kicky Nook at 20/1. He also kept a few growlers which would run at Tamworth and Bromford Bridge. There were others such as Admiral Scarf who kept a dinghy at Abersoch and Jumping Jesus who was a patent agent. We still have with us today the Galloping Hairpin, you know the excellent golfer who has the longest backswing in the business – nice to see you Tom!

Who will forget the Growler as I called him. You can, I am sure all see his black looks when anyone entered the bar when having a swig of his bottled Whitbread. I have seen Jimmy on a long evening including dinner sink forty-eight bottles of Whitbread – the gassiest of beers.

There have of course been many others, too many to mention. There is however no doubt that during my forty years the two most outstanding members we have had are our present Captain, John Beharrell, who won the Amateur Championship in 1956 and our Honorary member Charlie Ward whose wins on the professional circuit were legend. It was a pity he did not win The Open. I think I am right in saying that his highest placing was third which was a marvellous effort. Both of these two have been marvellous ambassadors for the Club. Talking of John, I remember playing him in the summer singles just after he had won The Amateur. I was five up on the 12th Tee and thinking what a scalp I was about to take when I topped my second shot at the 12th hole and lost the hole and the match two and one. I did however beat Geordie Fairweather and this was by a margin of ten and eight and this was my most memorable victory.

John's uncle, Ted Beharrell, was a very good scratch golfer but had the habit, on hitting a bad shot, of throwing his club some considerable distance to be picked up by his caddie. On one occasion he nearly killed me. He was playing a short pitch to the first hole when he played an awful shot. The offending niblick came whistling just over my head on the second tee, fortunately just missing me. In reverse I have always had on my conscience the fact that I might have been instrumental in speeding the demise of Cuthbert Pritchard. In the summer he always called in at the Club on his way home when he had three large vintage ports filled up with soda water. I asked him whether it would not be cheaper for me to get him some white port to quench his thirst. He agreed. I got him a case which he tried and liked – poor fellow died within the month! We sold the remaining bottles to John Hooper and as he seems to have survived my conscience is perhaps clear.

I have mentioned a couple of classic shots I have seen but I suppose the greatest was Bigwood's drive at the first when playing with Roy James in a foursomes match. The ball finished behind the eighteenth green – very difficult – you try it. Charlie fetched everyone out of the clubhouse to see it!

Then there was Trevor Heaton's drive at the sixteenth when his drive finished on the far side of the third in deep rough by Barns Farm below all those trees. The ball was found by his caddy – Frost – and his second was played with a brassie to the back of the green where it hit a pile of stones, came back to within two feet of the pin. He got his three and Warmie who played the hole beautifully lost it with his four and was furious. Frost was a good caddy for Trevor because he always seemed to find his ball in the rough and we thought he carried a leather mashie as the ball was always playable with a brassie. We had some good caddies in those days. There was one, Walter Pheasant, who looked after dear old Bob Hiam and was with him the only time in his life when he had a gross four at the fifteenth and wrote a marvellous four line verse about it and I just wish I had a copy.

While talking about members let us not forget those, whom I like to think of as Associates, namely the Artisans whose Captain, Frank [Brookhouse] is with us tonight. A most memorable body of men. I have been at their Annual Dinner every year since 1948. When I first started going they were held in the Bird Cage at the Royal Hotel. On those occasions we fixed various matches including a load of coal. There was the famous statement by Tom Warwood (the coalman), who, after playing in a mixed match, said, "If she could hit her drives as far as she hit her putts we would have pissed it!"

I thank them all for their help and friendship over the years because they have certainly been of help to me and I greatly appreciate being their President.

The reason I have been able to carry on is because we have always had very good helpers. I purposely do not use the word servants because they have been so good in what they have done in running the Club. I, of course, refer to the Professionals, Stewards and Head green keeper. When I started the ground staff consisted of the three Joneses and one other. They were a marvellous bunch and with us for so many years. Later Ginger Bevan joined us. I'm glad to say that he is still well and enjoying life. Alan Boraston joined us in 1954 and is still with us today and in fact is here this evening. He has given marvellous help and like all old timers "goes his own way". You ask him to do something, he nods, smiles and in about three weeks time you find it done. Extraordinary.

Our Professionals have always given us tremendous help in running the Club. They run the competitions and welcome visitors and societies to the Club. Mart Lewis who was one of nature's gentlemen from the old school was an excellent club maker and a real martinet. I always remember the dressing down he gave me when he spotted me playing a few practice balls up the eighteenth. It was all done in an immaculate manner, you could not take offence – in any case I was in the wrong – I never did it again.

Then there was Charlie Ward to whom I have already referred. He brought great fame to himself and the Club in tournaments with the selection for the Ryder Cup and his Master Golfers success. He was known as "the Whippet" and I remember when he played a round here in under two hours scoring 72.

I forget who he played with but I do know the said person said he would never play with him again. That is how we should play. I am glad to hear and I am sure others will be also that Arthur Gregory got round in the February Medal in 2 hours 20 minutes, really exhausting Teddy Grice on the way – well done Arthur.

We now have John Anderson who gives me excellent assistance in running the Club.

Stewards, we have had a few but not really so many. Jack and Lily Bailey. Jack was a happy chap who before the days of the present bar worked with a cheery smile from a hatch bar in the lounge. He helped me clear up several complaints such as a member who complained bitterly about the size of a sherry we served. He said "leave it to me" and put the same amount in a slightly wider glass. On the next Sunday I was complimented on the amount of sherry offered. Lily was known for her wonderful treacle tart which she made. I suppose our most notorious steward was Huntingdon-Jones. He was supposed to have been a Squadron Leader. He was very smooth and always regaling us with many tales of how to dry a decanter when it had been washed but we forgot to look into his other imperfections. He lasted only six months because he took a holiday by kind permission of Her Majesty for going off with all our gear and bankings. He appeared before our friends on the Aldridge Bench when it transpired that he had already been entertained by her Majesty on two previous occasions. I shall forgive him but never forget the club who gave us such a glowing reference for him!

We had two periods with that lovable rogue – Aucott – who if you had four drinks it was always nineteen shillings and seven pence whatever you had. When I asked him why, he replied "As long as there was change from a pound they seldom queried"!

It has always been known that Stewards at most clubs come with a bicycle and leave with a Jag. Times seem to have changed a little because now worldwide holidays seem to be the order of the day – with apologies to Bob and Paula [Leighton] but they have been a great help.

I have in my time as Secretary had the very good fortune to meet many splendid people in the golf world who I would not have met but for being secretary and I like to think that I have made some good friends. I have met many members of the press and I can assure you that they do not have to leave the clubhouse to write an excellent article on the day's play. I will give you an example, Eddie Griffiths, that doyen of Midland sports writers who called in one day when we had a small tournament and I asked why he had come. He said, "I thought I would call on my way to Stratford to report on an important Warwickshire cricket second eleven match." I entertained him in the usual way to which he had been accustomed. Some few hours later I found him fast asleep in Charlie's shop, never having left the Club. A wonderful report appeared in the paper next day about the cricket match!

I must refer to the ladies because I know I am thought to be a chauvinist pig which might be right but I love them dearly especially when they order a pot of tea for one with three cups and complain about the standard of catering after having cut the poor stewardess down to such a bottom price – bless them all. Before the war they were Permit Holders and had to apply for a permit each year. The system was however voted out in 1947 when they formed a Ladies Section in their own right. Bring back the old days did I hear someone say. No, seriously, they are marvellous and I consider that we look after them very well. In fact we had the English Ladies Championship last year with the final on a Saturday.

I have always said that being a golf club secretary is a way of life, not a profession and I have always found that those clubs who have a simple secretary and not a manager, manager/secretary or some other highfaluting name seem to be the happiest and friendliest clubs.

I have had so much out of golf and I hope and trust that I have been able to put something back into it.

Now all that I may have done would not have been possible without my dear wife Betty who has put up with me for thirty-seven years and has given me great support in all my trials and tribulations, and put up with me through thick and thin, sober and otherwise – I cannot thank her enough for being so understanding.

I would like to thank all those who have worked so hard to make this evening what for me has been so memorable.

Thank you all and to my personal guests and others who have been invited and my thanks for coming.

To finish with a heartening quote from my doctor: "Norman if you have been honorary secretary of this club for forty years then I have changed my thinking about drink – it cannot be bad for everyone." So gentlemen, get at it and thank you all for coming and especially for the honour you have accorded me this year in electing me your President.

* * * * *

Norman was given a standing ovation but collapsed a few minutes after delivering this tour de force and was taken to hospital where he was found to be suffering from exhaustion. As his doctor suggested, Norman did not do tired and emotional. He was rarely ill and had a clear-headed capacity for alcohol that scuppered medical edicts on drink and the dangers thereof. When he took over as honorary secretary in 1948, the Club had a bank overdraft of more than £1,500 and £11,000 worth of debentures outstanding; by 1996 Norman had built up a cash balance of more than £310,000. He was also captain, 1967-1969, honorary treasurer, 1973-1980 and president, 1988-1990. In his prime, when still working full-time as a partner in Whinney Murray, he used to call in at the Club on the way home from the office and he and other members would put the world to rights over a few drinks. That happy hour and a half from 5 p.m. to 6.30 p.m. now belongs to another world, battered into submission by the breathalyser, which was introduced in 1967, and longer working hours.

Little Aston was Norman's home from home but his authority stemmed from the backing of the committee and he also earned the devotion of the captains who served with him. Towards the end of the 1970s there was a run of captains who were under fifty, with families and demanding jobs and a two-year term of office would have been a daunting prospect without Norman.

David Moseley, who was captain during the seventy-fifth anniversary celebrations, said: "He was magnificent. Nothing was too much trouble. He made the captaincy a real pleasure." The week of the seventy-fifth, a hectic round of competitions and dinners, was nevertheless a civilised affair, with the captain and honorary secretary meeting at the bar at the start of each day to discuss proceedings over a silver tankard of champagne.

Norman did have his sticking points. From 1940-1946, he had served as an officer with the Royal Signals Corps attached to the Artillery Regiment stationed in India and Burma and it left an indelible mark. When it was suggested that the Japanese, who had a period of investing heavily in British golf clubs, might make the members an offer they could not refuse, Norman said simply: "They would never know."

Normal Russell celebrating twenty-five years as honorary secretary – with Maurice Bembridge

Receiving the salver from Dr. Victor Milne

David Pepper, John Beharrell (captain of the R&A), Norman Russell, John Scrivener (president of the English Golf Union) and Rodney James at the Staffordshire Dinner, 1998

Norman Russell celebrating fifty years as honorary secretary, with David Pepper and John Loader

Chapter Nine

Later Members

THERE IS only one person to start with when it comes to recording the golfing feats of Little Aston's members in the modern era, post-World War II for the purposes of this book, and that is John Beharrell, the Club's very own, home-grown Amateur champion and champion amateur. In all the long and distinguished history of the Amateur Championship there has been no more surprising or romantic story than the one that emerged at Troon, now Royal Troon, in 1956.

Beharrell had reached the semi-finals of the Boys Championship the year before but astonished the golfing world by becoming, at eighteen, the youngest winner of the Amateur. He was inspired, beating some of the best-known names in amateur golf including Charles Lawrie, Ian Caldwell, Gene Andrews, a very good American, and Dr. Frank Deighton. In the semi-finals, he defeated the Scot, Reid Jack, who was to win the title the following year.

In the final he beat Leslie Taylor of Ranfurly Castle by 5 and 4. Beharrell, four up at lunch, moved to six up when he holed a ninety yard pitch for an eagle 2 at the 7th, but lost the next four holes and had to check the score with the referee. He then won the 12th, or 30th, to be three up with six to play and the crisis had passed.

Rod Davies, the chief sports writer for the *Birmingham Evening Mail* and father of Dai, this book's co-author, drove non-stop through the night to get to Troon in time for the semi-final, there were no motorways then, and Beharrell's wonderful play delighted him and no less a critic than Leonard Crawley, a great all-round games player and golf correspondent for the *Daily Telegraph* and *The Field*, who wrote:

Beharrell's charming modesty and general deportment were the envy of every parent among the thousands who watched him … The new champion is beautifully built. Five feet ten tall with broad shoulders, a big bottom and strong legs, he must, I feel sure, be good at all games but owing to a serious illness in his early teens he was compelled to leave school and take to the fresh air and the game of golf alone.

John Beharrell receiving the Amateur
Championship Trophy from the captain of
Royal Troon Golf Club, June 1956

He has been admirably taught by Jack Cawsey [the professional at Pype Hayes] and he has picked up a wrinkle or two from Charles Ward, the greatest exponent of the short game in professional golf since the war, who is now Beharrell's home club professor at Little Aston. His balance, like that of all the world's greatest golfers of both yesterday and today, is superlatively good. He stands still when he hits the ball and he is still standing still and like a marble statue when the effort of striking is over.

Beharrell returned home to a civic reception at Sutton Coldfield Town Hall; played for England in the home internationals that year at Muirfield; and was elected winner of the Golf Writers' Trophy for "the most outstanding contribution to golf during the preceding twelve months". Even better, Little Aston made him an Honorary Life Member.

John has more than repaid the Club. He served on the committee in various capacities for twenty-seven years, was captain in 1987 and 1988 and played an invaluable role in steering the Club into the modern age when Norman Russell retired after fifty years as honorary secretary. John was the first chairman of the management sub-committee, a position he held for three years, spending countless hours at the Club to ensure that the transition to a new administrative set-up was as smooth as possible. He was president in the centenary year and over the years his contribution to the wider world of golf included being an England selector and in 1998-1999 captain of the R&A.

A bit about the Beharrells

The first Beharrell to be a member was John's uncle, George Edward, known as Ted, who joined in 1930 when he moved to work at Fort Dunlop in Erdington. His handicap fluctuated between 1 and plus 1 but although he represented Staffordshire and Midland Counties he never played in any championships. He could hold his own in the highest company and as chairman and managing director of the Dunlop Rubber Company often did. At the age of sixty-six, playing with Peter Thomson, a cultured

Australian who won the Open five times, he scored 66 round the New Course at Sunningdale.

Ted was a member of the committee and the green committee and brought a lot of society business to the Club through his links with the motor trade as well as accommodating the Dunlop Masters. He was captain of a far-sighted committee during the difficult years from 1941 to 1944 while helping maintain and oversee Dunlop's massive role in the war effort. He moved to London after the war and became captain of Sunningdale, where he liked to play four rounds at the weekend. Little Aston made him an Honorary Member in 1950 and he was knighted in 1961.

Jack and Mary Beharrell, John's parents, moved to Birmingham from Walton Heath just before World War II and joined Little Aston when the war ended. They used to play on a Sunday afternoon and John tagged along. He became a junior member in 1949 and spent the school holidays practising and playing. He pitched and putted for pennies with Charlie Ward and when he was fifteen beat the great man playing level. He also sharpened his game in matches with John Morgan, a Walker Cup player, and Bob Church, a good scratch golfer, who introduced him to competition of the highest calibre.

"John Morgan was an outstanding player," John said:

He was very much a class act and he was a very good friend of Ronnie White's (a member of Royal Birkdale who played in five Walker Cups). John and Bob Church took me up to Southport and Ainsdale and we had a threeball in the morning and in the afternoon Ronnie White joined us. He threw the ball onto the tee at the 1st, a long short hole of about 200 yards, and hit this 2-iron that finished six inches from the hole. Extraordinary.

In 1960, at the age of twenty-two, John married Veronica Anstey and they spent the second week of their honeymoon reaching the final of the Worplesdon Mixed Foursomes, where they were beaten, rather unkindly, by their bridesmaid Bridget Jackson and her partner Michael Burgess. "They hit the ball further than we did," Veronica recalled, "and the last two holes at Worplesdon are very long and they won on the last green, which was disappointing."

In 1955, at the age of 20, Veronica was a member of the LGU (Ladies Golf Union) Junior team that toured Australia and New Zealand and she won the Australian, Victorian and New Zealand titles during a seven month trip of a lifetime. The team won the Golf Writers' Trophy for their exploits and Veronica played in the Curtis Cup in 1956 and represented England but a bad car accident curtailed her career. "I was told I must never practise again and cut my golf down to a quarter of what it had been," she said, "so it was a short flash in the pan. My mind knew what to do but my body couldn't do it, so I gave it up."

Veronica Beharrell (nee Anstey)

Veronica won the Warwickshire Championship eight times and played out of Edgbaston competitively but Little Aston has been part of her life since she became a Beharrell and she had many happy times on the course:

We used to have a babysitter every Sunday afternoon [more often than not Charlie Ward's wife Gwyn] and whizzed up to play and we were always round in two hours ten minutes, not hurrying, just playing and getting on with it.

Mary Beharrell, who was the second honorary secretary of the ladies section, was made an Honorary Member in 1990 and died in December 2007 at the age of ninety-nine, just before she and the Club reached their centenary.

More players of note

John Llewellyn Morgan, who joined in 1952, was born in Llandrindod Wells in 1918 and learned his golf in that mountainous corner of mid Wales. He turned professional for a short period but regained his amateur status in 1948. His was an enduring talent, he won the Duncan Putter as late as 1968, but he was at his best in the 1950s. He won numerous Midland events and was Welsh champion in 1950 and 1951 and runner-up in 1952, and represented his country more than 100 times from 1948-1964 and then again from 1966-1968. He also played in three Walker Cup matches, in 1951, 1953 and 1955.

In 1953, at Kittansett in Massachusetts, the home side won nine points to three but John won both his matches. He and Gerald Micklem, who became one of the game's foremost administrators, beat Bill Campbell and Charlie Coe, who were regarded as unbeatable, by 4 and 3. Charlie Ward once described John as "the best putter, amateur or professional, in the country" and he was so majestic that Micklem said, "I don't think I have seen an exhibition of putting like it." *Golf Illustrated* called Morgan and Micklem the outstanding players in their team and John underlined this when he beat Coe by 3 and 2 in the singles. He also reached the last eight of the US Amateur, losing to Gene Littler, the eventual winner.

JULY 15, 1961

THE SPHERE

The clubhouse with the practice green in the foreground

BRITAIN'S GREAT GOLF CLUBS
LITTLE ASTON

Bearing one of the best-known names in Midlands golf, Little Aston is set in woodland about a mile from the centre of Birmingham. The club was founded in 1908 by Mr. C.F. Arnold, but did not become full owners of the course until 1925. Three years later the purchase of 12 acres near the 10th green established Little Aston in its present form. The course is 6,689 yards long, a notable feature being the large number of bunkers. In 1956, John Beharrell, a member of the club, became the youngest ever winner of the British Amateur Championship at the age of eighteen. The most recent major tournament played at Little Aston was the Dunlop Masters in 1958, won by Harry Weetman. The Professional, Charles Ward, has won many major tournaments including the Dunlop Masters in 1949. S.S.S. at Little Aston is 74.

Left: Charlie Ward giving a lesson to Ronnie Baxter, Centre: Freddie Mallett and Tom McMillan Jnr, Right: Mr. N.H. Russell, the honorary secretary at Little Aston, Mr. G.R. Baxter and Mr. T.M. Franks

Mr. J.E.N. Godrich and Colonel F.E.B. Jones

Hubert Lindop

Dr. Victor Milne and Dr. Hugh Livingstone

Richard Hill, Robin Tait, Tom Dippie and John Whitehouse

John Morgan with Brian Cooke

In 1955, just before the Dunlop Masters, John played four friendly rounds at Little Aston at an average of 66.5 (266); Harry Bradshaw's winning aggregate in the Masters was 277. A year later, in the Final Bogey, John was six up at lunch and all square in the afternoon. He came first.

John, who was always up for a hand of poker or game of liar dice after golf, died in 1991. His grandson Andrew Slater was on the committee during centenary year.

The Amateur x two

Trevor Homer slots in here because where else would you put a double Amateur champion? After a very long, sometimes tortuous and always salutary journey Trevor said ruefully: "Sometimes it's hard to take when you play 20 handicap golf and you remember that you used to be plus 2 but I've found I can enjoy social golf."

In 1972, as a young member of Walsall, he reached the final of the Amateur Championship at Royal St George's and after a nervous night during which he got "nicely drunk" beat Alan Thirlwell 4 and 3. Walsall made him a life member, and in 1973 he played in the Walker Cup at Brookline and Little Aston accepted him for membership. He won the Amateur again in 1974, beating Jim Gabrielsen of the United States in a tense final at Muirfield. One up playing the last, Trevor played his fourth shot before his opponent had played his second but won the hole with a 6.

He then made the mistake of turning professional after "an agony of indecision". He tried, and failed, to get his card in the United States, found the European Tour "not great" and tried his luck in South Africa. "I played rubbish all along the way," he said and after two and a half years recognised that it was time to walk away and go back into business. Norman Russell recognised a soul in torment and suggested he rejoin the Club, which he did but could not play in competitions until he was reinstated

Rodney James receiving the Staffordshire Open Championship trophy in 1963, aged twenty

as an amateur. "I had to wait three years while I got rid of my 'professional edge'," Trevor said – the inverted commas are his – and although he played some county golf for Staffordshire the glory days had gone.

Some fellows from Featherston Road

Rodney James was one of a raft of gifted juniors, many of them from the hotbed of golf that was Featherston Road in Streetly, who joined the Club in the 1950s. A talented sportsman and a particularly good cricketer, Rodney played golf for England in the home internationals of 1974 and 1975, having been first reserve in 1966. He was Staffordshire Boys champion in 1959; Staffordshire Open champion in 1963 and 1966 and leading amateur on four other occasions; Staffordshire Amateur champion in 1965; Midland Amateur champion in 1968 and 1972; and won the Harlech Gold Cross twice. In 1974 he won the Scrutton Jug for the best aggregate eight rounds in the Brabazon Trophy, the English Amateur Strokeplay Championship, and the Berkshire Trophy.

71

David Pepper (captain 1989-1991, president 2004-2006), former chairman of the General, Championship and Rules Committees of The Royal and Ancient Golf Club

Rodney, Club captain in 1985-1987, went on to perform sterling service as an administrator and was an England selector; the chairman of the Walker Cup selectors when Great Britain and Ireland won in the United States for the first time, at Peachtree in Georgia in 1989; and served on the R&A Championship committee in three decades and on the Implements and Ball committee, deliberating on equipment. One of his most important roles was supervising the pin placing at the Open.

Little Aston's James gang also included Rodney's brother Brian and sister Dianna, their parents Roy and Jean, who was Ladies' captain at the time of the fiftieth anniversary celebrations, and grandfather H.W. (Bert) Shipley, universally known as 'Ship', an architect in Walsall, who joined the club in 1924 and played for Staffordshire. Rodney's sons Anthony and Edward are low handicap golfers and granddaughter Isabella is a junior associate member.

David Pepper was another of the Featherston Road intake to attain distinction in the wider golfing world. In 1958 at the age of seventeen David won the Staffordshire Boys Championship, at Little Aston, by five shots with rounds of 89 and 80, the lowest round of the championship. Rodney James had rounds of 96 and 94; Lawrence (L.G.M.) Pepper had 101 and 100; and Trevor Homer, playing out of Calthorpe Park, now Great Barr, had 107 and 109. David was also fifth in the Carris Trophy that year and in 1959 reached his lowest handicap of 2. He was a member of the Repton team that won the Halford Hewitt in 1963 (when cousin Richard was also on the team) and 1986 and at the Harlech Easter Meeting of 1965 won the Winchelsea Foursomes with David Warmington, who will be happy to give you a blow by blow account of every shot they played over the six rounds. One of David P's proudest playing moments was returning the best gross score in the R&A Autumn medal in 1974. He tied with Dick Smith and Brian Chapman, both Walker Cup players who had the

Staffordshire County Finals, 1956. Staffordshire won the event with a team of six,
including Little Aston members Roger Bayliss, John Beharrell and Bob Church
(respectively second, third and seventh from the left)

misfortune to come up against Jack Nicklaus when they played in 1959 and 1961 respectively. David was third in the play-off.

It was as an administrator that David excelled. He started early, as treasurer of the Midland Junior Golfing Society in 1959, and progressed from there. At Little Aston he was treasurer for ten years, captain in 1989-1991 and president in 2004-2006. After joining the R&A in 1967 they made full use of his expertise and attention to detail and he became a fixture at the Open Championship, ultimately as chairman of the Championship committee with the duty of making the final speech in front of millions. He has had the rare distinction of being chairman not only of the Championship committee but also of the Rules of Golf committee and the General committee. He is a man held in high esteem but thankfully his modesty more than equals his ability.

David and his brother Lawrence (Lol) were introduced to the game by their parents Max and Jean, and their cousin Richard has been a member of the Club for more than sixty years. Angie, David's wife, was Ladies' captain in centenary year.

Patrick and Edward Hooper and Peter Denham, whose parents were all active members of the Club, completed the Featherston contingent of that era.

73

F.W.G. Church, a golden oldie

Bob Church, who came from Sheffield originally, was a scratch golfer for many years and a great golfing buddy of John Morgan. Bob loved to practise and was always looking for *the secret* but never quite managed to turn his dedicated dirt digging into success at the top level. He was a very steady player prone to streaks of putting brilliance and a great team man. He was a stalwart of Staffordshire golf and one of his best moments was when Staffordshire won the County Championship at Little Aston in 1956 beating Yorkshire and Surrey on consecutive days with a team featuring Charlie Stowe, Howard Thirlby, both Penn, Cecil Beamish, South Staffs, Roger Bayliss, South Staffs and Little Aston, another of the Club's England internationals, John Beharrell and Bob himself.

Bob seemed to get better as he got older and at the age of seventy-one travelled to America and won a competition that included former Walker Cup players of the calibre of Bill Campbell. Aged eighty-four Bob won Lawrence Batley's event for the over-80s with a gross score that bettered his age. His wife Barbara, far from being a golf widow, was a staunch member of the Ladies' section for nearly forty years.

Ann Booth is slipping in here, undoubtedly to her embarrassment, because she too was a Staffordshire stalwart, a player of real ability who represented England as a girl and as a senior but was never a full international, although she did make the reserve list in 1986, at the age of forty-one. She won the Staffordshire Championship seven times between 1965 and 1986, including three years in a row from 1970-1972 and was runner-up eight times. She played for the county first team continuously from 1962-1993; in 1962 and 1965 Staffordshire won the county championship and Kay Denham and Bridget Jackson, also members of Little Aston, were in the winning teams too; and in 1986 Ann was made a life member of Staffordshire County Ladies Golf Association. She was also county captain and an England selector.

Chris Poxon, who joined the Club from Whittington in 1990, has been another mainstay of Staffordshire golf, winning the county championship twice and he won the Midlands Foursomes three times, playing with Martin Biddle, of Warwickshire. Myles Pearson, a Staffordshire champion of more recent vintage, is embarking on a professional career.

Families from A-Z, more or less …

There is not room in the book to list all the members from A-Z and the positions they have held so apologies to anyone, worthy or otherwise, not mentioned by name; you are included in spirit simply by virtue of being a

Ann Booth (née Coxill) playing in the British Girls Championship

member. We will start towards the end of the alphabet with the Warmingtons not least because Thomas Warmington was there at the very beginning, a founder member, present at the Grand Hotel on Friday 15th May 1908. Alfie Warmington was captain in 1948-50 and president in 1956-1958 and David Warmington was president in 1996-98. David's wife Lesley was Ladies captain from 2004 to 2006, and their children Richard and Sally are also members.

The Andrews family cannot boast the length of service of the Warmintons but Neil, captain in 2005-2007, has ended up living, by happy coincidence, in a house with impeccable Little Aston connections: it was once owned by Charles Arnold, the man who started it all. Neil's brother Keith, a member of the Championship committee of the R&A who serves on the referees panel, was captain in 1993-1995 and their mother Cynthia, a Warwickshire county player and captain in her younger days, won the Staffordshire Veterans Championship in 1985 and later became president of the Staffordshire Vets. Neil was an Oxford Blue and his daughter Jenny was captain of the Oxford University Ladies team. Anne, Keith's wife, played county golf for Cheshire, Warwickshire and Staffordshire and served on the Board of the English Women's Golf Association. Daniel, David and Tim, sons of Neil and Keith, are also members.

The less serious side of the family's golfing tradition was embodied by Barrie, Neil and Keith's father, who pretty well appointed himself the Club's shadow captain in perpetuity, to keep an eye on the committee. The so-called shadow cabinet, a loose amalgam of like-minded seniors, only ever met informally, in the bar. "Father was fairly opinionated," Keith said, "and he liked to tell everyone what he thought and how the club should be run. Shadow Captain was very much a nickname, to try and shut him up; it didn't work but nobody took any notice and it became a term of affection."

Finally, not least because Jeremy was captain in centenary year, we come to the Cookes, fine hockey players who developed a passion for golf. At Little Aston there is a Cooke in every nook and cranny, with nine on the books in

Roy James, Barbara McMillan, Alfie Warmington, Binki Warmington, Tom McMillan, Jean James

centenary year. In fact, there have been only two years since 1937 when a Cooke has not been an officer or a committee member. Four Cookes have been captain, three have been president, one has chaired the green committee and three have chaired the house committee.

John, who joined in 1929 and became captain in 1947, was a good player and a passionate supporter of junior golf. He was elected an Honorary Member in 1981 and was awarded the MBE for services to industry in 1984. His brother Kenneth joined in 1946, was captain in 1983-1985 and was elected president just a year later. He and Heather, his second wife, were largely responsible for the creation of the Little Aston Geriatrics Society, which meets three or four times a year. Brian, John's son, became a junior member and eventually reduced his handicap to 3. He had two spells on the committee, twenty-four years in total and was captain in 1979-81, president in 1998-2000, then, later, chairman.

Jeremy, one of Kenneth's five children, is the latest Cooke to be entrusted with tending the broth and as a former honorary house steward he is well versed in looking after the needs of the inner man, and woman, and ensuring the comfort of members. He received exemplary guidance from his father-in-law, Ted Rose, a former member and noted bon viveur. The ladies in particular are grateful to Jeremy for upgrading their facilities although his friends insist there is no truth in the rumour that he recognised the need for improvements after falling asleep in their locker room at the end of an annual dinner.

Six foot seven in his stockinged feet, Jeremy was an accomplished hockey player who took up golf in the early 1970s. He is rarely comfortable in a high wind but hits the ball a long way and on his day can beat anyone.

The Club remains in safe hands.

Golden Jubilee dinner dance
Binki Warmington, Alfie Warmington,
Kitty Cooke, John Cooke

The Little Aston Golf Club

Golden Jubilee Dinner Dance
at the Town Hall, Sutton Coldfield
on Friday, 6th June, 1958

Evening Dress

Reception at 7.30 p.m.–8.0 p.m.   Dancing 8.0 p.m.–1.0 a.m.

Rodney James

David Warmington

Richard Pepper

Tom Dippie

John Beharrell

Arthur Gregory

John Church

Pam Dippie

Richard Hill

Brian Cooke

David Moseley

David Pepper

Peter Denham

Rachel Moseley

Tom McMillan jun

Chapter Ten

In Their Own Words

ARTHUR GREGORY, who died in 2010 at the age of ninety-eight, wrote this wonderful letter to John Beharrell on 26th June 2008. It was handwritten, legible, lucid and candid. The additions, in square brackets, are for clarification and, occasionally, correction.

> Dear John,
>
> It was very kind and thoughtful of you to send me the Brochure — thank you very much.
>
> I think I am now probably The Oldest Member (viz. P. G. Wodehouse!). I am approaching 97 now and I joined the Klub in 1948 when "Jinky" was Hon. Sec. — 60 years ago and I actively played over 50 of them.

I came to Walsall to practise from my home in St. Annes-on-Sea where I was a member of the Old Links, which was a lovely club to belong to in those days, many survivors of the Great War, who were great fun to play with. The professional was Phil. Rodgers, a double MM [Military Medal] holder who made his own clubs. I used to spend hours talking to him in his shop when I first joined as a Junior Member. At the end of War II my Regiment was stationed on the German-Dutch border. I had a recce round in my jeep and came across a 9-hole golf course with the pro in a wooden hut. He lent me a bag of clubs and ball to have a round. When I pulled them out of the drainpipe bag I found they were wooden shafts and the steel heads were stamped "P. H. Rodgers, St. Annes Old Links"!

I didn't know anyone at Little Aston but when we moved from Walsall to Streetly, I applied to join and was invited to have lunch with Jinky and the Captain, followed by a round of golf. I played off 9 at St. Annes and I suppose that's why I got in.

Jinky died only a few weeks later and John Cooke became Acting Hon. Sec. until the AGM in November when Norman Russell was appointed. [John was captain at the time and Norman was appointed immediately after Jinky's death]

That AGM was most acrimonious [1948 fine, 1949 acrimonious]. A group of members, led, I think, by Hubert Lindop, had decided to put up their choice (I think it was Alan Denham. He was certainly one of the group) for a vacancy on the Committee. The Notice for the AGM had specified the Committee's choice to fill the vacancy and the Group put forward a Resolution to compete against him.

I think the "Establishment" over-reacted to this. It had been hitherto not done. The Committee said they would resign en bloc if the Group's Resolution was passed. The Group were accused of "plotting" in the Four Oaks pub! Old Edge of Edge & Ellison Solicitors in Birmingham, was the President and in the Chair. He refused several times to allow the Group's Resolution to be put and words became quite nasty. The Group appeared to have anticipated the President's re-action and had arranged for a member supporter in the shape of A. J. Flint, a well-known Birmingham barrister, to speak. He stood up with a large tome containing The Companies Act and started quoting sections to Old Edge. The President finally gave way, the Resolution was put to the meeting and heavily defeated, its only support came from the few in the Group plus A. J. Flint! As a lawyer, I was quite interested in what went on but as a new member I kept my mouth shut! So ended an attempt to bring Parliamentary Democracy to the Club which did very well without it for the next 60 years anyway!

In those days, Sunday morning was the time when everyone turned up to play 4-balls and the lounge was crowded afterwards, as it is on Saturdays now. After being informed that I had been elected a member, I went up on Sunday morning and was, of course, not fixed up, not knowing anyone. I watched Mart. Lewis supervising the 1st tee, telling members when they could drive. One member took out a 1-iron to drive with and Mart told him he could not use an iron on "his" tees – he must take a wood. When the last four were preparing to go out, one of them approached me and asked me if I was a visitor. I told him I was a new member and he said, "If you are not fixed up you must join us. We will have a 5-ball, 3 against 2" and so I did.

I thought what a decent thing that was and what a good Club I had joined. I learned later that he was a member of the Committee but long gone now, of course, and I can't remember his name.

With regard to the comments in the Brochure, I think Norman Russell did a fine job, keeping LA on the right lines for 50 years. I did not always agree with him and he did not like not being agreed with but the comments are spot on. He didn't like me calling and referring to him as "The Ayatollah" either! With regard to Charlie Ward, the Brochure states that he was 6th in the Vardon Trophy but surely he won it round about the time you won the Amateur. There was always the photograph of the two of you with your trophies hanging opposite the bar.

We persuaded him to make up a 4-ball with us once and he went round in 65.

You couldn't help but like him. I arranged to have a lesson from him in mid-week once. We went to the vicinity of the Ladies' tee, he with his bag of balls and he sent a caddy down the 1st to pick up the balls. He started off, "Now let's see you hit one." I hit one dead straight down the middle. "Oh," he said, "You don't need a lesson. Just keep hitting them like that."! Going into the shop, I offered to pay for the "lesson" but he would have none of it, so I bought a new set of woods from him instead!

The Brochure deals – very diplomatically – with "The Ladies" question but there is no doubt that the Club's reputation concerning ladies was a joke with other clubs – all that not being allowed in front of the men's lounge window and not being allowed in the Car Park on Saturdays and Sundays. These rules led to some very hilarious situations.

I hadn't been a member very long and having played in a Sunday morning 4-ball, we were having a drink in the crowded lounge when one of the older members shouted out "a Woman, a woman peering at us through the window – where's the Secretary". Norman Russell went to the patio door and came back saying "They are asking for a chap named Gregory"! It was Buster Bleasby and his wife, Joanne, an old Army friend from the 1940s who had stayed on in the Army and just been posted to Sutton Coldfield. He had called at home and been told I was golfing at LA. I had to take them to the Four Oaks to celebrate our re-newed friendship.

The Oxford Circuit of the Bar held their Annual Meeting on a Sunday at the Club and one of the barristers from Nottingham brought his wife with him to pull his trolly. When John Anderson saw a woman on the course on a Sunday morning, instead of "turning a blind eye", he went to the trouble of getting in his car and driving down the course looking for a Committee member to report the awful news. He came across Ken Cooke who said "It's nothing to do with me. I am House Steward"! When the Bar players came in for a pre-lunch drink they made a big circle round a table on the terrace and when the Steward went out to take their drinks order, he came to the lady who said she would have a gin and tonic. The Steward had the temerity to tell her that he could not serve her where she was sitting in front of the men's lounge but if she would move to a table in front of the Ladies part of the Clubhouse he would do so. She said "I'll still have a gin and tonic" and didn't move. The Steward served her gin and tonic with the other drinks.

All this farce took place in the presence and hearing of "Scotty" Baker, a member of the Oxford Circuit Golf Society and then one of the top 3 Judges in the country, being President of the Probate, Divorce and Admiralty Division of the High Court. At the time, I thought that all the fuss about the lady wife caddy could not have done the Club any good.

The final farce came one Saturday afternoon when Roderick Chantrill arranged for his girl friend to meet him after his game of golf. I had played in a 4-ball with Jim Connor, Roderick and Guy Chantrill. Roderick had told his girl friend about the "no ladies on the Car Park at week-ends" rule and told her how to re-act. Ian Houston was Hon. House Steward at the time, I think. He happened to be in the Gents. toilet which had a small window looking out on to the Car Park and he saw Roderick's dolly bird seated at the wheel of an open sports car on the Car Park. He went out to move her off. "Madam," he said "I am afraid ladies are not allowed in this Car Park on a Saturday. Will you please move away." Roderick's instructions were put into force – she just looked at him and said "Bollocks". Houston was so shaken he made no reply and had to slink back to the Clubhouse! Roderick told me all this.

I sincerely apologise for this long letter but writing is about the only activity I have now except to shuffle a few yards to the loo with the assistance of a zimmer frame! I had hoped to attend the Centenary Dinner but it was not to be.

I have very happy memories of golfing at St. Annes Old Links and Little Aston. On a Summer day seated between the 8th green and the 13th, I used to say that it was the best place in the World to be.

Speaking or, rather, writing, of the 13th, I wonder if the Brewer's Weeping Spruce which I planted on the right of the green is flourishing? Norman Russell was furious with me. When he gave me a money voucher after winning the Charlie Ward Salver with John Anderson, I went to Notcutts at Shirley and bought the Brewer's Weeping Spruce tendering the LA voucher in payment! Notcutts telephoned LA to confirm its authenticity and Norman had to pay them instead of the pro. for something bought at his Shop!

I planted 2 Davidia Involucrata on the 15th but they both died – the rabbits ate the bark. I enclose cheque for £25.00 (which is about the cost of getting one from Burncoose Nurseries) and I should be grateful if you would get Andrew to plant one in a suitable place (they grow big, as you know) to celebrate the 100th Anniversary.

Thank you again, John, for your letter – I greatly appreciate it.

Wishing the members of the Club good golfing and good weather for the rest of the Celebrations and may the Club flourish for another 100 years!

With kind regards to Veronica and yourself.

Yours sincerely,

Arthur

Little Aston has never had a suggestion book as such but members used to put pen to paper, or paper in typewriter, on occasion for the delectation and delight of the honorary secretary. John Owen, a rugby man who played for England, was, and is, wittier and more whimsical than most and here is his version of events when he learned that he had signed for the wrong score in the March medal of 1991. His marker was John Slater:

Dear Norman

Thank you for your letter of 11 March and I am indebted to you for drawing my attention to the error concerning my handicap. Early in the round I mentioned to J Slater, my playing partner, that had we been playing in a Stableford, the deduction of one shot per hole on my card would have been a simple calculation even for one with mental powers so sadly reduced by age and infirmity. Clearly I was still guilty of over-estimating his mental capacity and being of a trusting nature I merely signed the card with which he presented me at the conclusion of the round.

I realise, even before you point it out, that the responsibility for checking the card is mine and I have therefore no cause for complaint. I regret that my own mental balance was still somewhat disturbed by the harrowing experience I had suffered at the 15th hole. In the expectation that you will derive some interest, if not pleasure, in hearing of this experience I am taking the liberty of repeating it.

I should say by way of background that, having completed the outward half in 38 shots, I was already in some anticipation of the laudatory if insincere comments that I would be receiving from fellow members on my return to the clubhouse with a net score of around 60. Some ill luck on the following five holes had slightly reduced these expectations but standing on the 15th tee I could afford to drop a shot a hole and still break even.

My drive was disappointing finishing as it did only ten yards from the tee and deep in the trees. Nevertheless a sideways chop and a reasonable iron left me where my drive should have gone for a total of only three. A superb 3 wood soared over the cross bunker but floated slightly on the breeze to finish just outside the trees to the left and no more than sixty yards short of the green. I still had a chance of a six, at worst a seven.

It was then that it happened.

As we approached the cross bunker I described the scene to Slater whose failing sight and lack of stature prevented him from seeing it for himself. A black mongrel crossing the public footpath had pounced on my ball and proceeded to worry it mercilessly. Its owner then took the ball from the dog's mouth and looking round to see that no one was near flung it several yards into the trees. When we finally arrived on the scene the dog and its owner were nowhere to be seen but we found the ball in an unplayable position deep in the trees.

In deference to his age, experience and handicap I sought a ruling from the said Slater who affirmed that the ball should be played where it lay but without penalty. Even in retirement and his dotage the advice of an estate agent should not be relied upon as later perusal of the rule book confirmed.

Calling on all the skill at my disposal I nevertheless managed to extricate the ball from the trees in only two shots and finally emerged myself just in time to see it in the jaws of a golden labrador which happened to be passing with a family of five. The owner declined my request to take the dog on to the green before forcing it to release the ball but instead took it from its mouth and thoughtfully placed it in a hole just off the fairway. My several attempts to propel it from there to the green appeared to afford considerable amusement to the family who had interrupted their walk to watch. The inability to give full vent to my feelings was an added strain.

The resulting ten at this hole disturbed my customary equanimity and several more shots were dropped on the final three holes. It is therefore of considerable comfort to learn that but for the thoughtlessness of my partner, my score should have been 75 rather than 76 and contrasts with his rather unfeeling remark that in all his considerable experience he had never seen such a variation in the two halves of a medal round.

Thank you again for your solicitude and it is reassuring to know that ne'er a sparrow falls but the Hon Sec is aware of it. The thought has done much to see me through the last few days.

Yours sincerely,

J.E. Owen

Chapter Eleven

Ladies

Y OU MAY have noticed that women have been popping up here and there throughout the book, mothers, wives, girlfriends, sisters, daughters, that sort of thing, but Little Aston, a most civilised place in most regards, has a mixed reputation when it comes to its treatment of women.

A lot of it is myth and legend but quite often the Club has not helped itself, with the enforcement of policies that seem petty in the extreme, especially when it comes to the car park and the terrace. That led to an appearance in Hansard in 1999 when Labour M.P. Derek Wyatt branded the Club sexist and resurrected the story, strenuously denied, that a woman was reprimanded, in writing, for parking in the car park and walking in front of the clubhouse to rush to the aid of her husband, who had suffered a heart attack.

Stuff and nonsense said the Club but there are plenty of women who remember run-ins on the terrace. The wife of one golf correspondent recalled "I know very little about the club except I got into severe trouble there, in the late 1970s, when I walked along the terrace! I had no idea that ladies were barred from it!" She shrugged and accepted the status quo. Her daughters and granddaughters would shrug and go elsewhere.

Arthur Gregory, who at the age of ninety-seven sent a beautifully handwritten letter, reproduced in chapter ten, to John Beharrell in centenary year, was embarrassed by such pettiness, "There is no doubt that the Club's reputation concerning ladies was a joke with other clubs – all that not being allowed in front of the men's lounge window and not being allowed in the car park on Saturdays and Sundays …"

John Owen, as so often, had his own take on the matter:

The popular conception of Little Aston is often centred on the alleged rule that prevents lady members from walking across the terrace in front of the men's bar. Much is made of this but in reality no such rule has ever existed. There is, however, a kernel of truth in this misconception and a story passed on through generations of Warmingtons may throw some light on it.

In the mid 1930s there was a member named Willie Pollock, a serial gambler, whose wife Mabel not only disapproved of this habit but also most of the other pleasures enjoyed by her husband. Legend has it that Mabel was a formidable woman and that Willie's life was far from easy.

There was a professional tournament at Little Aston and Willie Pollock offered odds of 10 to 1 against a victory by Midlands born hero Archie Compston. This was taken up by a good number of punters and with Compston well ahead of the field after three rounds Willie was staring in the face of a pay-out in excess of ten thousand pounds. Fortunately for him Compston, while still leading, hooked his approach to the 12th green into the marshy area that was superseded by the present lake and the resulting ten destroyed his chances.

Despite this narrow escape, Willie Pollock continued to promote betting activities and members would play cards for considerable sums mainly after but

260   GOLF ILLUSTRATED   August 20th, 1926

People Who Really Matter in Golf.

No. 9.—The non-playing lady who calls for hubby in the car.

sometimes even before a round of golf. They would also play "golf" using the sequential numbers on a pound note to determine who won each hole. Eventually, after too many spoiled dinners, Mabel took to hammering on the large window of the men's lounge to insist on Willie's immediate return home.

Whether through a fear that such tactics might be adopted by other wives or through genuine sympathy for the down-trodden Willie Pollock, it was determined that Mabel's interference had to be stopped. Rather than confront her head-on someone came up with the simple stratagem that if ladies in general were to be prevented from using that part of the terrace then by definition they would be unable to bang on the window. Accordingly the steward was instructed to see to it and the crisis was averted.

At the beginning it was probably practicalities rather than male chauvinism that led to the exclusion of women at Little Aston. After all, many of the members had wives who were members of Sutton Coldfield Ladies Golf Club and they often played mixed foursomes together, with the results reported in *The Birmingham Golfer*. However, the fledgling Club was reluctant to overextend itself financially when it came to accommodation and Mr. Farmer, the architect, was asked to amend his original plan and "reduce the size of the rooms and rearrange certain matters". Facilities for women were not incorporated.

The original Articles of Association stated "Words importing the masculine gender only shall include the feminine gender" but the phrase was removed when the articles and bye-laws were revised in 1913. Also, the original rule 38 stated, "Ladies are not eligible for Membership or play and must not be introduced to any part of the Club enclosure or buildings."

In April 1910, Charles Arnold tendered his resignation as honorary secretary but was persuaded to change his mind and the committee decided that he need not "enforce the strict reading of Rule 38" until the General Meeting had considered the matter. The suspicion is that enforcing the ban on women was perhaps creating difficulties between Arnold and Greatrex, who had three golfing daughters and was shortly to acquire, in Irene Precey, a daughter-in-law who was a feisty character and an enthusiastic and able golfer. She later gained a certain notoriety when she was honorary secretary of Sutton Coldfield Ladies in the 1920s and conducted such a heated correspondence with the honorary secretary of the men's club that Robert Fletcher, who wrote the history of Sutton Coldfield Golf Club, said that much of it was unsuitable for publication.

In July 1910, Mr. Caddick suggested striking out the word 'sons' and inserting 'children' in rule 31; and in rule 38 striking out the words 'are not eligible for membership or play and' and the words 'enclosure or'. Mr. Greatrex seconded the motion but Mr. Fyshe proposed the amendment "That it is undesirable to alter the constitution of the Club at the present stage of its existence". Mr. F.J. Clarke seconded the amendment, which was carried by forty-three votes to eight. The notion of daughters having the same rights as sons was presumably too radical at a time when Emmeline Pankhurst and her suffragettes were becoming a force and women in Britain were still eight years away from having limited rights to vote.

The Club's entry in *Nisbet's Golf Year Book* 1914 was unambiguous: "Ladies may not play". However, they had been allowed access to the course and the clubhouse as spectators on special occasions, such as the match between Oxford University and Birmingham in February 1914 and there are plenty of old photographs showing that women were conspicuous by their presence in the crowd at big events.

In June 1915 Mrs. Scott Jones, a member of Sutton Coldfield Ladies Golf Club, asked permission for ladies to play on one day a week but she was turned down on the grounds that such a decision would require a vote at an A.G.M.

Things started to change after the war and in February 1920, in advance of the Professional Meeting at the beginning of March, it was agreed that ladies were to be admitted to the course and clubhouse on the introduction of a member. In November, forty-four members, the Requisitionists, asked for a general meeting to discuss the possibility of ladies playing on the course. This was, in essence, the beginning of the end of Little Aston as an exclusively male golfing preserve.

A sub-committee of Messrs. Scarf, the captain, Barton, Fletcher and Lewis, the honorary secretary, was formed to consider the "subject of Lady Members" and reported no objection in principle to ladies playing on days other than Saturdays, Sundays and general holidays. The sub-committee's three suggestions, none of them "free from objection", were: "Ladies to be made full members of the Club … to play as visitors … to form an entirely separate Club …". The upshot was that on 11th December, at an Extraordinary General Meeting attended by seventy-six members, the Requisitionists were invited to nominate a small committee to meet the committee and "go into the matter in detail with a view of presenting a definitive report to a future general meeting".

In the meantime the Secretary, on the instructions of the committee, wrote to Greatrex and had discussions with his solicitor about extending the lease and subsequently resolved, in March 1921, to take no further action on opening the course to ladies.

They were swishing their clubs eagerly at the gates, however, and would soon be gathering on the first tee. In November 1921, Mr. Frank Bill, the honorary house steward, gave notice that he would move a resolution "to enable members to introduce ladies to the Club as visitors one day a week". In January 1922, at a Special General Meeting, attended by seventy members, Bill proposed and Scarf seconded a change to the bye-laws and regulations and the following bye-law was adopted, carried by an overwhelming majority:

That Members of the Club be allowed to introduce Ladies as visitors to the course and Club House for the purposes of play or otherwise one day in each week to be fixed by the Committee and not being a Saturday, Sunday or public holiday, and subject to such green fees and conditions as the Committee may from time to time determine.

Ladies were allowed to play on a Wednesday for a green fee of 1s. if playing with a member, 2s. if not. C.F. Arnold and H.E. Palethorpe were the first to be thanked for donating prizes for ladies and mixed competitions. This modest beginning was the catalyst for more changes and eighteen months later basic accommodation was provided for ladies in the clubhouse. Messrs. Streathers had an estimate of £47. 10s. 0d. accepted and there was "a door put in through the Secretary's room to the shower bath so the latter might be used for the convenience of the ladies".

Then, most momentous of all, in 1924, after discussions about the extension of the lease, the Club bought the freehold of the land from Greatrex. Initially, a new twenty-one year lease was accepted because a price of £12,000 for the freehold was considered too high and the terms of the lease stated: "Ladies to be at liberty to play on any day other than Saturdays, Sundays and public holidays." The freehold price was subsequently reduced

10/-

THIS INDENTURE made the _eleventh_ day of _May_ One thousand nine hundred and twenty-five BETWEEN THE LITTLE ASTON GOLF CLUB LIMITED whose registered office is situate at Little Aston in the Parish of Shenstone in the County of Stafford (hereinafter called "the Club" of the one part ARTHUR WHITEHOUSE GREATREX of Little Aston aforesaid Esquire (hereinafter called "the Vendor") of the second part and ARTHUR WILLIAM GREATREX and GILBERT GREATREX both residing at Little Aston aforesaid sons of the Vendor of the third part WHEREAS by an Agreement in writing bearing even date herewith and made between the Vendor of the one part, and the Club of the other part the Vendor has contracted to sell to the Club certain hereditaments at Little Aston aforesaid the greater part whereof are now in the occupation of the Club as Lessees thereof and are used by them for the purposes of a Golf Course and hereditaments AND WHEREAS upon the treaty for such sale it was agreed that it should be made subject to certain provisions enabling ladies to play Golf upon the said hereditaments but that such provisions should not be incorporated in the Conveyance of the hereditaments to the Club but should be embodied in a separate document NOW THEREFORE in pursuance of such agreement and in consideration of the premises The Club for themselves their successors and assigns hereby COVENANT and AGREE with the Vendor and the parties hereto of the third part jointly and with each and every of them separately as follows that is to say:-

1.   During such time or times as the said hereditaments

or any part thereof shall be used for the purposes of
playing Golf thereon ladies shall be permitted to play
Golf on the Course upon all days other than Saturdays
Sundays and Public Holidays when the Course is available
for Members of the Club and also to have the use of
such suitable portion of the Club House as the Committee
of the Club shall decide unless and until other
accommodation shall be provided for them. The right
may be suspended on Competition days or other special
days at the discretion of the Committee.

2.   Members of the Club may introduce ladies as
visitors to the Course and Club House for the purposes
of play or otherwise on any of the days aforesaid
subject to the payment of such Green Fees as the Club
shall from time to time determine but not exceeding
the Green Fees payable by male visitors.

3.   The Committee of the Club may grant to a lady
introduced by a Member and approved by them a Visitors
Permit lasting for a year available for the aforesaid
days on payment in lieu of Green Fees of such a sum as
the Club shall from time to time determine but not
exceeding one half of the annual subscription payable
by playing members of the Club.

4.   The Vendor shall during his lifetime have the
right to introduce ladies for play with him on Sunday
afternoons.

IN WITNESS whereof the Club have set their Common Seal hereto.

THE COMMON SEAL of THE LITTLE ASTON GOLF CLUB)
LIMITED was hereunto affixed in the presence   )
of :-   )
G Douglas Smith   ) Members of
Frank J Edge   ) ~~Directors~~.
) the Committee

Virgild Bignood   Secretary.

91

A painting of the clubhouse by George Willis Pryce (late 19th/early 20th century artist) showing a lady
Note the gang plank traversing

permit holder on the 18th green and others sitting outside the newly constructed extension circa 1928. the centre of the bunker

to £10,000 and the agreement was designed to secure the future of women at the Club, including as it did the proviso:

That the Club enter into a deed of covenant with Mr. Greatrex and his two sons that ladies are to be permitted to play upon the course and to have the use of such suitable portion of the club-house as the Committee shall decide until other accommodation be provided for them on all days of the week, other than Saturdays, Sundays and Public Holidays.

Furthermore, "Mr. Arthur Whitehouse Greatrex of Little Aston Park shall during his lifetime have the right to introduce ladies for play with him on Sunday afternoons."

A Special General Meeting was called for 25th April 1925 and the resolutions were passed unanimously. Messrs. Edge, Smith and Bigwood, the honorary secretary, were authorised to sign the Deed of Covenant on behalf of the Little Aston Golf Club.

Permit holders

It was a hugely significant date for the Club in more ways than one. The members now owned their course and a notice went up on the board pointing out that ladies would be allowed to play as visitors. In June, it was decided that they would be allowed to have yearly visiting permits at a fee of three and a half guineas each and within a month twenty-four ladies had become permit holders, including Mrs. W. Greatrex, the formidable Irene, nee Precey, Mrs. G. Greatrex, her daughter Isobel and Mrs. W. Bigwood, wife of the honorary secretary. That same month Greatrex presented a pair of silver bowls for a mixed foursomes competition of eighteen holes medal, ladies' handicap limit 24. The trophies are still played for every year and the competition is now held on a Sunday.

The minutiae of Club life now included references to the building of ladies' tees and the cleaning of ladies' clubs and in 1926 plans were made to extend the clubhouse to provide suitable accommodation for the ladies. They decided that "it would be necessary to have a lounge 20ft x 16ft, together with a locker room with 50 lockers". It did not take long for lavatories and a drying room to be added and there was plenty of discussion after Mr. Hobbiss had drawn up the plans. In July everything was delayed because of the coal strike and "the labour un-rest prevailing".

A sum of £2,000 was suggested for the additions, alterations and improvements and the sale to Scribbans of the walled garden and much of the lake for that amount earlier in the year financed the project. In a neat bit of business the Club, who had paid Greatrex £71 per acre when they bought the land, sold Scribbans his five acres, three rods and fifteen perches for about £335 an acre.

The building work was approved at an E.G.M. in October and "it was resolved that the work in connection with the Club House be proceeded with at the earliest possible moment". By May 1927 a telephone extension was being organised for the ladies' room and at the A.G.M. in September "a hearty vote of thanks was passed to Mr. Hobbiss" and he and Mr. Edge were presented with gold cigarette cases at a supper in 1928.

On 18th November 1929, the honorary secretary wrote to Scribbans about allowing him "to have a permit to introduce visitors to Little Aston without entering same in the Visitors' Book". It was, Wilfrid Bigwood stressed, "a new departure" but for a fee of thirty guineas per annum the Club could see its way to allowing Scribbans and members of his family living at the Hall to introduce visitors to the course "providing they are playing with members of the family". Scribbans did not quibble, sent the cheque and the annual permit was issued on 1st January 1930. The arrangement lasted until he died in 1935.

Aston Wood Ladies Golf Club

In the meantime, the ladies had set about organising themselves and on 5th August 1926, at a meeting at The Corner House, Four Oaks, home of the Bigwoods, a group of fifteen permit holders voted Irene Greatrex into the chair and Mrs. Bigwood proposed that "a Ladies Golf Union (LGU) club be formed in connection with Little Aston Golf Club". Mrs. Scott Jones, who was then captain at SCLGC, seconded the motion, which was carried unanimously. Mrs. Betteridge proposed, seconded by Miss Keeling "that the name of the Club be Aston Wood Ladies Golf Club (AWLGC)". A subscription of 10s. 6d. was to be payable on 1st July and the club was to be open to permit holders of Little Aston Golf Club only. Mrs. Greatrex was elected captain, an office she was to hold for fifteen years, Mrs. A.E. Wiley Ladies' secretary and Mrs. Douglas Smith and Mrs. Garner were elected committee members. A bank account was opened at Lloyds Bank, Sutton Coldfield and it was left to the committee to draft the "Rules of the Club".

The first committee meeting was held on 8th September, by which time the LGU had recognised AWLGC and awarded a standard scratch of 77. The committee ordered competition scorecards; arranged a golf meeting for 20th September, open to members only, eighteen hole medal in the morning and foursomes in the afternoon; fixed monthly medals for the first Monday in every month, except bank holidays, entry fee 1s.; organised a running bogey to be held daily throughout the year, entry sixpence; and ordered LGU tee markers from Mart Lewis, the professional. Mrs. Greatrex lent a clock for the ladies' lounge and Mrs. Garner presented notice-boards.

Early members of the Greatrex family

There were fifty-nine permit holders by July 1927 and thirteen of them turned up for the first A.G.M. of AWLGC at the captain's home, The Croft, Little Aston. The club rules were read and approved and Mrs. Scott Jones and Mrs. Horton were thanked for presenting, respectively, a silver salver for the senior final medal and a spoon for the junior medal. Senior and junior were the handicap divisions.

The men of Little Aston were allowed to mark extra day scores for the ladies and in September 1928 there was a qualifying round for the Charles Heeley Bowl, which is still going strong. More trophies were added to the collection, including twenty-four medal spoons. At the A.G.M. in 1928 there was a proposal to buy cigarette boxes as prizes for each division of the final bogey, cost not to exceed £5. Replica trophies, in this case silver match boxes, were often given out and kept by the winners. Despite all this expenditure the committee halved the subscription to 5s. for the year 1929-1930 and the number of permit holders increased from sixty-nine to seventy-four.

Hot water reached the ladies' cloakroom in 1929 and electric light at last illuminated the lavatories in 1933. The pioneering permit holders often played thirty-six holes a day, carrying their clubs. By the beginning of the 1930s the Open Meeting was so popular that the ladies were allowed to use the members' lounge for the day. The boundaries still had to be respected of course and the men responsible for inviting ladies into the clubhouse one Saturday were reprimanded and told to make sure it did not happen again. For Hagen and Shute's exhibition match in 1933, the permit holders were classed as visitors and had to pay an admission charge but use of the clubhouse was "specially extended to Ladies and limited to members, permit holders and friends".

In 1935, a new rule book was issued for the ladies' club and the name was changed to Aston Wood Golf Club, which appears on all the trophies presented between 1935 and 1945.

In 1937, a subscription was sent to support the Midland Championship and in 1938 the ladies took part in the Daily Telegraph Golf Competition and the Wakefield Cup. Staffordshire and Worcestershire were given courtesy of the course for a county match in April; there was a Daily Telegraph Ladies match in May; and in June a Midland Ladies team played a South African team. Mrs. Bigwood also organised events in aid of the N.S.P.C.C. and the LGU were keen to use the course. As early as 1934 they had asked permission for lady visitors from the Dominions and Colonies to be made honorary members for a week but were turned down because, not being a ladies' golf club, no such facility could be granted; a request to hold "the Open Championship" at Little Aston in 1936 was also declined because "the accommodation at our disposal would not be adequate to cater for the

Irene Greatrex 1952

requirements of such a competition, further, Club Rules only allow for play for ladies on Weekdays".

At the A.G.M. of 1937 Mrs. Kendrick, Mrs. Owen and Mrs. Tait, so influential after World War II, were all present but the ladies' minutes of 29th January 1938 were incomplete and unsigned and there were no more minutes until 9th January 1946.

Old attitudes died hard even in wartime. In October 1939:

> it was resolved that it was not a convenient time to recommend that for the duration of the war, Ladies be allowed to play at weekends on the Course ... but further consideration would be given to the matter the beginning of Spring.

In March 1940, the committee resolved that ladies might play on the course on Good Fridays and public holidays for the duration of the war but at a special meeting on 20th April, attended by sixty-five members, resolutions that would have allowed ladies to play on the course on Saturday mornings and Sunday afternoons were not carried. In 1940 eighty-four permits were issued; in 1941 it was down to fifty-four; and in 1942 it was thirty-two.

ASTON WOOD GOLF CLUB.

Name.. Competition...

Date.. Signature of Scorer..

Mark's Score		Yards	Par	Stroke Index	Score	Won x Lost— Ha'd o	Mark's Score		yards	Par	Stroke Index	Score	Won x Lost— Ha'd o
	1	353	4	13				10	411	5	3		
	2	389	5	5				11	296	4	10		
	3	459	5	7				12	439	5	6		
	4	291	4	1				13	147	3	17		
	5	153	3	15				14	278	4	16		
	6	398	5	9				15	483	5	2		
	7	350	4	4				16	333	4	8		
	8	351	4	11				17	312	4	14		
	9	133	3	18				18	363	5	12		
	Out	2877	37					In	3062	39			

Holes Won ....
Holes Lost ....
Result   ....

Ont   ....
In   ....

Total ....
Handicap ....
Nett ... ..

Par Score   76

The standard scratch of the ladies course was 76 between 1931 and 1947. The Permit Holders' LGU Club was often referred to as Aston Wood Golf Club, and engraved as such on some of the Club's trophies, should not be confused with the present neighbouring club of that name

Chapter Twelve

The Ladies' Section

MONEY, AND the need for more of it, contributed to a slight softening of the attitude towards women towards the end of the war when the Club's future finances were a matter of some concern, with the clubhouse alone needing extensive renovation and repair. On 28th April 1945 there was a meeting that was to have far–reaching consequences for lady golfers at Little Aston because "the prevailing opinion was that it was not possible to divorce Finance from the question of Ladies playing on the course on Sundays".

At a Special General Meeting on Saturday 26th May the following resolution was carried unanimously "That Ladies be permitted to play upon the Course on Sunday afternoons from 2.30 p.m. onwards subject to such conditions as the Committee may from time to time determine."

In June, the Committee resolved that:

Permit Holders should now be known as members of Little Aston Golf Club (Ladies' Section), Numbers restricted for the time being to one hundred, with no Entrance Fee. Annual Subscription £4.14s. 6d., and pro rata as for male members. Visitors: Green Fees to be charged as for male members. Number of visits limited to eight times.

The Articles of Association had to be amended in order to establish a section or branch of the Club to be called 'The Ladies' section' and at an E.G.M. on 27th October 1945 it was agreed, among other things, that:

For the purpose of registration the Club is declared to consist of 250 male members but the Committee may when they think fit, register an increase of such members provided that this regulation shall not affect the admission of Ladies or of junior temporary or non–playing members of either sex admitted in pursuance of any Bye law or Rule of the Club.

The Committee saw to it that they were "given very wide powers over the Ladies' section" and regulation (a) laid down the ground rules:

Ladies shall not be allowed to play upon the course or to use the Club House at any time on a Saturday, or on Sunday mornings. They shall not be eligible to attend or vote at any meeting of the Club or take part in the management of the Club or compete for any Club prize unless such competition is specifically made open to Ladies. The Committee shall not have any power to vary this regulation without the sanction of the members of the Club in General Meeting.

On 1st December 1945:

it was resolved to treat Monday, the 24th December, as a Bank Holiday and it was agreed that the Course be open to Ladies for play from 2 p.m. Play was also agreed on Wednesday, 26th December from 2 p.m. It was resolved that Ladies be permitted to play upon the Course on Sunday afternoons from 2 p.m. onwards for the months of December 1945 and January 1946.

Perhaps the winter months were lighter in those days.

The first ladies' committee was Mrs. J.H. Harper, honorary secretary, Mrs. M. Owen, captain, Mrs. D. Barker, Mrs. A. South, the former Ada Scribbans, and Mrs. P. Cozens and the new section blossomed with the limit of members increased to 125 in January 1946 and 150 in early 1949. By then there were 141 members of the Ladies' section and their accommodation and facilities were being stretched to the limit as Mary Beharrell, John's mother, who had taken over as ladies' honorary secretary, made clear in correspondence with Jinky Jinks. She questioned "the wisdom of increasing the membership so rapidly ..." More prosaically, she listed complaints about "our cloak–room. There is no hot water and no foot–bath and a long waiting list for lockers ...".

Jinky responded with his customary good humour:

With the new applications, they consist mainly of wives and relatives of members and this was the original basis laid down but, like all rules, it has been broken on occasion ... Now, with regard to the complaints and the following points about your cloakroom: There should be hot water but you will appreciate that the pipes have to come a considerable way and if the water is run off I think you will find, as we did by examination today, that when the water is run off a good supply of hot is available. It seems rather a waste but in view of the length of supply this course must be necessary to obtain the result.

Footbath: This is the first time I have heard that the ladies desire a footbath; it shall receive immediate attention.

Lockers: There should be several lockers vacant now and I should be glad if you would ask the lady members who use the tin cupboards to write their names on the labels which I shall put on the doors.

I have asked the Steward to immediately get an electrician to look at the electric plug operating the fire ...

In 1951, when the Midland Ladies Open Foursomes resumed after the war, at Brocton Hall, Mary Beharrell and Barbara Harper reached the final with a display of "courageous golf throughout a ding–dong semi–final" but were then beaten by Miss May Evershed and Mrs. Beryl Snape, two Staffordshire county players. Margaret Tait, who became a permit holder in 1937, was captain from 1947-1949 and one of the better players, with a handicap of 7. Kay Denham, who came to golf relatively late in life, joined in 1946 and proved a doughty competitor who became Midland champion in 1951 and

1962 winning Staffordshire team, Christine Bayliss, Ann Coxill, Susan Armitage, Angela Higgott, Marjorie Rickatson. Seated, Bridget Jackson, Jenny Stant, Kay Denham

Staffordshire champion in 1952 and 1955. She played for the Midland team throughout the 1950s and for Staffordshire for more than twenty years, including the county championship winning sides of 1962 and 1965. She was captain of Staffordshire in 1953 and became president in 1967.

The Ladies' section added an extra social and competitive edge to their game with matches against the ground staff and the artisans as well as other clubs. Annual matches against South Staffordshire, Sutton Coldfield, Moor Hall, Edgbaston, Trentham, Brocton Hall and Enville have endured for more than fifty years. The Little Aston ladies were also staunch supporters of Staffordshire and Midland events and won the Staffordshire Scratch League, formerly the Scratch Cup, seven times between 1950 and 1997. Members who played regularly in the scratch teams included Sally Adamson, Anne Andrews, Ann Booth, whose distinguished career is documented elsewhere

John Beharrell and Bridget Jackson at the Little Aston cocktail party, 1956

in the book, Pam Dippie, Jo Hollis, Rachel Moseley, Angie Pepper, Dee Power, Pauline Taylor and Ann Saunders. Anne and Rachel also served as Staffordshire and Derbyshire representatives on the Midland Inter County Scratch League.

Bridget Jackson, whose home club is Handsworth, was a member at Little Aston between 1954 and 1968. Her numerous playing honours included three Curtis Cup appearances and on the administrative front she became president of Staffordshire, ELGA, the English Ladies Golf Association, the LGU and Handsworth and an M.B.E. And she received an honorary doctorate from Birmingham University. She was also a founder member of the Midland Junior Golfing Society, as were John Beharrell and Veronica Anstey.

Ena Dixon–Green, granddaughter of Joseph Clarke, who had sold the land to Greatrex, was a stalwart of the Club for more than fifty years, from permit holder to Honorary Member. She was a bridge grandmaster and a much loved, larger than life character who could both inspire and intimidate as she helped improve the members' skills at the card table. More recently Heather

Lindop, Jo Bigwood and Kate Andrews have devoted much time and effort to running the bridge.

Special mention should be made of Muriel Kendrick, who was honorary secretary of the Ladies section' for nearly twenty years from 1950 and served with such distinction that she was the first woman to be made an Honorary Member of the Club, in 1966. She died in 1971 but the flag was not flown at half–mast because it was not until July 1994 that this courtesy was extended to the ladies. Noreen Grice was the first woman to be so honoured. Muriel's successor, Val Gilchrist, who retired in 1981, was also made an Honorary Member. In 1982 she presented a new window for the ladies' lounge, replacing the small panes with a picture window similar to the bay window in the dining room.

Juniors

Pam Dippie, who took over as secretary from Val, had been a member of the committee since 1964 and was a tireless supporter of junior golf. She arranged lessons and competitions and encouraged eleven to fourteen year olds to become holiday members, a category that no longer exists, and get a holiday handicap over nine holes. Many of her protégés became keen, skilful golfers who have continued to enjoy the game throughout their life and the Pam Dippie Trophy is contested by juniors aged sixteen years and under.

Anne Andrews, a tireless worker for Staffordshire and ELGA, took over as junior golf organiser in 1994 and ran a thriving group throughout the rest of the 1990s, with practice sessions on Sunday afternoons. However, on her retirement she warned of a dearth of juniors and after discussions with the men's committee it was decided to offer junior associate membership to children related to members, and their friends, who wanted to try golf. Twenty-six children joined. In 2002, Jon Gough and Cherie Jones organised a Junior Masters competition in the Easter holidays and eighty-four children, aged between eight and thirteen, took part. At that time more than thirty juniors attended Sunday coaching sessions. Later, Sue Porter reported the approach of another trough but there are now signs of a revival, with Mandy Davies running the juniors with the support of Chris Poxon.

The juniors of the 1950s and 1960s, who benefited from a post-war drive to recruit them and teach them the game, included people called Beharrell, Pepper, James and Streather, who grew up to become pillars of the Club and they appreciate the importance of introducing people to golf young and encouraging them to keep playing, girls and young women included.

For the record, the first junior to be elected was A.H. Horton soon after the course opened for play in 1909. Other Club notables who joined as juniors in the 1920s and 1930s included Trevor Heaton, W.R.P. Hayward,

The Juniors

The future of the Club

Taking things seriously

104

Geordie Fairweather and Peter Bigwood. Tom South, one of the founders of the Boys Championship in 1921, became a member of Little Aston and in 1945 married Ada Scribbans, widow of Harry, at St. Peter's Church.

Changed times?

Outside influences helped change the attitudes to women bit by bit. In 1976, the EGU sounded out the Club about hosting another major amateur tournament and asked if they would "offer better clubhouse facilities for ladies than at the last tournament and thus save the expense of marquees?" The committee agreed and said "We would be prepared to treat the main club lounge as a mixed bar for the duration of the tournament."

In 1988, the Club hosted the English Ladies Close Amateur Championship for the first time and the *Birmingham Post* had a bit of fun:

The two finalists will be the first women to play on a Saturday morning at Little Aston. One wonders, is the end of civilisation nigh?

The sky remained firmly in its place as Julie Wade, of Felixstowe Ferry, beat Susan Shapcott, of Knowle, at the 19th in a thrilling final. Ann Booth qualified for the match play stages and lost in the second round to Jill Thornhill, a Curtis Cup player.

Other breakthroughs took a little longer. In the mid 1980s, when Fiona Macdonald caused consternation by becoming the first woman to play for Cambridge University, some of the team's traditional opponents appointed her an honorary man for the day while others, including Little Aston, let it be known that there was no room for Fiona and the fixture. A suggestion that the Club could field Ann Booth was a non-starter: after all, the match was on a Saturday. Cambridge played without Fiona.

A decade later Alex Boatman made the Cambridge team and Little Aston proved just as intransigent, letting the university captain know that if they turned up with a girl in the side the fixture would be cancelled.

Then, in centenary year, Cambridge arrived with Louisa Tarn in their team and the only person really upset by her presence was Mark Davies, her opponent, who was beaten 5 and 4. He recovered quickly enough, knowing that his niche in history was secure.

Nowadays, lady members at Little Aston even have a vote, although the first A.G.M. at which they were permitted, 2002, was scheduled for a Saturday. It was not an indication of seismic change, just an oversight and the A.G.M. took place on a Monday, although it did revert to Saturday the following year. In his speech on behalf of the guests at the centenary dinner, Bruce Streather touched on the sometimes touchy subject of women:

Barbara McMillan, ladies captain 1964-66, driving at the 1st tee with a guest

No account of the members of the golf club would be complete without reference to the female members of the Club. Little Aston has a somewhat unfair reputation for restricting the privileges of lady members but really all that is happening is that the ladies know where they stand at Little Aston and they can now stand in an increasing number of places in the Club, including the men's bar ...

But unlike some clubs (and I would not of course mention Royal St George's or Rye in this respect), at Little Aston women get a better deal than dogs. Indeed, dogs are not allowed at Little Aston at all ...

So there you have it, the truth about the infamous sign: No Dogs is fact; No Women is fiction.

Chapter Thirteen

Mart Lewis: The First Professional

To all intents and purposes, M.J. (Mart) Lewis was Little Aston's first professional and began a tradition of long and distinguished service in a post that has always carried a certain cachet. Vardon had barely laid out his plans before professionals were applying for the job but in May 1909 Mr. Winder proposed and Mr. Jerrard seconded "that the professional to be appointed be a teacher, club maker and player and that a Greenkeeper, not being the professional, be employed". In the end an amendment, proposed by Mr. Barker and seconded by Mr. Sheldon, was carried: "That a professional be appointed who shall supervise the course and the men."

In June, it was resolved to engage H.E. Bean but Mr. Bean never was. A.W. Butchart was engaged at £1. 0s. 0d. per week but he left after a few weeks, putting in a claim for his travelling expenses and "wrongfully" retaining the caddie fees. The assistant F. Parsons took over pro tem, a professional called Gandin turned the job down and then, at last, in July 1910, Lewis was installed and the Club has been well served by its professionals ever since.

Martin James Lewis, known as Mart, born in Malvern, was one of seven golfing brothers who "knocked a ball around" on a public course before learning club making under his brother W. P. (Bill or Will) Lewis, the professional at Kings Norton. Mart then moved to Handsworth as assistant to Alfred J. (Alf) Lewis, another brother, who later moved to Sutton Coldfield. Mart was professional at Churchdown, near Cheltenham, and at Gatwick before his appointment at Little Aston, where he remained until his retirement at the age of seventy on 31st December 1949.

Mart, always smartly turned out in a tweed suit and matching cap, was a pillar of the Midland section of the PGA. He was a decent player but his forte was looking after the course and the members. He was a skilled club maker and had a small manufacturing unit in Clarence Road, Mere Green, where he made woods and irons with hickory shafts. He was also a knowledgeable

Mart Lewis and Charlie Ward at Mart's retirement match played between Max Faulkner and Wanda Morgan and Charlie Ward and Jean Donald

teacher, courteous and patient but a stickler for the proprieties. No one ever forgot a ticking off from Mart or transgressed again.

The professional's duties were many and varied and much of his income depended on his members. In 1913, the Club agreed to allow Mart to keep the caddie fees to supplement his wages providing he got himself a first-class assistant, who would be a good player and allowed to charge 2s. a round. Mart would be responsible for "the sweeping and keeping tidy the part of the ground frequented by the caddies". In April 1914, Mart wrote asking for "more support to his shop from members" and his wages were "increased 5/- for the future". World War I started on 1st August, Mart's assistant went off to war and by October 1915 Mart was asking leave to work on munitions. In November, the captain, Charles Heaton, "reported that he had made the arrangement with Lewis whereby he received 8/6 per week and 9/- for his assistant".

The war ended in November 1918 and in January 1919 Mart's wages were increased to £3 per week. In September, the Club agreed to give Mart the substantial sum of £5 towards his expenses to go to Walton Heath to compete in a tournament and in March 1920 "it was resolved that the Professional's playing and teaching fees be fixed as follows: per round 4/-; teaching 2/6 per hour". In September 1921 "it was agreed that M. Lewis's salary [note the upgrade] should be increased by £1 per week until June 30th 1922". However, "the Committee recommended a reduction in the playing fee to 2/6 a round".

To put those sums in context, here is an excerpt from a *Golf Illustrated* column, *Justice for the Professional*, of 22nd October 1926, the year of the General Strike:

… the financial position of the average golf professional is steadily becoming more and more precarious … In most cases he receives a small retaining fee. The average is probably under £1 per week. We have heard of instances in some of the smaller clubs in the provinces in which it is no higher than 10s. To be sure, a few of the leading men who are attached to big clubs receive as much as £4 a week – or even rather more – as retaining fee, in addition to being virtually assured of an extensive clientele for teaching and the sale of golf requisites …

Is it matter for surprise that the tendency grows stronger and stronger for ambitious young men to leave this country? The terms under which Percy Alliss [father of Peter] went to Berlin were announced some time ago – £800 per annum retaining fee, all the profits from his lessons and sales, a flat in the club-house rent free, and gas, coal, and electric light also gratis …

A professional with a reputation as a teacher – although not necessarily a great player – may be a considerable asset to a club. We have heard of one who brings £150 a year in green fees to his club because every visitor who comes to him for a lesson has to pay a green fee of 3s.6d. In short, he earns his retainer by attracting visitors.

In those terms Mart Lewis was relatively well paid and well looked after. He had a telephone extension installed in his shop as early as 1924 but must have thought of Alliss and his billet in Berlin in November 1928 when he was told that he could "install Electric Power in his shop provided he has a separate meter and defrays the cost of same".

Mart was also exceedingly well thought of. He was made an Honorary Member in 1932, at a time when most professionals were not even allowed into the clubhouse, and he was deeply touched by the honour as his letter to the committee made clear:

2nd March 1932

W. Bigwood, Esq

Dear Sir,

I thank you for your letter of the 29th ult and shall esteem it a favour if you will accept and also convey to the Committee and Members of the Club my sincere gratitude and thanks for the honour they have conferred on me in electing me an Honorary member of the Little Aston Golf Club.

I appreciate this far more than it is possible for me to express, not only for myself but also for the Profession to which I am privileged to belong, and who look on this honour as one of the highest compliments that can be paid to a Professional by the members of the Club to which he is attached.

Again thanking you

Yours faithfully,

(signed) M.J. Lewis

As the course supervisor, liaising with the chairman of green and the greenkeepers, Mart took a proprietorial view of the course, which he nurtured from its very early days, tweaking here, altering there but always maintaining its essential character and ensuring that it was a joy to play. Visitors invariably mentioned its immaculate condition and sang Mart's praises but, behind the scenes, everything was not always sweetness and light. At a meeting on 21st April 1935, the green committee considered the slightly ominous-sounding topic "Professional's Management of the Course" and decided that G. Douglas Smith should "inform the Professional that there is a strong feeling that will result in a change if more supervision is not given to the management of the Course".

Douglas Smith obviously worked his persuasive magic because in the *British Golfer* of May 1937 "Grasshopper" wrote about Sam King's victory in the Daily Mail Finals and said:

We who knew the Little Aston course expected a high standard of condition, and were not disappointed. Greens were splendid, and the fairways the best I have seen this year. Mart Lewis and his staff must have worked hard and long to have achieved such fine results in such an adverse season.

Grasshopper's views were echoed by the *Daily Mail* and the PGA in letters to the club.

In his time Mart had laid out the course at Bloxwich and he and Ted Matthews, the professional at Walmley, planned and built the muni at Boldmere but as he got older and his health deteriorated Little Aston starting thinking about a complete separation of the roles of professional and greenkeeper. Nothing happened, however, for Mart rallied and in August 1939:

the [Green] Committee decided, in view of the improvement in Mart Lewis' health, that they would postpone the engagement of a Greenkeeper. They also decided that the estimated expenditure for the coming year would be £1500.

A couple of weeks later war was declared.

On 1st February 1941 Mart, and four groundsmen, were granted a war bonus of 10s. per week which took Mart's wages up to £4. 10s.

In 1945, Charlie Ward became Mart's co-professional and Mart continued to work on the course and give lessons, with particular attention being paid to juniors. The Club gave plenty of thought to the senior professional's workload and noted in February 1946:

Mr. Mart Lewis will have his Co-professional away a lot during Summer months at important competitions, and, therefore, a good deal of extra teaching work etc. (there are many new members) and work involved in Summer meetings etc. will fall on him. As he grows no younger it is desirable that he should not have the additional burden of Course construction in the Summer months [April, May, June, July, August, September] when his plate will be quite full without it. We want rather to build up his strength in the Summer than to have him break down during that period. In case anything happened to Mr. Lewis, Mr. Ward would not yet be able to carry out all the things that Mr. Lewis does, and even if Mr. Ward could do them, he would have to give up his competition aspirations.

At the end of March 1946, the secretary was asked "to convey to Mart Lewis our appreciation for his winter's work" and in April Mart met with F. Bernard Clark, the chairman of green, Mrs. J.H. Harper, J.H. Harper, J.F. Cooke, A.C. Warmington and H.W. Jinks to discuss the provision of a golf nursery "to foster the golf spirit amongst Juniors …". They agreed to arrange classes for four juniors at a time, with one lesson of an hour once a week, cost 2s. per lesson per person.

At the end of 1947, however, Mart tendered his resignation but it was "unanimously resolved that this be not accepted". His health continued to be a worry but he proved well enough to have such a barney with F. Bernard Clark that Clark resigned as chairman of green and Mart was summoned before the committee on 8th January 1949 to explain himself. He apologised, claiming that he had in fact carried out the instructions of the green committee and that in his opinion the trouble was only over one particular hole. He said that he wished to retire on his seventieth birthday and until that time he hoped that he would be able to go on giving the Club the best of service. The upshot was that Mr. A.C. Warmington, the captain, assumed the chairmanship of the green committee and Mart agreed to carry out their instructions.

It was obviously a blockbuster of a meeting, 1949 seems to have been a rare year for controversy at the Club, but nigh on forty years of dedicated service outweighed the odd disagreement and a testimonial fund was set up for Mart, letters were sent to all the local clubs asking for contributions, and there was an exhibition match in his honour in April 1950 featuring Charlie Ward and Jean Donald against Max Faulkner and Wanda Morgan.

The 3rd hole

The short 5th

Approaching the 18th green

Chapter Fourteen

Charlie Ward: The Incomparable

CHARLIE WARD, for a decade or so after World War II, was indisputably one of the finest players in the country. Little Aston's diminutive professional twice won the Vardon Trophy, the equivalent of the modern order of merit, and Peter Alliss, who was just starting out on his career as Charlie was coming to the end of his, called him "One of our greatest post-war players."

Born in 1911, in Aldridge, the son of a miner, Charlie learned his golf by aping his elders, growing to love a game that many working class people thought, as he put it, "a little bit posh". In an interview just before he retired at the end of 1976, he told Dennis Shaw of the *Evening Mail* how he got started:

A pal and myself would play in the fields which are now Great Barr golf course. We knocked a ball as far as possible, dug a little hole, pushed in a stick and tied a rag to the top. Then we did the same again and again until we had our own little course. The ground was too rough for putting and we couldn't afford putters anyway. We simply tried to chip the ball straight into the hole.

Charlie started caddying at Sutton Coldfield, where his father was an artisan, then became an assistant to the professional Harry Sutton, whose advice was on the succinct side. "He gave me only two hints," Charlie said. "'You've got too many elbows for this game' and 'You've got to knock it down to get it up'. I had to puzzle out what Harry was on about for myself." The young man did that by practising obsessively. "On my day off I would go out and play by myself with four golf balls. If my scores were, say, 74, 76, 77 and 81, I would go out again to better them. If I couldn't, I would try again and perhaps again." He developed a reputation for speed, of swing and movement, they used to call him "Whippit Quick", and years later, in a tournament, he and his playing partner went round in two hours, beating their morning time by five minutes.

Charlie was an assistant, briefly, at Ladbrook Park, then moved on to Moseley. In the early 1930s, he won the Midland Professional Championship in successive years and in 1933 he and Bert Gadd, at the time the French Open champion, played in an exhibition match at Moseley against Densmore Shute, who had just won the Open Championship and Walter Hagen, four times Open champion, twice US Open champion and five times US PGA champion. This was heady stuff and Charlie and Gadd were duly beaten 6 and 5. Hagen, although past his best, won the first three holes on his own ball.

In 1937, Charlie moved to Torquay as professional at the Palace Hotel and in 1939 he was sixth in the inaugural Harry Vardon Trophy, awarded to the PGA member with the lowest stroke average in a series of designated events, subsequently the PGA Tour's order of merit. The winner was Reg Whitcombe, Open champion in 1938 and Charlie finished just ahead of Henry Cotton and Dai Rees. Then they all had their careers cut short by World War II, if they were lucky. Charlie, who was twenty-eight, joined the R.A.F. and spent time as a golf instructor back at the Palace Hotel, which had been converted into a military hospital for the rehabilitation of wounded R.A.F. officers. He ended the war at R.A.F. Wallingford, in Oxfordshire, with the rank of corporal.

In July 1945, the war in Europe ended and tournament golf resumed in a small way, with the News of the World VE Tournament at Walton Heath. Charlie won £30 for reaching the quarter-finals. The typical adult weekly ration then consisted of two ounces (50g) of butter; four ounces (100g) of bacon; one fresh egg per week and two pints of milk. A gin and tonic cost less than 1s. (10p) and if you knew someone who knew someone and you had the money, a Rolls Royce was less than £1,000.

In September 1945, the *Daily Mail* put up £1,575 for a seventy-two hole stroke play event at St Andrews and it was recognised that this was, in the absence of the official event itself, effectively the Open Championship. There were 172 entries, including six from America, and it was won by Charles Harold Ward, Corporal, for he was still in the R.A.F. He took away £200 and another corporal, one Max Faulkner, was second, one behind Charlie's total of 298. The field was as strong as it could possibly be at that time and Lloyd Mangrum, who was to win the US Open the following year, was sixth. Charlie later described the hallowed turf as "a bloody awful course" but he tended to do well there and when the Open resumed in 1946, at St Andrews, he finished fourth, alongside Cotton, Rees and Norman von Nida, five shots behind Sam Snead. Charlie was late for the presentation and Henry Cotton picked up his cheque for him.

As the tournament arm of Little Aston, Charlie was encouraged and championed by Ted Beharrell and it was under the auspices of Dunlop, who were keen to get the balls rolling again after wartime austerity, that Charlie and Dai Rees toured the United States in the winter of 1946/1947. "We were the first British pros to play the tournaments over there," said Charlie, whose R.A.F. training had not included leaving the ground:

I had to fly the Atlantic on my own and I was terrified because I had never flown before. Dai joined me a few days later. We were only allowed to take £75 out of the country but once in America we found ourselves guests of a club where our host announced that we were a couple of limeys over there to play their golf circuit and that we had very little money. The members had a whip round and presented us with 600 dollars. The Americans were bloody marvellous.

In Florida we stayed with Tommy Armour and he looked at our clubs and said they were not good at all. He then gave us brand new sets of his own make, big, heavy things that nearly pulled my arms off. Dai was third in Pinehurst and I was fourth in Florida but by the time we reached Miami our visas had run out. Tommy told us not to worry and go on playing golf. Over in California we played with Bing Crosby and Bob Hope and Bing took us round the film studios.

Charlie and Dai learned a lot on that tour. They realised that there was nothing between them and their hosts in terms of striking the ball but could not understand why the Americans were invariably two or three shots better. So at one event in Florida the British duo sat at the back of a green and watched about fifty players go through. "They missed as many greens as we did," Charlie said, "but every time they got down in two shots."

He took that lesson to heart and back home spent countless hours becoming the best man in the country from fifty yards and in. He would place a leaf on a green and had to hit it again and again, then he would go to the putting green with twenty balls and had to hole them all or start again with all twenty. At five foot four inches tall, Charlie, known as "the little man from Little Aston", had to rely on more than mere muscle. As well as his immaculate short game, he developed a method to keep up with his bigger and stronger peers. Using a very high tee he would place the ball just outside his left foot and, with an exceedingly deep faced driver, swing at the ball at warp speed. He did not achieve the carry of some of his contemporaries but imparted such over spin to the ball that it rolled quite far enough for him to compete. He was a match for almost anyone as his record in the Open showed.

In 1947, at Royal Liverpool, Hoylake, he shared sixth place, four shots behind Fred Daly; in 1948, at Muirfield, he was third, with von Nida, Roberto de Vicenzo and Jack Hargreaves, of Sutton Coldfield, six behind Cotton; in 1949, at Royal St George's, Sandwich, Charlie shared fourth place with Sam King, three behind Bobby Locke, who beat Harry Bradshaw in a thirty-six

Charlie Ward – the way to keep your head down

hole play-off; and in 1951, at Royal Portrush, C.W., as his fellow pros tended to call him, had a 68 in the last round to finish third on his own, five shots behind Faulkner.

Little Aston's members enjoyed testing themselves against one of the best players in the country and on one memorable occasion in 1947, he played with Norah Heaton against her husband Trevor and his partner, Alfie Warmington. The three amateurs had one of those days when they all played better than their handicaps and the men might have expected to win but although Norah managed to come in only once, with a stroke, they lost, by 5 and 4. Years later, reminiscing, Alfie suggested that Charlie must have gone round in under 60 that day. "Oh no," he said, "It was only a 62."

In 1948 and 1949, Charlie won the Vardon Trophy, effectively making him Europe's No 1. In 1949, back at St Andrews, he won the Dunlop Masters and, in addition to the prize money, was given a beautiful silver salver engraved with the names of all those he had beaten. It was a formidable list, including Fred Daly, Max Faulkner, Dai Rees, Harry Weetman and Harry Bradshaw. As the year's Master golfer and Vardon Trophy winner, Charlie was given a dinner in his honour by the *Birmingham Post and Mail* and the great and good from both amateur and professional ranks gathered at the Queen's Hotel. Tributes were paid by, among others, Frank Edge, the president of Little Aston and by Guy Bigwood, the president of the EGU. Henry Cotton and Dai Rees sent telegrams and a cablegram arrived from America from Ben Hogan, the non-playing captain of that year's Ryder Cup team.

Charlie, who had also played in the 1947 match, lost to Sam Snead in the singles at Ganton in 1949 but was in fine form two years later at Pinehurst, North Carolina. In the foursomes he and Arthur Lees beat Ed 'Porky' Oliver and Henry Ransom and in the singles Charlie drew Hogan, who had won the Masters and the US Open earlier in the year as well as attending the premiere of the film *Follow the Sun*, made to celebrate his exploits.

In the morning Hogan went round Pinehurst No. 2 in 67, five under par, and was only two up. He went to the turn in the afternoon in 33, and was still only two up. At the 10th he drove so far into the trees that he could only chip out sideways and was playing his third, from about 300 yards, before Charlie had played his second. The American launched his shot onto the green, some ninety feet from the hole and sank the

Charlie Ward with John Beharrell practising for the Open, Hoylake, 1956

massive putt for an incredible birdie. Charlie, also on in 3, missed his putt and instead of being only one down, as had seemed likely for the entire hole, he was three down. Hogan won 3 and 2 but freely admitted he would prefer not to have to go through it all again. That match, in November, was effectively Charlie's last great appearance on the international stage. He was aged forty and, as he said, "My game lost a little bit of its edge."

There was, though, to be one last hurrah. In 1956, in the British Professionals Close Championship at the Maesdu course in Llandudno, Charlie beat the formidable Scot Eric Brown in a thirty-six hole play-off after they had tied on 282. Brown led with a 66 to a 68 after the first eighteen but the forty-four year old Englishman came back with a 71 to 75 to take the title.

For years Charlie remained a force in Midland tournaments and in 1965 he won the PGA Seniors Championship, a victory that led to a challenge match at Formby against his American counterpart Sam Snead. Once again Charlie came within touching distance of beating one of the sport's all-time greats, coming back from three down with five to play but losing a desperately close match at the 37th. Tom McMillan jun. wrote about it in his memoirs:

A small party from Little Aston went to support Charlie. Arthur and Trina Schmiegelow, Bob Church and his wife, Barbie and I. At the end … Sam and Charlie were all square … The first hole on Formby runs parallel to a railway line, and very close. When Sam and Charlie arrived on the tee, there were a number of people sitting on the railway fence. Sadly, Charlie fluffed his drive. Sam hit the most enormous slice, which nearly hit the two-thirty train to Southport. It did hit, however, a young man sitting on the fence. It was a miracle it did not kill him. However, the ball bounced back and finished on the fairway. Sam won the hole and the tournament. He came and had a drink with us and he was so pro British it was embarrassing.

Charlie Ward, John Morgan, Trevor Heaton (captain 1950-1952) and Jack Hargreaves, professional at Sutton Coldfield, and member of Ryder Cup team 1951

A newspaper report of the incident was far less colourful and did not quite tally, it had Charlie topping his second shot and Snead slicing his second into the crowd from where he got up and down for a 4 Charlie could not match. Still, whatever the details the result was the same and later Little Aston presented Charlie, an inveterate smoker, with a silver cigarette box in recognition of his achievements that year. When he finally retired, in 1976, he had won more than seventy events in a glittering career that encompassed the Road to America, where he met Bing Crosby, Bob Hope and Dorothy Lamour, played against the best golfers in the world and earned the respect of them all.

Transition

Charlie had duly succeeded Mart, at a salary of £5 a week, with Joe Sutton as his assistant first of all, then later, in 1951, the joint professional. The arrangement was not entirely satisfactory, as the minutes showed, although it lasted until the end of 1955, when Joe left. There just was not room for the two of them and in the years that followed, Charlie's assistants included Carl

Roberts, who in 1960 was tragically killed in a car accident; Geoff Stinchcombe; the personable David Clay, who ensured that almost every member bought a new set of clubs, but quickly sought out more lucrative pastures and eventually owned his own club in America; the urbane Simon Fogarty who was tempted from Whittington Barracks but moved on to become professional at Blackwell and then at Royal Cape Town; and Maurice Bembridge, now on the board of directors of the PGA European Tour.

The shop and the running thereof remained a bone of contention and the truth was that Charlie, an outstanding player and good bloke, if inclined to be blunt, had no real interest in running the shop. He brought kudos to the Club by dint of his reputation and had many supporters but being a stay-at-home pro was not his forte and there were those who felt neglected, as the minutes record in just enough detail to be thoroughly intriguing:

22nd October 1953: Professionals. Considerable complaints had been received regarding the manner in which the professionals were running the Shop. A lengthy discussion took place on this matter and it was finally resolved that the Captain and Hon. Secretary should interview Charles Ward and express to him the very serious view that the Committee took over the running of the Shop at the present time, and that they should report back to the Committee at a later date.

25th February 1961: The Captain reported that the members of the Sub-Committee had met Mr. Ward to discuss his future with the Club and they were of the opinion that although during past months Mr. Ward's interest in the Club seemed to have waned that he was, in fact, still extremely interested in the Club and he stated that he considered that his future was with it …

27th January 1962: The Captain [Bob Hiam] was of the opinion that the present retainer paid to Mr. Ward was quite out of keeping with present day conditions and … should be increased from £7 to £12 per week … several suggestions and complaints regarding the Professional's service to members were put forward. However, the increase was approved …

2nd February 1963: The Honorary Officers recommend that the shop should be taken away from the Professional and run by the Club who would appoint a new Assistant who was keen and well versed in shop management and teaching matters …

15th March 1963: The Captain reported that Mr. Ward had stated that he wished to co-operate with the scheme outlined to him by the Honorary Officers …

11th May 1963: The Captain stated that the Secretary and himself had had a meeting with the Professionals at which several matters had been raised, and he would like the Committee's confirmation to what had been tentatively agreed:-

1: Charges: a) Lessons. The charge should be £1 per hour.
        b) Per Round. The charge should not be less than 25/- per Round.
2. Club Cleaning. The charge for club cleaning should be £2 per annum, payable in advance.
3. Shoe Cleaning. The charge for shoe cleaning should be £1 per annum, payable in advance.

The above charges were agreed and the Hon. Secretary was instructed to place a Notice on the Board.

Maurice Bembridge

Whatever the difficulties in 1963, the members still contributed £152 to a fund to help tide the professionals over during a period of sustained bad weather and in 1969 Charlie was made an Honorary Member and remained at the Club until he retired at the end of 1976. He was presented with a silver salver and with the deeds of 179 Clarence Road, Four Oaks, the house which he and his wife Gwyn, as sitting tenants, had bought in 1972 thanks to a loan of £4,000 from the Club. Gwyn, who was a hugely popular person at the Club, had often held the fort in the shop and was even allowed to play on the course during weekdays. The Wards retired to Torquay.

Maurice Bembridge: a trailblazer and ambassador

In many ways Maurice, one of Charlie's assistants, who was to play in four Ryder Cups from 1969-1975, was the forerunner of today's world travellers. He would play a full season of tournament golf in the United Kingdom and then, when events dried up in Europe, wing his way to South Africa, Australia and New Zealand.

Stockily built, most often to be seen with a pipe between his teeth, he was seemingly inexhaustible and an excellent player. He showed just how good when, in 1974, he got round Augusta National in the last round of the Masters in 64, equalling the then tournament record, set in 1965 by Jack Nicklaus. Maurice shared ninth place with Phil Rogers on 283, five shots behind Gary Player and Little Aston's tournament assistant, Maurice's official title, now has a permanent place in Masters' history because all those who set a course record are immortalised by having their names inscribed on a metal plaque mounted on the wall of a huge drinking fountain in a lovely shady area in between the 7th and 15th holes.

Out in 34, two under par, Maurice started back birdie, birdie, birdie: "I just couldn't miss, whatever I did. Putts started going in from all over the place." He hit a decent drive at the 13th but as he approached the ball noticed that "Pappa", his local Augusta caddie, was standing well away from it. A snake, a

John Anderson on the 2nd tee with the old 17th behind

deadly water moccasin, was lying close to the ball. "I took my 2-iron, zapped it and threw it into the creek," Maurice said. He then used the 2-iron more conventionally, hitting the ball to twenty feet for another birdie. He also birdied the 15th and at the 18th he hit his second at least forty feet past the hole, on the top tier of that fearsome green:

I was just trying to lag the putt somewhere near the hole and like everything else on that back nine, it went in. I felt like saying, 'Sorry, it's just happening. It wasn't me Sir, I didn't do it.' Many years later Peter Alliss was still calling it "one of the greatest rounds compiled by a British golfer".

Maurice was with the Club from March 1967 until January 1976 and loved his times at Little Aston:

They were the happiest of my youth. Everyone was so helpful to me, it was an eye-opener. Everything was great for the years I was there – even down to the treacle tart in the clubhouse. I've never found anywhere to match it ever since.

John Anderson and Brian Rimmer

John Anderson took over from Charlie in 1977 and was a wonderfully gifted golfer and exemplary club professional, who stayed for twenty-six years before retiring from professional golf and regaining his amateur status. He now plays off what he himself calls "a comfortable handicap of ten" at Ladbrook Park, where he first worked at weekends cleaning clubs and shoes in exchange for lessons before being taken on as assistant.

John was a contemporary of Tony Jacklin and was easily good enough to compete on the European tour. In 1967, having been given £1,000 in sponsorship by James Hartley, a member of Ladbrook, he had several top ten finishes and led the Pringle tournament at Royal Lytham and St Annes after 55 holes but the railway that bounds the course on the right of the front nine got him, as it has done so many others, and he did not win. The following year a move to the John Jacobs Golf Centre at Esher in Surrey proved counter-productive as a swing change scuppered his game, although his teaching skills benefited.

In 1969, he started teaching in Båstad in southern Sweden and stayed there for three years, coming home to work as a labourer one winter and a postman the next. He got married, to Penni, in 1970 and became the professional at Shrewsbury in 1971. One of his fondest memories was winning the Staffs and Shropshire Alliance in 1972 over thirty-six holes at Little Aston when he and Ces Langford beat Charlie and Tom Gilchrist by three shots.

John moved to Hill Valley, a new course, in 1975 and helped to promote it by playing tournaments in East Africa, with some success, and qualifying for the Open at Carnoustie. "I got quite a bit of airtime," John said, "because a) I was playing with the leader for two rounds and b) Peter Alliss was co-designer of Hill Valley." Two years later he settled down at Little Aston, giving great service to the Club and regularly winning local events, including the Midland Open and the Staffordshire Open, the latter three years in a row, from 1977-1979. Over the years his assistants were Stuart Smith, Nick Littlehales, Ian Sadler, Mark Budz, Stuart Bottrill, Ross Anderson and Tom Parker.

Brian Rimmer, the current professional, took over from John in 2003. He is a teacher and player of rare quality and had hardly put his foot in the door before he reduced the Little Aston course record to 63 competing in the PGA Plumb Centre Pro-Am. He also won the Staffordshire Professional Championship that year and he and David Cox came first in the final of the Lombard Trophy in Portugal, a national event for club pros and their members that takes a lot of winning. Brian proved he is a handy partner to have when he and Michael Adamson won the 2005 Gulf Air International Pro-Captain Challenge in Bahrain and then he won the title again two years later with Neil Andrews.

To date Brian, who started his career as assistant at Burton-on-Trent followed by spells as professional at Oaklands Golf and Country Club,

Brian Rimmer

Anglesey, St Thomas's Priory and Trentham Park, has won the Staffordshire Professional Championship six times and been Staffordshire Open champion twice. Some of his proudest moments were representing Great Britain and Ireland in the PGA Cup, the club pros' equivalent of the Ryder Cup, in 1992 at the K Club and in 1998 at The Broadmoor in Colorado Springs, and winning the Club Professional Championship at Northop in 1997. He also won the Sun City World Pro-Am in South Africa.

Married to Iola, he has been captain of the Midland Professional Golfers' Association and is much in demand as a coach and, of course, a playing partner.

Chapter Fifteen

Nature and Nurture:
Greenkeepers, Artisans and Stewards

IN OCTOBER 1937, the Greenkeeping Research Association in Bingley, Yorkshire, invited the Club to send the greenkeeper to a conference and George Beharrell, the chairman of the green committee, was tasked with choosing the representative "provided the man selected is not employed in the Professional's shop". Jones, foreman and Bevan, groundsman were chosen but when the next invitation arrived, in February 1938, "M.J. Lewis had intimated his desire to attend. It was resolved to leave the matter in the hands of T. McMillan senior to decide." By July:

it was resolved to recommend the engagement of a head Greenkeeper at wages of not exceeding five pounds per week and that M.J. Lewis be relieved of the responsibility of the course. The general Committee to decide what reduction should be made to the wages of Lewis but they make a suggestion of 30/- weekly.

In the end it was not until Mart Lewis retired that the roles of professional and greenkeeper were separated and in January 1950 E.H. (Ernie) Jones, previously the foreman, became the head greenkeeper. He and his brother Bert (G.A.) had joined the Club in 1919, on the recommendation of their younger brother Cecil (C.E.), who had been taken on earlier and the Joneses began the now legendary dynastic greenkeeping traditions of Little Aston, with longevity, loyalty and skill the key factors.

When Ernie died in 1959, Bert succeeded him and only Cecil, the longest-serving but youngest brother, did not become head of the greenstaff because he was a shade too old when his chance came. Altogether their full-time service to the Club amounted to 135 years and Cecil, who was also known as Bobby, after the legendary R.T. Jones, because of his skill as a player, continued to work part-time for many years after his official retirement. He was particularly proud of having initiated the Groundstaff v Ladies match, which is a highlight of the calendar to this day. He began as a caddie, aged ten, in 1912 at a fee of eightpence a round and when he started on the ground staff in 1918 he was paid 18s. for fifty-three and a half hours a week.

It was hard, physical work and in his memoir, *Sixty Years of Golf at Little Aston*, Cecil listed the "full complement of men and machines: two elderly men, two elderly horses, two fairway mowers, one reaping machine and three hand-mowing machines for tees and greens". The horses were provided by Ansells Brewery "on condition that they ended their days at Little Aston".

By 1919, there were eight groundsmen and Cecil recalled the work that ensued:

Three greens were redesigned, the 1st, 9th and 14th and new bunkers were made, including the cross bunkers at the 14th. In 1921, a drought that lasted from April until October was the cause of a great number of grass fires on and around the course. From the 10th hole to the 16th was ablaze. The fire even crossed the fairways. Out of these fires came a new innovation to Little Aston. Seeds from silver birch trees as far away as Streetly settled on the sparse patches and a species of tree was added to the course of which it had been devoid previously.

New machinery was introduced in the 1920s:

Two horse drawn triple mowers were purchased from Ransomes for the fairways and the rough, which had been previously cut by a reaper once a year. This was a big step forward, rough could be cut at regular intervals and the fairways mown every week.

Cecil remembered men as well as machines, painting a lovely picture of the life of the Club:

The Duke of Windsor, when he was Prince of Wales, played over the course twice. Amongst the Club's most distinguished members were Sir Hallewell Rogers and Sir Ernest Canning who both served as Lord Mayors of Birmingham during their membership … There were quite a few colourful characters who graced the course in the old days. Lieutenant-Colonel C.F. Fiddian-Green who would arrive in his carriage drawn by two horses with a coachman and a flunkey attired in scarlet complete with top hat and cockades. Frank "Tiny" Edge in contrast would be on his reinforced high pressure tyred bicycle followed by Alfred Cheatle in his "Chuff Chuff" dressed in a long motor coat and hat with ear flaps. Most members came on cycles in those days and a shed was built to accommodate them. Others came by train and walked from Streetly Station. There were no buses then …

Cecil and Ernie were the only men kept on for the duration of World War II, assisted by 400 sheep, who kept the grass down, and members who occasionally mowed the greens to help out. The Club worked hard on the course after the war and Henry Cotton, writing in *Golf Illustrated* on 29th September 1955, sang its praises:

This course must have the best fairways in the world. I naturally have not seen them all but I have never seen better and more weed-free turf anywhere, dry all the year round too. Ganton and Gleneagles and Hoylake are in the running for top places but even they must be runners-up alongside Little Aston.

For many years there were four Joneses on the staff, A.C., who was not related to the others, had joined in 1935, and they obviously knew their stuff. Bert, who died unexpectedly in 1965 four days after cutting new holes for the last day of the Martini tournament, was described by John Cooke, the chairman of the green committee, as "a perfectionist who was easy to work with. He will be sadly missed".

It was a big ask to keep up with the Joneses but the Borastons' length of service, fifty-five years and counting, has established them as part of the fabric of the Club. Greenkeeping was not the science it has become when Alan was first attracted to its charms. He was working as a junior gardener at The Hall, next door, when he struck up a friendship with Jim "Ginger" Bevan who was on the Club's green staff and when, in 1948, Ginger moved to Sandwell Park, he persuaded Alan to join him. Alan moved to Little Aston in 1953 and when he eventually became head greenkeeper at Little Aston he brought Ginger back onto the staff. Ginger put in forty-five years of service in all and was the man who carried the Prince of Wales's clubs when he visited in the 1930s. Ginger, who kept the 10s. note that his Royal Highness rewarded him with, describing it as "a king's ransom", never forgot one other thing about his distinguished bag "He swore!".

Alan proved a worthy successor to the meticulous Bert Jones, being a stickler for detail and cataloguing in his diary the day-to-day execution of his duties. He specialised in minutiae and even put on record what he had spent on oil and petrol for his machinery. Forty-one pounds in one year! He was a stickler for appearances too, as his son Andrew recalled: "My Dad never did me any favours. He was anxious that I should not appear to be receiving any preferential treatment and so he went out of his way to make things tough for me. I really did start at the bottom." This training was augmented by visits to the Warwickshire College of Agriculture at Moreton Morrell and by long sessions of study for his City and Guilds greenkeeping qualifications. He attended trade seminars, kept himself abreast of most of the modern trends and was eventually installed as his father's deputy. It proved a timely promotion.

In 1988, Alan had the first of two heart operations and Andrew took charge. Temporarily, it happily transpired. Alan recovered his health and there was no question of his transforming the job into a sinecure. "He worked as hard as he ever did," Andrew said. "That was his style, good, old-fashioned greenkeeping. His heart and soul were in this golf course. It always came first."

It was pride in his job and pride in the course that drove Alan, during one isolated disagreement with the Club, to the verge of resignation. A faction of members were of the opinion that Little Aston's greens were too slow, that they were not cut short enough and, against their groundsman's emphatic recommendations, ordered them shorn to a slicker level. This caused them to turn bare and Andrew recalled "Dad

From left, Andrew Boraston, Head Greenkeeper, Craig Hartley,
John Barsley, James Newbold and Steve Yates

David Gibbons

did come close to resigning." Fortunately, quiet diplomacy prevailed, Alan carried on and in good time the greens improved. No subsequent problems occurred, apart from the year that a chemical company provided a moss killer that, on a lot of greens, killed rather more than the moss! On investigation the chemical company was found to be at fault and the moss killer was removed from the market.

Sadly, Alan's second operation in 1998 was not as successful as the first and he died on 2nd May. His funeral was attended by committee and members alike and more than 200 people overspilled the church. Compliments were overwhelming.

Alan's methods and philosophies live on with his son, who of all the course carers was the only one born to the job. For as long as he could remember, in school holidays and on summer evenings, he had been his father's little helper. He had swished greens, he had cleared leaves, he had caught fish in the lake by the 17th and, when no one was around, had swung a crafty club or two. The golf course was his second home. Within a week of leaving school he was where he is today, on very familiar ground:

I think I'm able to step back a bit more from this job than my father could but I hope that I keep up his standards, that I can avoid making a mess of all his hard work. I'd like to think that he would think that I'm still doing the job. I'm happy with the course, but not one hundred per cent happy; it's dangerous to think like that. There's always something that can be done.

The Artisans

Little Aston is lucky enough to having a thriving link with the Aldridge Artisans' Golf Association at a time when artisans are a dying breed, going the way of the caddie and disappearing from all but a few clubs. Just how has that happened? What changed? "The world," said Frank Brookhouse with characteristic acuity. He is in his seventies and has been an artisan for fifty-five years, having started as a caddie but gone are the days when his father, Frank senior, who worked in a dairy, could earn 15s., about as much as he earned in a week at his job, caddying at the weekend.

The Aldridge Artisans started life in 1898 as Sutton Coldfield Working Men's Golf Club, open to the park keepers employed in Sutton Park, greenkeepers, stewards and caddies. Club professionals, who had often started as caddies, were members too but membership was restricted to thirty-five in total. They played at Sutton Coldfield in exchange for the work they did on and around the course and from early on were also allowed to play at Little Aston, where many of them caddied and, in later years, helped out at major tournaments. "Pre-war caddies were paid 1/10d in the morning and 2/- in the afternoon, with tip 1/- minimum," Frank said:

We knew who the bad tippers were and would always hide at the back when they came looking for a rat [caddiespeak for caddie] but Mart Lewis made sure they were shared around and you couldn't escape. Mart paid you your fee and the player paid you your tip.

Frank started playing at Great Barr, called Calthorpe Park in those days, in the school holidays, paying 1s. a day and getting three rounds in. Golf became a passion and caddying was a congenial way of earning some money, learning how to conduct yourself in all sorts of company, making lifelong friends and, in some cases, acquiring a job. Frank remembered one lad who came from a very poor family and could not get work until he started caddying for the boss of Imperial Metal Industries, a very big concern. He gave his caddie a job in the warehouse and the lad worked his way up until he was running the warehouse, making good money, with 100 men under him, but he still caddied on a Sunday. Later, there were those who looked at what he was earning and said he should no longer be an artisan. John Matthews, whose father Jack was caddie master at Sutton Coldfield from 1895-1950, was a caddie too but grew up to run his own garage business and when he applied to join the Artisans and rolled up to Streetly in his Jag, Jack Hargreaves, the professional, voted against letting him in. Others did not and John, who was also Charlie Ward's nephew, is still a member.

As the world changed and park keepers and caddies became fewer and further between, artisans' clubs started disappearing too and in 1978 Sutton Coldfield Working Men's Golf Club looked as though it might cease to exist

The Aldridge Artisans at their annual match against the Club. To the left of John Beharrell, centre, is Don Davies. To his right are: Bob Cox (head), Frank Brookhouse and John Matthews

altogether. Instead, the members changed their name to Aldridge Artisans' Golf Association, most of them had been at school in Aldridge, and thanks to the good auspices of John Lewis, a member who used to play for West Bromwich Albion and Norman Russell, who became their president, the artisans found themselves a new home at Little Aston. They offered to pay a small subscription but were told that "under no circumstances would payment be accepted".

"We're allowed to play early Sunday or on Monday afternoon in the winter," Frank said:

In the summer it's Monday or Friday after half past four or Sunday early. Just once a week, though. We help out on the course about once a week, as and when. We don't drive the machinery and we don't cut across the greenkeepers, we're there to help them out where needed. We do bunkers mainly and divoting. We always divot on a Sunday and it doesn't take any longer than a round of golf if you've got fifteen blokes who know what they're doing, spread out across a fairway. It's a fine art. At tournaments we'll do car parking and the scoreboards, that sort of thing.

Norman made sure that the Association was affiliated to the Staffordshire Union of Golf Clubs and attended the county dinner and it is now the only Artisans' section affiliated to the county. Numbers are falling nationwide but it is important to Little Aston and clubs of the stature of Royal Birkdale, Royal

Liverpool, Southport & Ainsdale and Walton Heath to maintain their traditional links with the artisans and the game's roots. It is a proud history and the Aldrdige Artisans duly celebrated their centenary in 1998. At one time they boasted two Ryder Cup players in Charlie and Jack Hargreaves and used to be able to turn out a team of twelve who were scratch or better. Nowadays, the lowest handicap is 8 but the players are as competitive as ever, with sixteen trophies to play for, including the Collyer Cup, the oldest, which was presented in 1926, and numerous matches, including one against the ladies, who rate it one of the highlights of their season.

The annual presentation and dinner is held at the Club and the guests include many of the Aldridge Artisans' Golf Association's vast number of vice presidents, all usually past captains of Little Aston or members of the committee. There were twenty-eight at the last count, fifteen of them active and they personify the close ties between the members of the Club and the Artisans, all men of golf to the tips of their spikes. A newspaper article describing artisans as "second-class citizens" did not reflect the experience of men like Frank Brookhouse and John Matthews, who said simply "There is too much respect for that."

The starter's hut, a masterpiece of reconstruction

Frank Brookhouse tells the story:

We had stumbled across a fifty-two year old bathing hut, made out of elm, in the woods near the 17th hole. It had at one time belonged to Scribbans, the bakers, who owned Little Aston Hall. We moved the hut, put in new foundations and then used the original wood for most of the shed, fitting a complete new roof and floor, new windows and doors. The members of Little Aston GC were amazed at the way the old hut had been transformed into such a fine building. For this we must thank Pete Roberts who did the bulk of the rebuilding work and ex-brickie Charlie Cox, seventy-four years young, for the foundation work. Also, thanks to Reg Lewis, Tom Jelves and Dan Davies.

The Stewards

Looking after the inner needs of golfers is a bit of a niche business. It is not, generally, at the haute end of cuisine either in terms of culinary requirements or earning power but members and visitors still expect the best, preferably for not very much, and keeping everyone well fed and watered and content is a balancing act requiring rare dexterity and tolerance of a high order. Being honorary house steward has been no sinecure as one incumbent discovered when he tried improving the level of customer service with the mantra "a pie, a pint and a word to the wise". It did not last long after one member, having received his pie and pint, said: "And a word to the wise? Don't eat the pie."

The Starter's Hut

Perhaps because of the more intimate, nurturing, emotional nature of the job, Little Aston's stewards and house staff have lacked the longevity of their outdoor colleagues although there was a certain amount of stability in the first forty years. Mr. and Mrs. Walker lasted from 1909, when the clubhouse opened, until 1925, when they stood down because of his failing health and they were held in such high regard that the Walker Fund raised the sizeable sum of £105. 7s. 0d. In 1926, Mr. and Mrs. Bailey were appointed and looked after things until Ethel Bailey resigned after her husband's death in 1937. She was persuaded to return twelve months later and stayed until 1945. The grateful members each contributed two guineas to her retirement fund.

At the beginning the Club was run as a gentleman's club, with the smoking room the focal point. Plentiful supplies of spirits and port were essential and in the early days beer was drawn from the barrel and served in personalised silver or pewter tankards, a tradition that petered out after World War II.

Jack and Lily Bailey succeeded their namesake Ethel and lasted as steward and stewardess until 1952. Mrs. Ensell, their second-in-command, took charge until the Aucotts arrived in 1953. They resigned in 1956 and for the next four years the Pailthorpes looked after things until the short, ill-fated tenure of Mr. and Mrs. T.R. Jones, who lasted only six months. In July 1961 Mr. Jones, who was known as Hurlingham, absconded with the day's takings

Alfie Warmington with the Club's steward and his wife, Mr. and Mrs. Bailey, who were taken on the bus for the Hollinwell match to provide "appropriate nourishment on the journey"

from the Public School Meeting and, perhaps even worse, Peter Bigwood's winnings on the Derby sweepstake. Jones was arrested and charged and turned out to be a con man with a criminal record.

The next appointees moved to Wales after only nine months but the Aucotts returned. Arthur Aucott had a good sense of humour and a supply of tall tales and his wife was revered for her treacle tart. When they retired in 1968, their son Graham, who had often helped out in the bar, and his wife Doreen took over and stayed until their own retirement in 1979.

Bob Leighton, who had a heart condition, two wives and a rather short fuse, coped well enough until his health deteriorated and Denise Rayward, an accomplished chef, was appointed, combining the roles of steward and stewardess. Her food was outstanding, if not to everyone's taste, but she left for Woodhall Spa after a few months. Sue Hesson took over the kitchen and Julian Frutos became steward, with his wife Maria assisting; they were succeeded by Peter and Miriam Moore; then in 2004 Wayne Foulger, one of the bar staff, was promoted to steward and Rob Boyne was put in charge of the cooking and remained until his unanticipated resignation two years later.

Praise be, Wayne was still here in centenary year and the catering was in the capable hands of Carl Luke, who had been a chef at Fairlawns Hotel.

In the middle of all this toing and froing "the two Pats", friendly, efficient, courteous and interested, deserve a special mention for providing some welcome stability. Pat Humes aka "Blonde Pat", fair-haired and smiling, arrived in 1981 and worked mostly behind the bar and Pat Noakes, known as "Dark Pat", dark-haired and smiling, was on duty mainly in the dining room from 1982 until she retired in 2004. In fact, Blonde Pat was joined by her husband Ray when he retired from the police force in 2002.

The members remain eternally grateful. Thank you all.

Chapter Sixteen

Events: Amateur

T HE CLUB'S first major national event was the third English Amateur Championship in April 1927, well, strictly speaking it was the English County Championship held just before the main event. There were four players per team and Surrey won with an aggregate of 650, with Worcestershire second on 668. Bernard Darwin, of *The Times*, disliked such laborious preparation but he did approve of the venue:

Little Aston is a course that demands all the practice that anyone can give it, for it is both good and difficult. It is seldom that one sees a course on which the tee shot that is ill struck is so ruthlessly and so regularly trapped. Long, straight driving is, as it should be, of the greatest value, but with the strong, cold wind that has been blowing it is not easy of attainment.

The course is decidedly long, measuring 6,400 yards, but the ground has plenty of run in it, and there is no reason for the moderate hitter to slog his soul out. The greens are pleasant, and of a moderate pace, but they want a good deal of knowing, otherwise the ball has a habit of curling away unexpectedly and finishing a highly disconcerting distance from the hole. There are plenty of fine trees, but, for the most part, their bark may be said to be worse than their bite. The trees do the frightening and the bunkers do the trapping, and the latter do a good deal of it ...

There were blizzards on the first day and Mart Lewis had to lay in a new supply of winter mittens. In the second round there was no snow and *The Times* dutifully recorded: "The earliest matches saw the defeat of the comparatively old gentlemen of the tournament ... Mr. (Michael) Scott was putted out of his match and Mr. Darwin putted himself out ..." There were no by-lines then but Darwin was the golf correspondent being characteristically scathing about his own play. And when C.W. Timmis, a schoolboy from Leasowe, had six 3s in the first twelve holes of the second round, Darwin called it "a really heartbreaking achievement".

Mr. T.P. (Thomas Philip) Perkins, of Castle Bromwich, beat Mr. J.B. Beddard, of South Staffs and a country member of Little Aston, by 2 and 1 in the final, watched by about 1,500 people. Perkins, two down with seven to play, won the next four holes to turn the match around and proved it was no

T.P. Perkins, winner of the 1927 English Amateur Championship, on the 5th tee

fluke by winning the Amateur in 1928 and playing in the Walker Cup, where he was hammered by Bobby Jones. They also met in the final of the US Amateur and Jones won crushingly again. Perkins turned professional and finished joint second in the 1932 US Open.

Darwin, who refereed the final, was impressed by Perkins and lauded Little Aston: "[I have] a knowledge of golf courses extensive and peculiar and I do not believe that there is in this country an inland course which is a more severe test of golf."

At the Midland Counties Meeting in September 1935 the amateur and professional course records were broken, the former by Dr. W.M. Robb of Moseley with a 68 and the latter by Bert Gadd with 66. The reporter from the *Birmingham Post* was astonished:

I cannot recall a more brilliant burst of scoring in any Midland competition – professional or amateur – and Little Aston is not the course on which one expected it to be accomplished. When Pixton did his 71 [1928], it was regarded as a great achievement; Stanley Lunt's 69 [1933] as uncanny.

The English Amateur was back at the Club in 1948 with an entry of 200. H.J. Roberts, of Sandwell Park, who had beaten the favourite Charles Stowe, of

Michael Lunt, Geoffrey Marks, Trevor Homer, former Walker Cup players, at Little Aston

Penn, in the semi-finals, was six up after ten holes of the final but his game fell apart and he was beaten 2 and 1 by Alan George Beaufoy Helm, of Stinchcombe Hill.

Women's golf also started to feature, with a Curtis Cup trial early in 1948 and the following year Charlie Ward, Jean Donald, Frances Stephens and Jeanne Bisgood played an exhibition match that raised £400 for the Curtis Cup funds. Full-blown international golf arrived on 13th June 1950, with England versus Australia, six players a side, and the papers called it a test match. It ended in a three-all draw, with Frances Stephens, Elizabeth Price and Jeanne Bisgood winning the first three matches for England and the Aussies the last three, two of them at the 20th.

In 1956, Staffordshire won the English County Finals with members John Beharrell, Bob Church and Roger Bayliss in the side but the home team was not quite so fortunate in the English Women's County Finals in 1967. Lancashire, who fielded five internationals, won and Staffordshire were second. Ann Booth won three of her six matches.

In 1970 the top amateurs returned for the Brabazon Trophy, now officially the English Open Amateur Stroke Play Championship and the winner was Rodney Foster, from Bradford, with 287, two shots ahead of Scott MacDonald, of Dalmahoy. Geoff Marks, Trentham, was third on 291 and Michael Bonallack, Thorpe Hall, fourth on 292. In the 1979 Brabazon, David Long, of Shandon Park, birdied the last two holes to finish on 291, one shot ahead of Ian Marchbank, Auchterarder, and Ian Bradshaw, Eastham Lodge.

The Club hosted its third English Amateur in 1985 and eighteen year old Roger Winchester, of Sidmouth, completely unheralded, won the title, beating Paul Downes, of Coventry, in the semi-finals and Peter Robinson, of Knebworth, by one hole in the final. Winchester said he had never previously won a thing, not even his club's monthly medal.

In May 1988, the English Ladies Close Amateur Championship was held at the Club for the first time, the details of this historic occasion are in the ladies section chapter 12, and in August there was the inaugural English Open Mid-Amateur Championship, for men of thirty-five and older. Peter McEvoy, of Copt Heath, one of Britain and Ireland's all-time great amateurs, won by twenty shots with rounds of 68, 76, 70 and 70.

In his time, McEvoy had shared the course record of 66 with fellow amateurs Downes and Anthony Wall, two better than Cobie Legrange's then professional record of 68 but those scores were shattered during the Brabazon Trophy of 1994. Eighteen year old Gary Harris, from Broome Manor, set the new mark with a 64 in the third round, despite dropping a shot at the 2nd. He had nine birdies in all, including four in a row from the 8th and finished 3, 3, 3. He won the title by six shots from Warren Bennett, of Ruislip, with a total of 280 – 72, 70, 64, 74. Chris Poxon, a member who was one of Staffordshire's outstanding players for many years, was ninth, on 292, with rounds of 74, 71, 77 and 70.

It is not often that you get a sneak preview on your home course of massive talents like Sergio Garcia, Paul Casey, Luke Donald, nephew of long-standing member Geoff Binks, and Henrik Stenson, to mention just a few of the participants in the British Boys Championship of 1994. But they were not yet the men they were to become and the finalists have not so far made a significant impact on the adult game. Chris Smith, Scarborough South Cliff, seven down after thirteen holes of the thirty-six hole final against Chris Rodgers, Royal Mid-Surrey, and still five down at lunch, mounted an incredible recovery in the afternoon and won by 2 and 1. Smith can boast that he beat Garcia; Biagio Paocillo of Italy that he defeated Casey; Matthew King, Toft Hotel, that he bested Donald; and Robert Duck, Northamptonshire County, that he did for Stenson. Garcia was only fourteen and a tiny tot but he reached the last eight and won the title three years later. Since then he, Stenson, Donald and Casey have played a big part in the Ryder Cup and established themselves at the top of the game. Others to win as professionals were Carl Pettersson, Simon Dyson, Kenneth Ferrie, Alastair Forsyth, Gregory Havret, Graeme Storm, Jose Manuel Lara and Richard Finch.

The women were back in 1996 for the English Ladies Close Amateur Stroke Play Championship. Sarah Gallagher, of Trentham Park, led from the start after an opening 69 at Sutton Coldfield and had rounds of 73, 74 and 74 at Little Aston to finish seven shots ahead of Elaine Ratcliffe, Sandiway, and Joanne Hockley, Felixstowe Ferry. In 1998, the Ladies Open Amateur

Championship, the country's premier women's amateur event, was won by Kim Rostrom, of Clitheroe, who beat France's Gwladys Nocera by 4 and 3 in the final. The rain was so torrential that the greenstaff had to go ahead of the players to squeegee each green and only that and the course's natural sandy sub-soil prevented play being abandoned. In June 2005, Chris Stirling, of Meon Valley, won the English Senior Ladies Stroke Play Championship, with Carolyn Kirk, of Ganton, second and Rosemary Watters, Porters Park, winning the over sixty-fives' trophy.

At the other end of the age scale, in September that year, Yorkshire won the English Boys County Finals, beating Warwickshire on a countback. Warwickshire lost to both Yorkshire and Essex in the foursomes but beat them, and Gloucestershire, in the singles. Warwickshire's eighteen year old captain Andrew Sullivan won his three matches and was simply sensational against Daniel Brooks, of Essex. It is doubtful that any words can do full justice to Sullivan's start and John Beharrell settled for "quite remarkable".

At the 388 yard 1st hole, Sullivan drove beyond the flag and sank the putt. People were still wondering if the 1st had ever been driven before when Sullivan reached the 2nd green with an 8-iron. And holed the putt. There was sheer disbelief when he hit a 9-iron to four feet at the 3rd and sank that putt too. Eight shots for the first three holes. Five under par. Fourteen Open champions and many other stellar players had tackled Little Aston down the years but not one had made a start like that. Sullivan continued to play golf of the highest order but although he was out in 29, he was only one up, with Brooks having a birdie at the 6th and an eagle 2 at the 7th. He was five under par when he lost on the 15th, with Sullivan nine under.

In 2006, Liz Bennett, of Brokenhurst Manor, won the English Ladies Stroke Play with scoring that was a little more sedate. She finished on 290, two under par, with rounds of 75, 72, 70 and 73, two shots ahead of Sophie Walker, of Kenwick Park. The best round of the championship was a 68, five under par, by Florentyna Parker, of Royal Birkdale.

Over the years the Club has also hosted numerous Staffordshire and Midland events, most notably the Midland Open Amateur Championship, which was held here in tandem with Sutton Coldfield every year from 1976 until 2000, bar 1979. Winners included McEvoy, Downes, Michael Hassell, Gary Wolstenholme, John Bickerton, David Howell, Harris and Donald.

It is too early to say how the boys who contested the 2008 British Boys Championship, which graces the centenary pages, will turn out but keep your eyes peeled.

Chapter Seventeen

Events: Professional

BIG PROFESSIONAL events were first played at Little Aston in the 1930s, although the Club hosted the Midland Professional Autumn Meeting as early as 1913. Exhibition matches were popular and two of the biggest names in British golf, Percy Alliss, father of Peter, and Abe Mitchell, the player depicted on the lid of the Ryder Cup trophy, visited the Club in 1932. A year later the flamboyant American, Walter Hagen, who did so much to raise the status of professionals, and his compatriot Densmore Shute, the Open champion, were the stars.

National professional events began in earnest at Little Aston in 1937 with the Daily Mail £2,000 tournament. Henry Cotton, later Sir Henry, who was to win the second of his three Open Championships three months later, was the main attraction. It was recorded that:

well over 1,000 spectators were on the course, an orderly crowd in the main, but when Cotton set out, Mr. Bigwood had to make an appeal on the first green for spectators not to click cameras in the hearing distance of players.

Plus ça change.

Sam King, from Knole Park, won with final rounds of 67, a new course record, and 69 for a total of 283, four shots ahead of Cotton. Charlie Ward, representing the Palace Hotel, Torquay, finished on 299. "The competitors," it was said, "were loud in their praise of the course and of the perfect arrangements made by the club officials for their convenience."

There was innovation too. Henry Longhurst, who went on to become a peerless television broadcaster, wrote in his autobiography *My Life and Soft Times*:

I believe I can claim to have done the first 'live' outside [radio] broadcast on golf when the BBC set up a glass box on stilts at some vantage point far out on the Little Aston course outside Birmingham overlooking two greens and three tees. In a way we were not unsuccessful. We saw plenty of play, chopping and changing from one hole to another, and had an added piece of good fortune when a past Open Champion, Arthur Havers, completely fluffed a short approach shot in front of our window. Perhaps he was unnerved by the thought of being on 'live' for the first time in history.

Some reliable geographers think that Longhurst's perch was between the 4th and 7th greens but in his memoirs Tom McMillan jun. recollected:

A small scaffolding tower was erected between the 1st tee and the 2nd green. I was there, along with a lot of other people. After lunch, I remember that Henry had some difficulty climbing up the ladder to the top of the twenty foot high tower. There was some anxiety about his safety, and hauling him up by rope was suggested, but turned down.

They say the palest ink is better than the finest memory.

In June 1939, the Penfold Professional League, inaugurated the previous year, was played at the Club. It was the brainchild of Little Aston member, A.E. "Dick" Penfold, a ballistics expert, described by *Golf Monthly* as "modest about his great achievements … he can give down-to-earth information upon any one of the thousand questions of the flight theory of golf balls". He was head of Golf Ball Developments Limited, near Bromford Bridge and his intention was to give the players more match play and aid Ryder Cup selection. The twelve players who led the averages for the Vardon Trophy the previous year played each other head to head over eighteen holes, two matches per day, two points for a win, one for a draw. At stake: £1,000 in total, £200 to the winner and £45 to the twelfth man. Cotton and Charles Whitcombe tied with eighteen points each, Cotton losing two matches and Whitcombe losing one and halving two of eleven.

The next tournament at Little Aston was the Dunlop Masters in October 1947 and it was the scene of yet another first. On the day before the tournament a hand-picked team of members was chosen to play a fourball alliance competition against professionals due to play in the tournament. It was, in essence, the first Pro-Am to be played in this country. In the tournament itself Arthur Lees and Norman Von Nida, Australia, tied on 283 and Lees won the thirty-six hole play-off, and £300, with rounds of 71, 70 to Von Nida's 76, 69. Charlie Ward was fifth on 287.

Two years later at the Lotus Saxone event, Charlie raised hopes of a home win when he started with a 66 to lead by a shot. He and Max Faulkner were tied for the lead on 137 going into the last day, thirty-six holes in those days, and Charlie was a shot ahead of Faulkner after three rounds. In the end Charlie needed two pars to win but found a poor lie off a good drive at the 17th, bunkered his approach and took five. He took another five at the 18th and finished second.

Penfold re-entered the tournament scene at Little Aston in 1950 with another innovative event, the PGA LGU Foursomes. The leading professionals and the leading women amateurs all played one round each at

The Dunlop Masters 1955, the 1st tee

Bobby Locke, four times Open champion   *Peter Thomson, five times Open champion*

Sutton Coldfield and Little Aston, with the top thirty-two of each sex qualifying. There was then a draw for partners and a knockout mixed foursomes completed at Sutton Coldfield. Kay Denham and Margaret Tait, both members at both clubs, qualified but were beaten in the first and second rounds respectively. The winners were Norman Sutton, Leigh, and Mrs. Joan Gee, Chevin.

The 1954 Daks was won by Peter Alliss, then a tall, dark, handsome young man, after an agonising wait. "In those days they didn't put the leaders out last and I was out first with Bernard Hunt," Alliss said:

We did two rounds in a total of three hours 54 minutes and I did 68 and 69 or something like that [it was 67] and Bernard wasn't much more. We were both totally relaxed and enjoying our game as much as two Sunday morning club golfers. I finished with 279 and had the deadly wait for Bobby Locke to finish.

The South African, who had already won three of his four Open titles, came to the last needing a par to tie but his stock-in-trade was a carefully controlled draw off the tee, his ball duly clattered into the huge old oak tree on the right and the great man took five. Alliss was ecstatic "I had won my first major open event and £400. It was a sweet moment for me." It was not so sweet for Charlie Ward, who was beginning to miss the putts that hitherto had always gone in and his good rounds were tending to come singly rather than in fours. He started with a 69 but the next three rounds were 76, 74, 73 and not only was he thirteen strokes behind Alliss, he was two behind John Llewellyn Morgan. Bob Church finished on 302.

The Irishman Harry Bradshaw was a popular winner of the Dunlop Masters in 1955. Six years earlier he had suffered his "ball-in-the-broken-

Henry Cotton (centre) on the 2nd hole playing in the Dunlop Masters. Note the former groundsman's cottage top right

bottle" fate at the Open at Royal St George's and the British public were sympathetic towards him. Bradshaw had driven into a carelessly discarded bottle, broken half way down, and his ball lodged in the bottom half. In those days the edict "play the ball as it lies" was rather stricter than now and roving referees were few and far between, so Bradshaw elected to, literally, take a smash at the thing. He ended up in a tie for the championship with Locke but lost the play-off. The crowds at Little Aston were said to be "the biggest outside any tournament other than the Open, and were splendidly marshalled". Bradshaw won well, with rounds of 69, 70, 71 and 67 for a total of 277, four ahead of Cotton.

It was a bittersweet event for Alliss, who finished fifth and felt that his performance would secure his Ryder Cup place despite the heartbreak of the match at Wentworth in 1953 when he and Bernard Hunt, both rookies, were deemed to have lost the cup. The team was announced and there was no Alliss, so he drowned his sorrows before going back to where he was staying, nearby, with the Foster Wards, members who had become friends. At the dinner table it all got too much and he burst into tears. "Not too many people saw me ... but I felt a total fool the next morning." His hostess got a very large bunch of flowers. Alliss was to play in eight Ryder Cups in all, including the win at Lindrick in 1957 and the tie at Royal Birkdale in 1969.

Edward Hooper, Club member for forty-nine years, when aged twelve, collecting Henry Cotton's autograph

In the Dunlop Masters of 1958 the winner was the big Shropshire lad, Harry Weetman, born in Oswestry. He led from the start after an opening round of 67, one ahead of Locke and two ahead of Cotton and subsequent rounds of 68, 70 and 71 increased his margin to four shots over Locke and six over Cotton, who never did manage a victory at Little Aston. It was a happier hunting ground for Alliss, who produced a timely burst of brilliance to win the 1962 Schweppes Close Championship. At lunch on the final day he was three behind Dave Thomas and two behind Ralph Moffitt, of Coventry Hearsall. Thomas collapsed to an 80 but Moffitt was leading until Alliss surged to the front with five successive birdies from the 12th. He finished with two 4s for a 71 and a winning total of 287.

There were some distinguished performances by the amateurs in the field. Alex Holmes, then of Walmley but later Little Aston, finished on 308, while Michael Lunt recorded a score of 295, to finish seventh, beating no fewer than five of the previous Ryder Cup team. Tony Jowle of Moseley holed his 2-iron tee shot at the 9th and got the maximum prize available at that time, a voucher for £29. 19s. 11d. Harry Middleton, a professional from Ireland, holed an 8-iron at the 5th and won £1,000, the same as the first prize, from the sponsors.

Bernard Hunt, winner of the Dunlop Masters, 1955

Little Aston was a natural home for the Dunlop Masters given the huge Fort Dunlop presence in nearby Erdington and the members with Dunlop connections; the tournament was back in 1963. The stellar field included Open champions in Thomson, Locke and Nagle and Bob Charles was to win the Open later that same year at Royal Lytham & St. Annes. Add in Alliss, Rees, Thomas, Hunt and Christy O'Connor and there could hardly have been a better entry for a British event. The players were tested by some severe rough but after two rounds O'Connor led with two 69s, two ahead of Hunt and three in front of Moffitt, who again upstaged all the international stars with rounds of 75, 66, 71 and 70, setting a target of 282. Hunt, who needed to finish 4, 4, 4 to win, missed a three-footer at the 17th to take 5 and ended in a tie.

What followed was another Little Aston first, with a play-off over four holes instead of the customary thirty-six. The layout of the 1st, 2nd, 17th and 18th is perfect for such a denouement and Hunt played the four par 4s in 14 to Moffitt's 17 and won £2,000.

In 1965 the Martini International was won by Peter Butler, a local lad and Ryder Cup player from Harborne, with a total of 275. Rounds of 70, 69, 67 and 69 left him four shots ahead of Jean Garaialde and Hunt in joint second place. Charlie Ward, who had a 67 in the third round, finished with a total of 288. Two Club members also took part: Rodney James had two rounds of 76 and David Pepper was called in as a marker for Neil Coles when Ross Newdick, a New Zealand professional, fell ill after the first round. David recalled Coles going round in 69 "despite my efforts. He hit the hole and stayed out five times". Also putting in an appearance was Dave Musgrove, Garaialde's rookie caddie, "dressed up proper" as he put it, in collar and tie. Musgrove went on to win four majors, two Open Championships, with Severiano Ballesteros and Sandy Lyle, a Masters, with Lyle, and a US Open, with Lee Janzen. And it all started at Little Aston.

The Penfold Swallow tournament took place in May of 1966, although it very nearly did not. Four days before it was due to start the fire brigade got a call saying that the field behind the 10th green was ablaze. The firemen duly turned out, drove down the service road at the side of the course, along the 10th fairway and stopped just short of the green. They found a farmer burning stubble, with everything under control and the driver of the fire engine turned round, on the green! He left tracks about thirty feet long and up to a foot deep, not to mention trepidation about the tournament taking place. Jimmie McDowall, the Club captain, told the *Birmingham Evening Mail* that repair work on refilling and returfing the damage "would take five men about five days to complete" but Alan Boraston and his team did a wonderful job in taking turf from the fringes of other greens and by placing the pin at the back, the hole was playable.

Dave Thomas, who shared the lead after a first round of 68, went on to win, playing the last nine holes in a splendid 33, for a total of 281, to beat Hunt, something of a course specialist, by one. He had a 25 foot putt for a play-off but hit the hole and stayed out.

By now professional tournament golf in the British Isles was starting to be about more than just golf. The attendant tented villages, with their exhibitions and retail sales, the corporate tents and the catering facilities meant that more and more people wanted to come and watch and they wanted to come in their cars. But Little Aston had insufficient room for all the paraphernalia required, let alone enough room to park all the cars, and it was becoming obvious that a rich history of generous support for the professional game was going to have to come to an end.

It did so at the Dunlop Masters in September 1969 with a field that was probably the most distinguished in the Club's history. Tony Jacklin was just two months into his reign as Open champion, before going on to win the US Open nine months later, Peter Thomson, five times Open champion, was back and Billy Casper, winner of the US Open in 1959 and

The Birmingham Post

Tuesday, March 8, 1966

**Lighting-up times;
6.28 p.m. to 6.9 a.m.**

Charlie Ward (left), the Little Aston professional, and Rodney James, the Staffordshire amateur champion, inspect the damage caused by a fire engine which drove on to the 10th green at Little Aston Golf Course on its way to a fire.

Fire engine rips up the tenth

Birmingham Post Sutton Coldfield Staff

A FIRE ENGINE, on its way to a blaze, was driven across the tenth green at Little Aston Golf Course, ruining the turf. Last night, faced with strong complaints from angry club officials, a Staffordshire Fire Brigade officer apologised to the captain, Mr. James McDowall.

The incident happened after firemen from Rushall had been sent to a fire near the golf course.

Mr. McDowall said last night: "It will take about five days' work by five men to repair the green and will mean that other work on the course which is now becoming urgent after the mild winter will have to wait.

"Greens and fairways need cutting and we have to get ready for the Penfold Swallow tournament which starts here at the beginning of May. The tenth green will be playable by then but will not be in as good a condition as the other 17."

Apology

Mr. McDowall said that a fire brigade officer had apologised to him for the incident. Asked whether the club would claim compensation from the brigade he declined to comment.

Mr. C.H. Ward, the club professional, said that the fire engine had left tracks up to 30 yards long and a foot deep on the green.

"Some of the turf will have to be replaced but where the marks are not too severe they will be prised out.

"This is the first time a fire engine has gone over one of our greens. Horses have galloped over the greens in the past, but it is only half a day's work forking out the impressions left by their hooves."

Stubble blaze

The fire officer who saw Mr. McDowall said last night: "We are looking into the matter. We are always concerned when damage is caused to anyone's property."

He said that it was dark when firemen drove over the green on Sunday evening.

They had at first thought that a wood fringing the tenth green was on fire, but it turned out that a farmer was burning stubble in a nearby field.

"As far as compensation is concerned it is a matter for the county council and the golf club."

A Staffordshire County Council spokesman said last night: "We have not had a claim from the golf club."

145

1966 and runner-up in the Masters at Augusta in 1969, he was to win the title in 1970, was also playing. In America at the time Casper, though understated and much under-rated, was overshadowed only by the big three of Palmer, Player and Nicklaus. As the tournament unfolded only Jacklin, of the stars, had any influence on proceedings, and even that was minimal. Cobie Legrange, a relatively unheralded South African, set himself apart from the rest by opening with rounds of 69, 68 and 70 which gave him a six shot lead over Butler and ten over Jacklin.

It was quite a performance by Legrange, who had gone through three caddies in practice before Charlie Ward fixed him up with John Lewis, one of the artisans and a good player, with the words "And if he's no good, he'll hit the bloody ball for you." Legrange's swing was not a thing of beauty and the *Birmingham Post* described it thus:

It would have been remarkable in a playground. He would move the club head back a few inches, stop, sway onto his right foot, move the club again, stop, and finally start the backswing about two feet away from the ball. Experienced professionals were going pale watching.

The headlines rather cruelly dubbed him "C-C-C-Cobie" but the swing held up and a final round of 74, for 281, was good enough to see him home by three from Butler. Maurice Bembridge, not long an assistant at the Club, finished seventh.

Jacklin, who finished with a 68 to share third place with the evergreen O'Connor, inevitably attracted the largest crowds, beautifully managed by well-organised stewards, many of them from the Artisans' section. And the Open champion gave everyone something special to cheer right at the end when he hit a 9-iron second shot straight into the hole for an eagle 2 at the 17th, causing perhaps the biggest roar ever heard at Little Aston. It was a fitting way for the top professionals to say thank you and farewell.

In August 1970, the PGA wrote asking if the Club would like to hold the Classic International Tournament the following year but they declined because "in view of the lack of car parking space it was considered that the Club would not be able to offer the facilities which the promoters would require …". In January 1972:

the Secretary reported that he had been approached by the PGA to find out whether the Club would be prepared to stage a major professional tournament in 1973 and possibly every other year thereafter. It was felt that however much the Club might wish to hold professional tournaments that with the non-availability of large car parking areas in the immediate vicinity it was not feasible to do so. It was however felt that the Club should still try and stage major amateur events.

So that was the end of the big professional occasions, although the course has continued to test the local professionals and those who have to brave regional qualifying for the Open.

Chapter Eighteen

The Centenary Celebrations

T HE CENTENARY celebrations were, in a word, brilliant. The years of planning, the attention to detail, the expense and the sheer hard work were all worth it and the result was, as Brian Cooke, the chairman, put it, "a good week of fun". Work started in March 2002 and reached fruition in June 2008, 21st-28th, with a hectic social whirl of golfing, wining, dining and dancing towards the bicentenary. A good, if exhausting, time was had by all, the final night was a triumph and Brian thanked all concerned, specifically Jon Gough and Lisa Ward of Events Unlimited, the professional organiser who was in charge of the entertainment; Mike Adamson and Tim Hampton, who arranged all the golf and table plans; Angie Pepper and her team who arranged all the ladies' events; and David Moseley, the instigator of the church service.

There were heartfelt thanks to all the other committee members who played a big part in the years of build up: John Beharrell, John Sambrook, Norma James, Mandy Davies, Philip Davies, Neil Andrews and Jeremy Cooke. And there was a special vote of thanks to Glyn Ridley, the Club manager, who rose to the challenge of co-ordinating a massive project with calm good humour. Jeremy, the captain, was the other Cooke at the heart of the occasion, supported by his wife Sarah, as the Club dispensed largesse to friends and fellow golfers from organisations big and small, from near and far, celebrating 100 years of fun, friendship and competition.

On the first day of Centenary Week, at the Men's Centenary Dinner, Bruce Streather, a former member who became captain of Sunningdale and is the oldest man to win the President's Putter at Rye, spoke on behalf of the guests and his speech encapsulated the love and the laughter of a very special place. Here is an edited version of what he said, starting with his first visit at the age of twelve:

My mother had been deputed to take me to the Club but due to her rather poor sense of direction coupled with the fact that the Club had been founded by camouflage experts

147

rendering it the second most difficult to find in England (after Woking) we arrived late and she left me in the car park. I took my bearings, noticing first that there was no door to the clubhouse! I made my way slowly round the side where I found a glass door slightly ajar and entered cautiously. There was a noise of a TV emanating from a small adjoining room so I shouted rather softly 'Hello' and poked my head into the room. I saw an old black and white TV in the corner and rising from a battered seat a smallish figure with a flat cap on his head and wearing a rumpled brown cardigan. It was the great man himself, Charles H. Ward and he gave me what he was always to give me in the years that followed, namely a very warm smile. "Can I help you?" he enquired. "Well," I said, "I've come to play golf with Roderick Chantrill but I'm a little late." "Roderick's on the putting green," Charlie replied. "But I'll show you to your father's locker. You can change your shoes and then go straight out on to the course."

Roderick was a larger than life character. He knew everyone, was a wonderful raconteur and never said an unkind word about anyone. All in all a great person to be with – off the course. On the course, however, he had two failings. The first, which plagued him in his early years, was his inability to hold onto a golf club when a shot displeased him. Indeed some time later he dispatched his putter into the lake beside the 17th green and there it remains probably covered by the several tons of earth that now make up that new green. Later as he grew bigger – and bigger – he always took a caddie. And whoever the caddie was, he invariably upset Roderick's fragile temperament.

Unaccountably Roderick and I took four and a half hours to play, word got back to my father and I was assigned to play with Graham Grove, who was known as Greyhound Grove. He was more interested in the time a round took than the score. If you asked Graham how he had done, he would respond, "Two hours forty two minutes" or "Two hours forty eight minutes, held up by Hugh Cave."

Perhaps my own attitude to the Club can be best summed up by the words of Bobby Jones when giving his speech accepting the freedom of St Andrews. He said, "If you were to take out of my golfing life everything save for the times I have spent at St Andrews I would still have had a full golfing career." That's exactly how I feel about Little Aston. Indeed probably more so because it's great to return to one's roots. So thank you members of Little Aston for your wonderful golf course, for your humour, for the consistent warmth of your welcome to me over the years and for the many acts of kindness which you have always shown me.

The Competitions

Day 1

The theme for the week was variety: something for everybody. It started off, in rather disappointing weather, with a Men's VIP Invitation, teams of four, with the two best balls to score, except on the par 3s and on the 18th where every score counted. The winners, with 94 points, were John Hilliard, Roger Boak, Mark Davies and Tony Fitzpatrick, all members. They finished three points ahead of Paul Stafford, David Moseley, Dan Andrews and John Nosworthy, the captain of Copt Heath, who were second on a countback from John Beharrell, Geoff Hackett, Nigel Lloyd and former Walker Cup stalwart Geoff Marks. Keith Andrews, Mike Knott, Tom Moseley and David Appleton of Formby came fourth, courtesy of a superior back six after tying on 86 points with Chris Poxon, Tony Norcott, Simon Pettit and James Garvey.

The winners were indebted to Davies, who had three birdies on the first nine and Hilliard, who played the back nine in level par gross, revived by the obligatory dose of Pimms after the 8th. All four made telling contributions at the 18th, inspired by a martial ditty played by the Rugeley Power Station Brass Band.

Day 2

There were joint winners of the Centenary Salvers, a mixed greensomes medal, when Mike and Sally Adamson, off 10, and Keith and Anne Andrews, off 7, returned nett 70s. Geoff Wyatt and Biddy Brough were third on 74. On a distinctly windy afternoon the winners, playing together, all played solid, sensible golf, although the Andrews, already the holders of the Greatrex

Hole	Marker's Score	Blue Yards	White Yards	Yellow Yards	Par	Stroke Index	Score A	Score B	NETT POINTS	Ladies Red Yards	Par	Stroke Index
1		392	392	378	4	13				368	4	13
2		446	446	410	4	5				392	5	5
3		514	503	490	5	7				442	5	7
4		317	317	314	4	1				271	4	9
5		161	161	153	3	15				137	3	15
6		423	423	410	4	9				385	4	1
7		362	362	346	4	4				313	4	4
8		410	392	376	4	11				342	4	11
9		193	193	178	3	18				143	3	18
OUT		3218	3189	3055	35					2793	36	
10		444	432	426	4	3				391	5	3
11		393	393	363	4	10				296	4	10
12		485	485	484	5	6				437	5	6
13		183	161	156	3	17				130	3	17
14		342	326	300	4	16				262	4	16
15		549	549	517	5	2				473	5	2
16		419	398	375	4	8				313	4	8
17		380	380	370	4	14				339	4	14
18		400	391	374	4	12				328	4	12
IN		3595	3515	3365	37					2969	38	
OUT		3218	3189	3055	35					2793	36	
TOTAL		6813	6704	6420	72					5762	74	

COMPETITION

DATE · TIME · ENTRY NO. · Handicap · Strokes Rec'd

Player A · Player B

PAR 72 SSS 74 · PAR 72 SSS 73 · PAR 72 SSS 72 · PAR 74 SSS 74

RESULT · HANDICAP · NETT

Marker's Signature .... Player's Signature ....

Card of the course, 2008

Bowls, coped less well with the notorious near halfway refreshments. Having had birdies at the 3rd, 6th and 8th, they double bogeyed the 9th and Keith said "I think we have to put it down to the Pimms."

Day 3

The ladies had a shotgun start for the Coronation Salver, which was played in conjunction with the Ladies Centenary Salver. Sandra Boak, a 27 handicapper, scored 38 points to win by four from Rachel Moseley, who pipped Janet Denham on the better back nine. The trophy, donated by Ladies' captain Angie Pepper, will now be competed for annually. "I'm so thrilled to have my name on it first," said Sandra, who revealed that there was no Pimms for the ladies, only squash.

Day 4

Angie devised a novel format for the Ladies VIP Invitation competition, ensuring that everyone got round, showered and powdered in good time for the Centenary victuals in the marquee. The men had taken five and a half hours to complete their rounds but the women, playing foursomes in teams of four, with everybody in each quartet playing six holes with each partner, took two hours less. Julie Otto, nee Wade, the guest speaker and star player, off plus 1, inspired her team of Angie, past captain Louise Cooke and Cherie Jones to victory with 66 points. They were two points ahead of Helen Gough, the South Staffs captain, Sue Barker, the Staffordshire Veterans captain, Pauline Taylor and Jill Picton-Jones. Julie Brown, the Staffordshire captain, Mandy Davies, Sandra Boak and Joan Jones were third with 61 points, a point ahead of Christine Waters, Copt Heath, Jane Drury, Margaret McAllister and Cicely Gale.

Also on the Thursday

Most clubs have their collections of, usually, retired individuals who gather together once or twice a week and play for a small kitty. Sometimes they adorn themselves with wry or humorous acronyms but at Little Aston, on Thursdays, they just turn up. Eighty-eight of them turned up to play on Centenary Thursday and a dozen more were there for lunch. It was some competition to win. Mike Adamson and his partner Philip Eve came in with 46 points and beat John Beharrell and Mike Leadbetter thanks to a better back nine of 25 points. Bryan Fehilly and Fran Murray were third, with 45.

Day 5

Jo Hollis, Tim Hampton and Nigel Withers won the Ladies, Men & Artisans competition with a score of 79, one point better than Louise Cooke, Philip Eve and Graham York. Jeannie Carpenter, Geoff Wyatt and Nigel Winn were third on 77.

Day 6

On the final day of celebrations Nigel Lloyd and Jamie Burns tied with 38 points in division one of the Men's Centenary Competition, with Nigel taking the title with a better back nine, 18 points to17. Jon Gough was third with 37. Jim Crow took the division two prize, also on countback, after he and Fran Murray both returned 38 points. Jim's back nine of 21, to 19, proved the tiebreaker. John Aucott was third with 36.

The Boys Amateur Championship

In August, 11th-16th, there was golf of a different standard altogether in the Boys Amateur Championship. There were 256 competitors, one from Australia, one from the United States and one from the United Arab Emirates with the rest from all over Europe, including Karlis Broders from Latvia, who reached the fourth round. He was joined in the last sixteen by players from Ireland, England, Scotland, Belgium, Germany, Switzerland, Denmark, France, Italy and Portugal and in the end it was the Portuguese, Pedro Figueiredo, who triumphed. He beat Fraser McKenna, of the Balmore club, on the northern outskirts of Glasgow, at the 39th hole of a titanic final.

Figueiredo, from the Quinta Do Peru club south of Lisbon, holed from two feet for a birdie 4 at the 3rd, the third extra hole, after McKenna, who had been bunkered in two, missed from five feet. It was cruel on the Scot who had been one up playing the 36th and looked odds-on to win a seesaw match until his opponent holed from forty feet.

Jeremy Cooke paid tribute to all the competitors: "They have been a credit to their generation."

Women's Seniors Home International

An altogether older generation brought the centenary celebrations to an end with surprisingly competitive women's seniors' home internationals in cold, blustery conditions at the end of September. Wales won, beating Ireland, Scotland and England, to complete an historic double, their younger women had won the home internationals at Wrexham earlier in the month, and Jeremy Cooke stood up stoically to some teasing, if pointed, heckling at the party afterwards.

England, who had got into the habit of winning this series with five victories out of five, set Ireland on the way to the wooden spoon with a seven and a half points to a half hammering and Wales won four of the five singles to beat Scotland five points to three; England then beat Scotland six points to two and Wales tonked Ireland seven points to one; in the decider Wales won all three foursomes against England and resisted a sterling fight back by the home side to win five points to three. Scotland lost only two games as they beat Ireland five and a half points to two and a half. The Irish, beaten but unbowed, based their party piece afterwards on *Molly Malone* and professed themselves glad just to be "alive, alive-o". Wales, who had holed most of their putts, failed, in a flurry of oversized plastic leeks and daffodils, to hold most of their notes and Joan Neville, the president of the Ladies Golf Union and herself Welsh, said: "Wales is the land of song but there are exceptions to every rule."

*Patrick Cadman, Mark Eddy and Anthony James,
at the Men's Dinner*

Jeremy Cooke, captain 2007-2008

*Judy Hodgkinson, David Moseley and Marita Roxburgh,
at the Ball*

*Ian Boak, John Hilliard and Jon Wood, on the first tee prior
to the Centenary Stableford*

*Mandy Davies and Amanda Bingham,
appropriately dressed for the
Centenary Salvers on Ladies Day*

Jo Hollis, captain 1997-1999,
"the non conformist"

Angela Pepper, captain 2006-2008

Lucille Wood, Mandy Poxon, Laura Clancy, Angela
Smith and Lulu Pettit, at the Ladies' Lunch

Ladies in play on the eighth green

Sally Adamson, Anne Andrews, Keith Andrews and
Michael Adamson, joint winners of the Presidents'
Salvers with the President following the presentation

Men's Captain's Day 2008

Lady Captain's Day 2008

Chapter Nineteen

Centenary Service at St Peter's

**St Peter's
Little Aston**

**Service to mark
the Centenary of
Little Aston Golf Club**

Tuesday 24th June 2008

T HE VICAR OF St Peter's and his wife have long been given Honorary Membership, so a service of thanksgiving during Centenary week seemed appropriate. The church, decorated with golf related floral displays by Heather Lindop and Cherie Jones, was packed for an occasion that was full of joy and emotion. The Reverend Phil Moon, a doughty 20 handicapper, led the service and the Reverend Brian Weaver, who plays off 17, gave the address.

In his prayers, Phil Moon gave thanks for all those who had worked so hard to develop the Club:

We thank you, Heavenly Father, for the vision, hard work, and commitment, of our founders ... We are grateful for all who have continued this work. Our club officials, committee members, administrators, so that 100 years on, we can both see and enjoy the fruits of their labours.

... We thank you for the natural beauty of our golf course. For the trees, plants, grass and the abundance of wild life. We remember, before you, all who have worked to maintain and develop the whole area. For our head greenkeepers and those who over the years have assisted them, for their dedication and good humour. We thank you also for the help given to maintain our course by the Artisans.

We know how easy it is to take the work of others for granted. We are grateful for all, who over the years, have kept the clubhouse going. We thank you for their service behind the bar, in the dining room, in the locker rooms and the pro's shop. We appreciate their cheerfulness, encouragement and their sympathy.

We thank you for the game of golf. For the friendship and friendly rivalries we enjoy. For the help and support we can give one another and the opportunity we have for exercise, refreshment and enjoyment. We are grateful for our community that includes both Senior Members and Juniors, Ladies and Gentlemen and Artisans. Also the many visiting teams and societies and others, who throughout the year use our facilities.

Finally, Heavenly Father, we thank you for all your blessings. We look back with gratitude for the past 100 years ...

Finally, if not quite in the correct order of the church service certainly in order of seniority and service to the Club, we quote the testimonies of three members: John Beharrell, president of the Club, Jeannie Carpenter and Richard Chapman.

John

Quite a number of members of Little Aston Golf Club have been lucky enough to have accumulated memories of the Club over a time of 50 years and a lucky few for even a longer time.

Each and every one of the members will be ever grateful for the determination, drive and foresight of the previous generations who both created the club and have kept it on a steady path. Then there are those members who steered the Club both through the First and Second World Wars. They were difficult times and everything could have slipped away. Let us hope that our founders would be proud that their vision has enabled the Club to celebrate its centenary this year with the club in good heart.

Indeed so much pleasure and enjoyment have been given to members of differing generations which makes this service a special and most appropriate thanksgiving for the Club.

One of my great thrills was receiving my first matched set of second-hand irons. They were made by Forgans of St Andrews whose factory overlooked the 18th green. I sent off for their catalogue and on the back page David Forgan had written – some one hundred years ago – a verse headed 'Golf' and I quote:

It is a science – the study of a lifetime, in which you may exhaust yourself but never your subject.

It is a contest, a duel or a melee, calling for courage, skill, strategy and self-control.

It is a test of temper, a trial of hono(u)r, a revealer of character.

It affords a chance to play the man, and act the gentleman.

It means going into God's out-of-doors, getting close to nature, fresh air, exercise, a sweeping away of the mental cobwebs, genuine re-creation of the tired tissues.

It is a cure for care – an antidote to worry.

It includes companionship with friends, social intercourse, opportunity for courtesy, kindliness and generosity to an opponent.

It promotes not only physical health but moral force.

These words have remained with me and as the world moves on let us pray that these sentiments will be carried through for the next one hundred years allowing the current generation and future generations many more happy times at Little Aston Golf Club.

Jeannie

When I was asked to follow the President at this service by adding my reflections on Little Aston, I instantly asked the question 'Why me?' Then I was reminded that I am the third of four generations of family members starting with my grandfather Tom McMillan who served on the committee before the last war and was president in 1950 -1952. He was followed by father Tom, now in his 97th year, who was captain of the Club at its half century, president eight years later and is now an honorary member. My mother was captain of the ladies section in 1964 and after her premature death in 1970 was buried here in the churchyard at St. Peter's. I myself was married here in 1971.

My first recollections, at a very young age, come not from the Golf Club itself but from the wonderful teas my mother provided for her bridge playing golf friends, the remains of which I would devour on my return from school. I can also remember the Club steward Arthur Aucott coming to us for parsley from our garden as we lived only 400 metres away, followed by his son Graham to collect mint for the pimms.

As a teenager I was involved in Sunday lunches at the club where I had to be on my best behaviour in the dining room (not easy and yes, they did allow the young in for lunch in those days). I can recall adopted aunts and uncles Hiam, McDowall, Warmington, Milne and Cooke to name but a few. Tasting the cranachan, a dessert for Burns Night, was my first introduction to alcohol.

Bob Hiam, Rachel Moseley's father, took me under his golfing wing which may account for my backswing as he was an excellent hockey player! His approach to the drive was to wave the head of the club six inches above the ball and then take it by surprise! I played friendly golf occasionally at Little Aston but as with many young mothers with a growing family and other commitments it was just exercise with good friends on a beautiful course and the fun of introducing my youngest son Andy to the game.

For almost the whole of my life Little Aston Golf Club has been there but in the early days it was only on the fringe of my activities. It was, however, one of the members, Ramsey Wood who told me of a job far away in the north of Scotland which accounted for my absence for some years until I returned when my mother became ill. After she died father moved to Sussex where as a member of Rye he became involved in the creation of the now world famous CRAFT Club. For those who have not come across the tie the initials C R A F T stand for "Can't Remember A Flipping Thing" (the polite version I believe!). Actually, despite his advanced years father is still very much in touch with the celebrations here at Little Aston and was extremely sad that he was physically unable to attend this service and the dinner last Saturday.

Life is a strange thing and going full circle I now find myself with the honour of being next year's lady captain. It is certainly not for my golfing prowess, being totally inconsistent. But it helps not to let the opposition know this, and certainly doesn't help your partner, if you have one. As one poor member learnt to their chagrin I can play, and I quote from P.G. Wodehouse, "like a submarine ploughing through the rough on the 1st hole and occasionally coming up for air and finally appearing on the green"; and another time actually arriving on the 5th green one inch from the flag (almost equal to my mother who had a hole-in-one there).

Memories of happy times spent at Little Aston are in abundance but above all I think it is the warmth of friendship which the Club has always generated both on and off the course that comes through strongest. Times spent together in such a beautiful setting are something quite special and for which we should be extremely grateful.

And so, for family and friends who have gone before, partners, teammates, opponents and acquaintances, I give thanks for everything that Little Aston means to us, the memories we hold and the fun we have enjoyed together which I hope will continue for many years to come.

The next generation

My name is Richard Chapman. I have been a member of Little Aston Golf Club for about one year. I am nine years old and I am one of the youngest members of the Club.

I am grateful that I have a granddad who has the time to teach me and my brother Edward to play golf. I was very honoured when I was accepted to join the Club.

I normally play in the school holidays and sometimes I have a lesson with a pro. It is always fun to put on my special golf clothes and my Little Aston cap.

I like playing iron shots, just like Jim Furyk. I can now hit the ball around 180 yards with my driver off the tee. The holes are always very well kept even the bunkers. Putting is hard with the different slopes. You need to be very careful!

Every time I come to the Golf Club I meet people who are very friendly. After a good round of golf I like to have a glass of coke in the casual bar. Pat usually looks after us and always asks how my brother is doing in the Lichfield Cathedral Choir. I have also been in the dining room where there is lovely food to eat.

Let us thank God for a beautiful place to play. Let us thank God for time to play with our families and friends. Let us thank God for all the wonderful people who bring the golf club alive. Let us give thanks for the game of golf to enjoy.

Amen

St Peter's church window decorated for the service

Appendices

Little Aston First Committee Meeting at Sandycroft, Streetly, on Wednesday 20th May 1908

Elections for full membership

Pro: by: Mr. Winder and sec: by: Mr. Fletcher & resolved that: all Gentlemen to whom circulars were originally sent be elected members without ballot provided their application be sent in writing before the 15 of June.

Resolved that the following Gentlemen be elected original members of the Club:

1	C.F. Arnold	26	A.E. Horton
2	W.N. Arnold	27	H. Jerrard
3	O.V. Arnold	28	B. Lorrimer
4	W. Bellamy	29	A.H. Lewis
5	H.T. Buckland	30	Walter Lewis
6	Frank Barker	31	James Lacy
7	Gilbert Barling	32	A.L. Lloyd
8	T. Betteridge	33	G. Lewis
9	Wyndham Brodie	34	Clive Levi
10	W. Briscoe	35	J.S. Nettlefold
11	G. Finhimann Clarke	36	E.G. Pearson
12	Alfred Caddick	37	S. Powis
13	A.E. Cheatle	38	H.S. Player
14	Leonard Clarke	39	B.V. Smith
15	Walter Edwards	40	F. Sampson
16	H.M. Eddowes	41	J. Sheldon
17	L.A. Evans	42	I.G. Sheldon
18	Frank Edge	43	J.M. Taylor
19	G. Fowler	44	W.J. Taylor
20	P.J. Fisher	45	R.H. Thornton
21	E. Haywood Farmer	46	T.A. Vaughton
22	C. Haywood Farmer	47	Walter Wilkinson
23	A. Fyshe	48	Thos. Warmington
24	J.A. Fletcher	49	A.E. Wiley
25	F.C. Hardy	50	F.H. Winder

On the 28th of May 1908, the following were also elected original members:

51	T.W. Essex	59	F.T. Cozens
52	W.H. Tonks	60	G. Greatrex
53	J.B. Russell	61	W. Briscoe [name crossed out, presumably because he had already been listed at 10]
54	A.W. Greatrex		
55	A.N. Thacker		
56	H.C. Windle	62	A.W. Yardley
57	W. Greatrex	63	Sir Hallewell Rogers
58	A.W. Heaton		

Spellings and initials are a bit tricky not least because they are often different in later entries in the minutes so 100 per cent accuracy is not guaranteed but we have done our best. The vast majority of these men were members at Sutton Coldfield Golf Club at this time. Eddowes hosted Sutton's inaugural meeting on 8th October 1889; Barling, a doctor, was captain in 1899; Fyshe had been honorary treasurer; Hardy was the current honorary secretary; Lloyd was a former honorary treasurer and secretary and was to be captain from 1909 until 1913; Vaughton would be captain from 1914-1918; and Winder had been honorary treasurer and secretary in the early 1890s. In June, J.E. Pritchard and E.E. Lamb also joined Little Aston. Lamb was captain at Sutton from 1906-1908 and Pritchard, who was honorary treasurer from 1901until 1914, also acted as Little Aston's honorary auditor from 1908-1922.

* * * * *

The close links between the clubs were apparent in a couple of matches against the artisans, officially Sutton Coldfield Working Men's Golf Club, in 1911. In the April game, fourteen of the parent club's team of seventeen were also members of Little Aston and in November Little Aston played the artisans at Streetly.

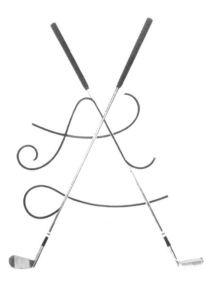

Presidents and Captains

Presidents

1909-1914	E. Ansell	1970-1972	J. Foster-Ward
1914-1921	Sir Hallewell Rogers	1972-1974	G.R. Baxter
1921-1923	W. Wilkinson	1974-1976	R.C. Hiam
1923-1925	F.E. Barker	1976-1978	J. McDowall
1925-1929	T. Ansell	1978-1980	P. Grove
1929-1932	C. Heaton	1980-1982	J.H. Sangster
1932-1936	J. Wylie	1982-1984	P.G. Bigwood
1936-1944	F. Scarf	1984-1986	F.W.G. Church
1944-1948	W. Bigwood	1986-1988	K.N. Cooke
1948-1950	F.T. Edge	1988-1990	N.H. Russell
1950-1952	T. McMillan snr	1990-1992	T.R. Gilchrist
1952-1954	J.B. Russell	1992-1994	W.J. Jinks
1954-1956	G. Greatrex	1994-1996	B.C.B. Pickles
1956-1958	A.C. Warmington	1996-1998	D.A. Warmington
1958-1960	R.G. Horton	1998-2000	B.J. Cooke
1960-1962	W.T. Heaton	2000-2002	D.O. Moseley
1962-1964	F.B. Clark	2002-2004	V.G. Milne
1964-1966	J.F. Cooke	2004-2006	D.I. Pepper
1966-1968	T. McMillan jun	2006-2008	J.C. Beharrell
1968-1970	V.E. Milne	2008-2010	J.R. Sambrook

Captains

1908-1911	C.W. Milligan	1948-1950	A.C. Warmington	1981-1983	D.O. Moseley
1911-1913	T. Pollock	1950-1952	W.T. Heaton	1983-1985	K.N. Cooke
1913-1917	C. Heaton	1952-1954	J. White	1985-1987	R.D. James
1917-1919	Geo. Heaton	1954-1956	J.R.H. Peat	1987-1989	J.C. Beharrell
1919-1920	H.C. Ansell	1956-1958	T. McMillan jun	1989-1991	D.I. Pepper
1920-1922	F. Scarf	1958-1960	J. Foster Ward	1991-1993	V.G. Milne
1922-1923	F.E. Barker	1960-1961	G.R. Baxter	1993-1995	F.K. Andrews
1923-1925	G. Douglas Smith	1961-1963	R.C. Hiam	1995-1997	W.E. Newnes
1925-1928	J. Wylie	1963-1965	V.E. Milne	1997-1999	J.D. Eddy
1928-1929	C. Heaton	1965-1967	J. McDowall	1999-2001	J.R. Sambrook
1929-1932	B. Lorrimer	1967-1969	N.H. Russell	2001-2003	T.R. Hampton
1932-1934	G. Greatrex	1969-1971	P. Grove	2003-2005	M.T. Adamson
1934-1936	W. Bigwood	1971-1973	T.R. Gilchrist	2005-2007	A.N. Andrews
1936-1941	W. Archdale	1973-1975	P.G. Bigwood	2007-2009	J.G. Cooke
1941-1944	G.E. Beharrell	1975-1977	B.C.B. Pickles	2009-	A.N. Jones
1944-1946	R.G. Horton	1977-1979	F.W.G. Church		
1946-1948	J.F. Cooke	1979-1981	B.J. Cooke		

Lady Captains

1946 Mrs. M. Owen
1947 Mrs. M. Tait
1949 Mrs. M. Heath
1952 Mrs. N. Heaton
1954 Mrs. G. Goslett
1956 Mrs. J. James
1958 Mrs. M. Heath
1960 Mrs. L. Morley
1962 Mrs. M. Firth
1964 Mrs. B. McMillan
1966 Mrs. V. Gilchrist

1968 Mrs. P. Dippie
1970 Mrs. D. Hinde
1972 Mrs. J. James
1974 Mrs. P. Foster-Ward
1976 Mrs. F. Franks
1978 Mrs. C. Hill
1980 Mrs. W. Walters
1982 Mrs. D. Fisher
1983 Mrs. H. Lindop
1985 Mrs. R. Moseley
1987 Mrs. A. Pickles

1989 Mrs. L. Cooke
1991 Mrs. J. Cadman
1993 Mrs. J. Denham
1995 Mrs. P. Eddy
1997 Mrs. J. Hollis
1999 Mrs. J. Milne
2001 Mrs. N. James
2002 Mrs. A. Andrews
2004 Mrs. L. Warmington
2006 Mrs. A. Pepper
2008 Mrs. J. Carpenter

Competition Winners – Men and Juniors

Final Medal – Edward Ansell Cup
Mens thirty-six hole singles handicap stroke play medal, played in May

Presented by the first Club President, Mr Edward Ansell, in 1911

1911 J.G. Sheldon
1912 G. Greatrex
1913 R.S. Mackenzie
1914 T. Pollock Snr.
1923 F.W.J. Merlin
1924 J.A. Fletcher
1925 P.G. Kelsey
1926 A.C. Warmington
1927 T. Pollock Jnr.
1928 V.H. Pinson
1929 R.W. Fisher
1930 W.R.P. Hayward
1931 S.H. Scribbans
1932 W.T. Heaton
1933 R.H. Baker
1934 J.F. Cooke
1935 W. Pollock
1936 N.H. Russell
1937 A.C. Warmington
1938 A.G. Blarney
1939 G. Fairweather
1947 G.C. Richards
1948 P.W. Tait
1949 H.J. Podmore
1950 A.H. Gregory
1951 H.J. Hooper
1952 R.S. Hill
1953 P.W. Tait

1954 T.S. Withington
1955 J.L. Morgan
1956 J.M. Whitehouse
1957 F.W.G. Church
1958 F.W.G. Church
1959 D.A. Warmington
1960 J.L. Morgan
1961 B.J. Cooke
1962 C.W.J. Seldon
1963 R.D. James
1964 R.A.G. Chantrill
1965 D.I. Pepper
1966 R.D. James
1967 R.A.G. Chantrill
1968 J.L. Morgan
1969 J.L. Morgan
1970 R.D. James
1971 A.H. Gregory
1972 P.H. Grant
1973 D.I. Pepper
1974 M.M. Milne
1975 A.H. Walters
1976 A.P.S. Grant
1977 B.C.B. Pickles
1978 F.K. Andrews
1979 B.G. Streather
1980 I.R. Gill
1981 M.M. Milne

1982 W. Holmes
1983 R.D. James
1984 R.R. Gelling
1985 P.A. Beharrell
1986 A.W.S. James
1987 D.R. Brander
1988 I.R. Gill
1989 J.H. Cadman
1990 H. Grundy
1991 R.J. Wyatt
1992 B.A. Anderson
1993 A.W.J. James
1994 L.D.G. Pepper
1995 D. McAllister
1996 J.D. Milne
1997 F.K. Andrews
1998 B.M. Nicholson
1999 S.M. McIntosh
2000 P.A. Stafford
2001 S.M. McIntosh
2002 S.J. Gale
2003 S.J. Gale
2004 G.I. Hackett
2005 N.H.P. Lloyd
2006 G. Newton
2007 P.A. Stafford
2008 T.R. Ford
2009 S. Oswald

Final Stableford – H. H. Sherwood Bowl
Mens thirty-six hole singles handicap stroke play Stableford, played in July.

Presented by Harold H. Sherwood in 1947

1924 A.V. Greenstreet	1957 J.L. Morgan	1984 M.T. Adamson
1925 C. Macbeth	1958 J.C. Beharrell	1985 A.J. Slater
1926 W.R.P. Hayward	1959 F.W.G. Church	1986 J.H. Cadman
1927 V.H. Pinson	1960 G.F.D. Edwards	1987 J.M.G. Eddy
1928 A.C. Warmington	1961 J.L. Morgan	1988 J.M. Waters
1929 A.H. Horton	1962 R.D. James	1989 B.G. Eddy
1930 A.C. Warmington	1963 N.H. Russell	1990 B.G. Eddy
1931 W.R.P. Hayward	1964 R.A.G. Chantrill	1991 R.A. Anderson
1932 A.G. Blarney	1965 T.R. Pepper	1992 R.A. Anderson
1933 A.G. Blarney	1966 G.S. Grove	1993 R.A. Anderson
1934 G.E. Beharrell	1967 F.W.G. Church	1994 D.R. Brander
1935 W. Archdale	1968 P.H. Grant	1995 C.G. Poxon
1936 J. Docherty	1969 G.S.C. Trench	1996 C.G. Poxon
1937 H.H. Sampson	1970 E.C. Hinde	1997 J. Wood
1938 R.P. Lindner	1971 D.I. Pepper	1998 M.J. Leadbetter
1939 A.C. Warmington	1972 J.L. Morgan	1999 P.A. Stafford
1946 G.J. Hughes	1973 B.G. Streather	2000 G.I. Hackett
1947 P.W. Tait	1974 B.C.B. Pickles	2001 S.M. McIntosh
1948 J.R. Beharrell	1975 J.L. Morgan	2002 B.M. Nicholson
1949 D.G. Collins	1976 J.R. Sambrook	2003 P.P. Bradshaw
1950 D.G. Collins	1977 D.O. Moseley	2004 N.H.P. Lloyd
1951 G.B. Partridge	1978 P.H. Grant	2005 D.J. Browse
1952 J.M. Whitehouse	1979 P.H. Grant	2006 F.K. Andrews
1953 J.L. Morgan	1980 M.J.D. Everton	2007 G.Newton
1954 T.S. Withington	1981 R.S. Hill	2008 P.A. Stafford
1955 F.W.G. Church	1982 F.K. Andrews	2009 G. Newton
1956 J.L. Morgan	1983 A. James	

Junior Handicap Cup

Presented by Mr. R.G. Horton

Eighteen hole medal under handicap, open to members of twenty-five years of age or under at the date of the competition.

1938 N.H. Russell	1972 M.J.D. Everton	1992 A.W.S. James
1946 R.T. Barnie-Adshead	1973 I.R.T. Dippie	1993 S.M. McIntosh
1947 A.M. Barnie-Adshead	1974 A.H. Walters	1994 R.A. Anderson
1948 A.M. Barnie-Adshead	1975 I.R.T. Dippie	1995 S.M. McIntosh
1949 A.R.A. Wood	1976 A.P.S. Grant	1996 M.L. Fielding
1950 R.S. Hill	1977 A.P.S. Grant	1997 M.L. Fielding
1951 J.M. Whitehouse	1978 M.J.D. Everton	1998 T.J. Andrews
1952 J.M. Whitehouse	1980 I.B. Stirling	1999 T.J. Andrews
1953 J.C. Beharrell	1981 D.C. Sambrook	2000 M.L. Fielding
1954 T.R. Pepper	1982 D.C. Sambrook	2001 M.L. Fielding
1956 R.G. Garman	1983 P.H. Cadman	2002
1957 L.G.M. Pepper	1984 M.E. Hill	2003 J. Hateley
1958 B.J. Cooke	1985 J.H. Cadman	2004 O. Lloyd
1959 R.D. James	1986 A.J. Slater	2005
1960 R.D. James	1987 B.L. Butler	2006
1961 J.M. Dorr	1988 C. Crosland	2007
1962 B.G. Streather	1989 R.J. Wyatt	2008
1963 G.S. Grove	1990 R.J. Wyatt	
1969 B.G. Streather	1991 R.J. Wyatt	

Summer Fourball Match play – Charles Heaton Memorial Salvers
Mens eighteen hole fourball handicap match play.

Inaugurated by the Club in 1933 in memory of Charles Heaton

1933 W.T. Heaton and J.H. Mansfield
1934 C.S. Buckley and A.C. Warmington
1935 R.W. Fisher and H.H. Sampson
1936 G.E. Beharrell and W. Pollock
1937 J.T. Colman and H. Willshaw
1938 R.H. Baker and H.H. Sampson
1946 I.E.K. Giles and J. Seedhouse
1947 J.F. Cooke and G.J. Hughes
1948 T. McMillan Jnr. and J.M. Leach
1949 F.D. Murray and E.A. Denham
1950 R.W. Pollock and D.D. James
1951 J.H. Sangster and J. McDowall
1952 H. Livingston and S. Davidson
1953 R.S. Hill and J.M. Whitehouse
1954 J.L. Morgan and J.F. Cooke
1955 J.R. Beharrell and J.C. Beharrell
1956 T.R. Pepper and R.M. Tait
1957 J.L. Morgan and J. McDowall
1958 J.L. Morgan and J. McDowall
1959 B.J. Cooke and D.A. Warmington
1960 F.W.G. Church and J.F. Cooke
1961 J.L. Morgan and J. McDowall
1962 R.D. James and B.J. Cooke
1963 D.I. Pepper and P.J. Denham
1964 T.R. Gilchrist and L.W. Blundell
1965 R.D. James and B.J. Cooke
1966 J. Seedhouse and K.N. Cooke
1967 G.F.D. Edwards and D.O. Moseley
1968 T.R. Pepper and H.W.M. Cave
1969 T.R. Pepper and H.W.M. Cave
1970 K.N. Cooke and J. Seedhouse
1971 R.A.G. Chantrill and B.C.B. Pickles
1972 J.C. Beharrell and J.R. Sambrook
1973 J.L. Morgan and P.H. Grant
1974 F.K. Andrews and J.G. Cooke

1975 R.R. Gelling and G.S. Grove
1976 I.R. Gill and P.J. Denham
1977 A.N. Andrews and T.R. Pepper
1978 J. Beattie and T.A.S. Charles
1979 I.C.F. Riach and A.A. Johnstone
1980 W.R. Jordan and A.H. Walters
1981 D.A. Peel and P.L. Butler
1982 W.R. Jordan and M.J.D. Everton
1983 G.E. Wyatt and D.M. Drury
1984 I.R. Gill and M.J. Quantrill
1985 F.K. Andrews and D.R. Brander
1986 B.J. Cooke and A.A. Johnstone
1987 J.C. Beharrell and P.A. Beharrell
1988 B.J. Cooke and P.A. Bingham
1989 T.R. Hampton and D.G. Carpenter
1990 F.K. Andrews and D.R. Brander
1991 W.E. Newnes and D.R. Brander
1992 M.J. Ost and W.R. Jordan
1993 F.K. Andrews and M.J.D. Everton
1994 S.M. McIntosh and R.A. Anderson
1995 J.R. Sambrook and A.N. Jones
1996 B.W. Knight and T.R. Pepper
1997 G.E. Wyatt and D.O. Moseley
1998 F.K. Andrews and S.J. Gale
1999 G.I. Hackett and S.M. Baker
2000 A.C. Morris and B.M. Nicholson
2001 S.M. McIntosh and A.J. Slater
2002 A.C. Morris and B.M. Nicholson
2003 R.J. Wyatt and J.D. Milne
2004 M.G. Davies and J.R.J. Pugh
2005 G. Newton and D.J. Gawthorpe
2006 G.J. Spalding and N.H.P. Lloyd
2007 M. Clancy and T. Cowgill
2008 M. Clancy and T. Cowgill
2009 M. Clancy and T. Cowgill

Summer Singles Match play – John Wylie Cup
Mens eighteen hole singles handicap match play.

Presented by John Wylie in 1935

1926 S. Lunt
1927 F.J. Hemming
1928 D.A. Clark
1929 W.T. Heaton
1930 A.H. Horton
1931 M.K. Foster
1932 J.F. Cooke
1933 W.R. James
1934 G.E. Beharrell
1935 M.K. Foster
1936 N.H. Russell
1937 J.M. Leach
1938 L.G. Reid
1946 G.P. Tinker
1947 P.W. Tait
1948 G.B. Partridge
1949 H. Livingston
1950 P.W. Tait
1951 J.H. Sangster
1952 J.H. Sangster
1953 H.E. Jackson
1954 J.L. Morgan
1955 J.M. Whitehouse
1956 J.L. Morgan
1957 P. Miller
1958 J.L. Morgan

1959 J.M. Leach
1960 J.C. Beharrell
1961 J.L. Morgan
1962 T.R. Pepper
1963 D.I. Pepper
1964 R.D. James
1965 R.D. James
1966 G.F.D. Edwards
1967 R.A.G. Chantrill
1968 D.O. Moseley
1969 J.L. Morgan
1970 J.L. Morgan
1971 D.I. Pepper
1972 T.H.P. Dippie
1973 J.L. Morgan
1974 T.R. Pepper
1975 J.E.G. Stubbings
1976 T.R. Hampton
1977 T.R. Hampton
1978 J.C. Beharrell
1979 J.C. Beharrell
1980 T.R. Hampton
1981 J.C. Beharrell
1982 W.E. Newnes
1983 D.I. Pepper
1984 R.D. James

1985 A.A. Johnstone
1986 A.N. Andrews
1987 T.R. Hampton
1988 J.E.G. Stubbings
1989 D.I. Pepper
1990 A.N. Andrews
1991 D.I. Pepper
1992 F.K. Andrews
1993 F.K. Andrews
1994 R.D. James
1995 T.W.B. Homer
1996 A.W.S. Jones
1997 B.M. Nicholson
1998 D.R. Brander
1999 S.M. Baker
2000 F.K. Andrews
2001 S.J. Gale
2002 S.M. Baker
2003 P.A. Stafford
2004 S.M. Baker
2005 A.Farrer
2006 S. Oswald
2007 G. Newton
2008 A.C. Morris
2009 P.A. Stafford

Walter Wilkinson Memorial Cup
Mens thirty-six hole singles handicap stroke play medal, played in July.

Presented in 1923 by Mrs. Walter Wilkinson in memory of her husband who died in office as president 1921-23

1923 W. Bigwood	1956 A. Schmiegelow	1983 B.J. Cooke
1924 M. Smith	1957 J.L. Morgan	1984 D.M. Drury
1925 W.R.P. Hayward	1958 F.W.G. Church	1985 D.R. Brander
1926 A.V. Greenstreet	1959 B.J. Cooke	1986 D.R. Brander
1927 H.V. James	1960 J.L. Morgan	1987 J.M.G. Eddy
1928 F.H. Sampson	1961 K.N. Cooke	1988 A.J. Slater
1929 W.R.P. Hayward	1962 D.A. Warmington	1989 P.A. Stafford
1930 A.H. Horton	1963. D.A. Warmington	1990 D.R. Brander
1931 W.R.P. Hayward	1964 J.H. Bradbury	1991 D.R. Brander
1932 A.C. Warmington	1965 R.D. James	1992 F.K. Andrews
1933 C. Martin	1966 R.A.G. Chantrill	1993 F.K. Andrews
1934 R.P. Lindner	1967 B.J. Cooke	1994 E.C.S. James
1935 J.F. Cooke	1968 R.D. James	1995 C.G. Poxon
1936 J.P. Mackey	1969 P.H. Grant	1996 C.G. Poxon
1937 K.W. Chaundy	1970 J.M. Leach	1997 A.J. Slater
1938 J.M. Leach	1971 B.G. Streather	1998 P.A. Stafford
1939 J.P. Mackey	1972 M.J.D. Everton	1999 S.M. Baker
1946 G. Fairweather	1973 B.G. Streather	2000 F.K. Andrews
1947 F.D. Murray	1974 B.C.B. Pickles	2001 R.J. Wyatt
1948 I.A. Heath	1975 F.K. Andrews	2002 B.M. Nicholson
1949 E.A. Withington	1976 A.P.S. Grant	2003 P.A. Stafford
1950 G.B. Partridge	1977 F.K. Andrews	2004 P.A. Stafford
1951 H.J. Hooper	1978 B.G. Streather	2005 J.G. Hilliard
1952 J.R. Beharrell	1979 R.D. James	2006 T.R. Ford
1953 A.J. Homer	1980 B.G. Streather	2007 G. Newton
1954 F. White	1981 R.D. James	2008 R. Meek
1955 No Play	1982 B.G. Streather	2009 J. Burns

Winter Foursomes Match play – John Cooke Tankards
Mens eighteen hole foursomes handicap match play.

Presented by John F. Cooke in 1962

1962-1963 J.F. Cooke and E.L.S. Sanders
1963-1964 R.D. James and B.J. Cooke
1964-1965 G.F.D. Edwards and M.S. Lee
1965-1966 J. L. Morgan and N. H. Russell
1966-1967 A.D.W. Thomson and G.S. Grove
1967-1968 R.D. James and B.J. Cooke
1968-1969 D.I. Pepper and D.A. Peel
1969-1970 B.G. Streather and J.E.G. Stubbings
1970-1971 B.G. Streather and J.E.G. Stubbings
1971-1972 R.D. James and T.M. Franks Snr.
1972-1973 R.D. James and T.M. Franks Snr.
1973-1974 B.G. Streather and J.E.G. Stubbings
1974-1975 J.L. Morgan and R.J.C. Pugsley
1975-1976 D.I. Pepper and B.J. Cooke
1976-1977 F.K. Andrews and M.J.D. Everton
1977-1978 J.L. Morgan and P.H. Grant
1978-1979 J.L. Morgan and P.H. Grant
1979-1980 J.R. Sambrook and D.O. Moseley
1980-1981 I.C.F. Riach and B. Andrews
1981-1982 G.S. Grove and K.N. Cooke
1982-1983 W.G. Streather and B.G. Streather
1983-1984 T.R. Hampton and D.I. Pepper
1984-1985 I.R. Brander and D.R. Brander
1985-1986 T.G. McBride and D.M. Drury

1986-1987 A.A. Johnstone and P.R. Bromage
1987-1988 T.R. Hampton and D.I. Pepper
1988-1989 I.R. Brander and D.R. Brander
1989-1990 A.A. Johnstone and A.N. Jones
1990-1991 W.E. Newnes and I.R. Brander
1991-1992 D. McAllister and G.S. Grove
1992-1993 J.G. Cooke and W.R. Jordan
1993-1994 S.M. McIntosh and R.A. Anderson
1994-1995 P.L. Butler and J.N. Roxburgh
1995-1996 C.G. Poxon and E.C.S. James
1996-1997 I.R. Brander and D.R. Brander
1997-1998 A.N. Andrews and D.J. Andrews
1998-1999 I.R. Brander and D.R. Brander
1999-2000 J.C. Wood and C.G. Poxon
2000-2001 G.E. Wyatt and B.J. Cooke
2001-2002 J.C. Beharrell and S. Jones
2002-2003 P.J. Ingham and S.J. Gale
2003-2004 S. Jones and J.C. Beharrell
2004-2005 F.K. Andrews and J.C. Wood
2005-2006 A. Farrer and G. Ridley
2006-2007 M. Sanders and A.D. Swift
2007-2008 D.M. Drury and G. Newton
2008-2009 J. Hobday and E.M. Holden-White

Winter Singles Match play – Thomas Ansell Challenge Cup
Mens eighteen hole singles handicap match play.

Presented by Thomas Ansell, President, in 1926

1926-1927 S. Lunt	1953-1954 F.W.G. Church	1989-1990 D.R. Brander
1927-1928 W.H. Bowater	1954-1955 T.R. Pepper	1990-1991 P.A. Beharrell
1928-1929 P.H. Sampson	1955-1956 J.C. Beharrell	1991-1992 D.I. Pepper
1929-1930 K.W.C. Dobson	1956-1957 F.W.G. Church	1992-1993 A.W.S. James
1930-1931 H.H. Sampson	1957-1958 T. McMillan	1993-1994 R.D. James
1931-1932 W. Bigwood	1958-1959 J.L. Morgan	1994-1995 F.K. Andrews
1932-1933 G.E. Beharrell	1959-1960 R.M. Tait	1995-1996 F.K. Andrews
1933-1934 L.G. Reid	1960-1961 J.L. Morgan	1996-1997 J.E. Owen
1934-1935 J.F. Cooke	1961-1962 J.L. Morgan	1997-1998 F.K. Andrews
1935-1936 C.L. Hodgkinson	1977-1978 J.C. Beharrell	1998-1999 P.A. Stafford
1936-1937 R.W. Fisher	1978-1979 J.C. Beharrell	1999-2000 E.C.S. James
1937-1938 G.E. Beharrell	1979-1980 F.K. Andrews	2000-2001 B.M. Nicholson
1938-1939 R.P. Lindner	1980-1981 D.I. Pepper	2001-2002 A.N. Jones
1945-1946 G.J. Hughes	1981-1982 T.R. Hampton	2002-2003 O.C. Darby
1946-1947 P.G. Bigwood	1982-1983 J.H. Sangster	2003-2004 J.G. Hilliard
1947-1948 F.D. Murray	1983-1984 C.B. Lindop	2004-2005 B.J. Cooke
1948-1949 G.C. Richards	1984-1985 M.T. Adamson	2005-2006 W.R. Jordan
1949-1950 P.W. Tait	1985-1986 M.T. Adamson	2006-2007 P. Brownhill
1950-1951 G.R. Baxter	1986-1987 J.C. Beharrell	2007-2008 M. Sanders
1951-1952 P.W. Tait	1987-1988 C.E.A. Hooper	2008-2009 G. Newton
1952-1953 W.T. Heaton	1988-1989 J.C. Beharrell	

Club Championship
Mens thirty-six hole scratch stroke play medal, played July.

Presented by Norman Russell
The winner receives an antique, oversized golf club displayed permanently in the clubhouse

1968 A.W. Holmes	1982 B.G. Streather	1996 C.G. Poxon
1969 J.L. Morgan	1983 R.D. James	1997 C.G. Poxon
1970 J.M. Leach	1984 R.D. James	1998 C.G. Poxon
1971 B.G. Streather	1985 F.K. Andrews	1999 C.G. Poxon
1972 P.H. Grant	1986 D.R. Brander	2000 C.G. Poxon
1973 B.G. Streather	1987 P.L. Butler	2001 C.G. Poxon
1974 R.D. James	1988 F.K. Andrews	2002 B.M. Nicholson
1975 J.L. Morgan	1989 P.L. Butler	2003 B.M. Nicholson
1976 J.C. Beharrell	1990 C.G. Poxon	2004 P.A. Stafford
1977 R.D. James	1991 C.G. Poxon	2005 C.G. Poxon
1978 I.C.F. Riach	1992 C.G. Poxon	2006 S.M. Baker
1979 R.D. James	1993 R.A. Anderson	2007 M. Pearson
1980 R.D. James	1994 C.G. Poxon	2008 M. Pearson
1981 R.D. James	1995 C.G. Poxon	2009 C.G. Poxon

Milligan Bowls
Mens eighteen hole foursomes handicap stroke play Stableford, played October

Presented by Colin W. Milligan, the first Club Captain

1909 [Autumn] W.J. Davis and E.R. Routledge
1910 [Spring] L.A. Evans and T. Duesbury
    [Autumn] E.J. Smith and A.E. Cheatle
1911 [Spring] S. Powis and H. Jerrard
    [Autumn] T. Duesbury and W.S. Brown
1912 [Spring] W.J. Davis and W. Bennett
    [Autumn] W.L. Lewis and G. Greatrex
1913 F.C. Carr and E. Evershed
1914 W.L. Lewis and G. Greatrex
1920 C.B. Wright and B. Seymour Jones
1921 G. Greatrex and A. Whitlock
1922 S.I. Fillingham and C. Crosland
1923 F. Scarf and H. Foster
1924 A.V. Greenstreet and T. Betteridge
1925 H. Jerrard and B. Lorrimer
1926 T. Pollock and F.W.J. Merlin
1927 F.J. Hemming and C. Macbeth
1928 S.H. Sherwood and C.T. Pritchard
1929 W.T. Heaton and W.R.P. Hayward
1930 A.C. Warmington and W. Pollock
1931 W. Archdale and G. Greatrex
1932 R.H. Baker and A.G. Blamey
1934 T. McMillan Snr. and J.L. Milne
1935 R.W. Fisher and D.A. Clarke
1936 W. Archdale and W.T. Heaton
1937 L.G. Reid and G. Fairweather
1938 G. Fairweather and H. Clark
1939 G. Fairweather and H. Clark
1946 W. Pollock and R.W. Fisher
1947 A.H. Horton and N.H. Russell
1948 G.J. Hughes and R.W. Fisher
1949 A.R.A. Wood and H.J. Podmore
1950 H. Livingston and S. Davidson
1951 T. McMillan jun and G.R. Baxter
1952 R.S. Hill and J.M. Whitehouse
1953 P.W. Tait and G.S. Mackay
1954 F. White and F.W. Mallett
1955 N.H. Russell and R.C. Hiam
1956 J.L. Morgan and F.W.G. Church
1957 J. McDowall and I.H. Houston
1958 J. McDowall and A.J. Homer
1959 G.R. Baxter and E.C. Hinde
1960 J.M. Whitehouse and A.P. Withington
1961 F.W.G. Church and B.J. Cooke
1962 F.W.G. Church and T. McMillan jun
1963 J.L. Morgan and N.H. Russell

1964 R.A.G. Chantrill and G.C. Chantrill
1965 P.H. Grant and L.W. Blundell
1966 T.H.P. Dippie and R.S. Hill
1967 R.A.G. Chantrill and A.D.W. Thomson
1968 J.L. Morgan and T. McMillan jun
1969 P.H. Grant and B.C.B. Pickles
1970 J.L. Morgan and L. Bramhall
1971 H.M. Pepper and D.I. Pepper
1972 P.H. Grant and B.C.B. Pickles
1973 P.J. Denham and J.W. Gray
1974 G.R. Baxter and E.C. Hinde
1975 D.I. Pepper and B.J. Cooke
1976 B.C.B. Pickles and D.O. Moseley
1977 T.R. Hampton and J.E. Gawthorpe
1978 B.J. Cooke and J.E.G. Stubbings
1979 P.H. Grant and D.A. Peel
1980 T.R. Hampton and D.I. Pepper
1981 M.T. Adamson and P.A. Bingham
1982 M.J. Leadbetter and J.G. Cooke
1983 M.T. Adamson and J.R. Sambrook
1984 J.L. Morgan and F.W.G. Church
1985 A.R.A. Wood and A.W.J. Jordan
1986 R.D. James and A. James
1987 A.N. Jones and P.H.B. Cadman
1988 T.H.P. Dippie and R.S. Hill
1989 D.O. Moseley and B.C.B. Pickles
1990 J.E. Owen and T.R. Pepper
1991 T.R. Hampton and R.A. Anderson
1992 D.M. Drury and P.C. Eve
1993 D.O. Moseley and T.E. Moseley
1994 W.E. Newnes and R.W. Burnett
1995 P.A. Bingham and M.D. Maloney
1996 T.E. Moseley and A.J. Slater
1997 T.R. Hampton and D.O. Moseley
1998 W.E. Newnes and J.H. Smith
1999 J.G. Hilliard and S.M. McIntosh
2000 J.C. Wood and M.E. Hill
2001 D.O. Moseley and F.K. Andrews
2002 J.R. Sambrook and B.A. Macmillan
2003 A.D. Swift and P.R. Sambrook
2004 J.C. Wood and S. Pettit
2005 B.J. Cooke and G.E. Wyatt
2006 J.K. Gough and S. Pettit
2007 A.N. Jones and F. Marks
2008 J.E.G. Stubbings and R. Pitt
2009 A.N. Jones and A.N. Andrews

Mixed Foursomes Match play – Foster Ward Salvers
Mixed eighteen hole foursomes handicap match play, played April-September

Presented by Mrs. Pauline Ward in 1973 in memory of her husband, Foster Ward

1973 A.N. Andrews and Miss U. Holt
1974 Dr. and Mrs. P.H. Grant
1975 Mr. and Mrs. B.J. Cooke
1976 Dr. and Mrs. T.H.P. Dippie
1977 Mr. and Mrs. B.J. Cooke
1978 Mr. and Mrs. F.K. Andrews
1979 Mr. and Mrs. M.L. Booth
1980 R.D. James and Mrs. J. James
1981 R.D. James and Mrs. J. James
1982 R.D. James and Mrs. J. James
1983 R.D. James and Mrs. J. James
1984 Mr. and Mrs. P.J. Denham
1985 Mr. and Mrs. D.I. Pepper
1986 Mr. and Mrs. F.K. Andrews
1987 Mr. and Mrs. F.K. Andrews
1988 Mr. and Mrs. F.K. Andrews
1989 Mr. and Mrs. D.I. Pepper
1990 Mr. and Mrs. F.K. Andrews
1991 Mr. and Mrs. R.D. James

1992 Mr. and Mrs. F.K. Andrews
1993 Mr. and Mrs. D. McAllister
1994 Mr. and Mrs. P.J. Denham
1995 Mr. and Mrs. D. McAllister
1996 Mr. and Mrs. R.D. James
1997 Mr. and Mrs. D. McAllister
1998 Mr. and Mrs. A.N. Andrews
1999 Mr. and Mrs. D.I. Pepper
2000 Mr. and Mrs. S. Gale
2001 Mr. and Mrs. F.K. Andrews
2002 Mr. and Mrs. F.K. Andrews
2003 Mr. and Mrs. R.D. James
2004 Mr. and Mrs. F.K. Andrews
2005 Mr. and Mrs. C.G. Poxon
2006 Mr. and Mrs. J.C. Wood
2007 Mr. and Mrs. M. Clancy
2008 Mr. and Mrs. J.C. Wood
2009 Mr. G. Newton and Ms. C. Jones

Mixed Foursomes Stroke play – Greatrex Challenge Bowls
Mixed eighteen hole foursomes handicap stroke play medal, played in May

Presented by Arthur W. Greatrex, the original owner of the golf course land, in 1926, who sold the land to the Club on the condition that ladies may play

1926 W.R. James and Miss Fiddian Green
1927 G. Greatrex and Mrs. Scott Jones
1928 G. Greatrex and Miss D. Billing
1929 A.V. Greenstreet and Miss G. Meredith
1930 Mr. and Mrs. T. Betteridge
1931 W.R.P. Hayward and Miss I. Greatrex
1932 Mr. and Mrs. B. Fenton
1933 Mr. and Mrs. B. Fenton [Bowls won outright and re-presented]
1934 Mr. and Mrs. M.K. Foster
1935 Mr. and Mrs. M.K. Foster
1936 H.W. Shipley and Mrs. A. Sheldon
1937 F.H. Timings and Mrs. W. Archdale
1938 R.G. Horton and Miss G. Harcourt
1939 Mr. and Mrs. J. White
1946 Mr. and Mrs. E.A. Denham
1947 Mr. and Mrs. E.A. Denham
1948 Mr. and Mrs. E.A. Denham
1949 H.C. Homer and Mrs. I.H. Houston
1950 R.W. Pollock and Miss M. Eley
1951 Mr. and Mrs. F.V. Coslett
1952 Mr. and Mrs. I.A. Heath
1953 Mr. and Mrs. I.A. Heath
1954 R.M. Tait and Mrs. P.W. Tait
1955 Mr. and Mrs. I.A. Heath
1956 J.L. Morgan and Miss M. Eley
1957 T.R. Pepper and Mrs. J. White
1958 P.W. Tait and Mrs. E.A. Denham
1959 J.L. Morgan and Mrs. T.M. Franks
1960 Mr. and Mrs. L. Bramhall
1961 Mr. and Mrs. J. Boden
1962 P.J. Denham and Mrs. E.A. Denham
1963 N.H. Russell and Mrs. I.A. Heath
1964 J.L. Morgan and Mrs. T.M. Franks
1965 Mr. and Mrs. E.A. Denham
1966 N.H. Russell and Mrs. A. Morley
1967 T.R. Gilchrist and Mrs. I.A. Heath
1968 Mr. and Mrs. E.C. Hinde
1969 P.G. Bigwood and Mrs. R.W. James
1970 Dr. and Mrs. V.G. Milne

1971 Mr. and Mrs. T.M. Franks
1972 Dr. and Mrs. T.H.P. Dippie
1973 Mr. and Mrs. J.C. Beharrell
1974 Mr. and Mrs. G.E. Fisher
1975 Mr. and Mrs. B.J. Cooke
1976 Dr. and Mrs. T.R. Gilchrist
1977 Mr. and Mrs. D.O. Moseley
1978 Mr. and Mrs. D.O. Moseley
1979 R.D. James and Mrs. R.W. James
1980 R.D. James and Mrs. R.W. James
1981 Mr. and Mrs. F.W.G. Church
1982 K.N. Cooke and Mrs. M.L. Booth
1983 Mr. and Mrs. J.C. Beharrell
1984 Mr. and Mrs. B.J. Cooke
1985 Mr. and Mrs. M.T. Adamson
1986 Mr. and Mrs. B.J. Cooke
1987 Mr. and Mrs. D.I. Pepper
1988 Mr. and Mrs. F.K. Andrews
1989 Mr. and Mrs. D.A. Warmington
1990 J. Slater and Mrs. B.L. Brough
1991 Mr. and Mrs. M.T. Adamson
1992 D.O. Moseley and Mrs. B.L. Brough
1993 Mr. and Mrs. F.K. Andrews
1994 Mr. and Mrs. R.D. James
1995 M.T. Adamson and Mrs. A.M. Holroyde
1996 M.T. Adamson and Mrs. A.M. Holroyde
1997 J. Slater and Mrs. B. Brough
1998 Not known
1999 Mr. and Mrs. F.K. Andrews
2000 Mr. and Mrs. D.O. Moseley
2001 S.M. McIntosh and Mrs. A. Saunders
2002 A.N. Jones and Miss J. Andrews
2003 M.G. Davies and Mrs. D.J. Gawthorpe
2004 M.T. Adamson and Mrs. A.M. Holroyde
2005 D.J.E. Thomas and Mrs. S.J. Porter
2006 M. Clancy and Mrs. D. Bradshaw
2007 Mr. and Mrs. G.R. Hands
2008 Mr. and Mrs. F.K. Andrew
2009 J.C. Wood and Mrs. M. Smith

Mixed Greensomes Stroke play – Coronation Salvers
Mixed eighteen hole greensomes handicap stroke play medal, played July

Presented by Will Archdale, Captain, to mark the Coronation of King George VI in 1937

1937 G. Fairweather and Mrs. A.E. Wiley
1938 G. Fairweather and Mrs. A.E. Wiley
1939 T. McMillan Jnr. and Mrs. E. Kendrick
1946 Mr. and Mrs. E.A. Denham
1947 Mr. and Mrs. A.C. Warmington
1948 F.D. Murray and Miss M. Eley
1949 T. South and Mrs. H.H. Sampson
1950 R.W. Pollock and Miss M. Eley
1951 Mr. and Mrs. H.J. Hooper
1952 Mr. and Mrs. K.N. Cooke
1953 W.T. Heaton and Mrs. M. Kendrick
1954 W. Pollock and Mrs. E. Patterson
1955 Mr. and Mrs. K.N. Cooke
1956 Mr. and Mrs. R.W. James
1957 Mr. and Mrs. H.J. Hooper
1958 T.R. Pepper and Mrs. M. Pepper
1959 Mr. and Mrs. L.G. Firth
1960 J.L. Morgan and Mrs. T.M. Franks
1961 J.L. Morgan and Mrs. T.M. Franks
1962 R.D. James and Mrs. H. Pratt
1963 Mr. and Mrs. E.A. Denham
1964 J.L. Morgan and Mrs. T.M. Franks
1965 J.L. Morgan and Mrs. T.M. Franks
1966 P.J.M. Smith and Mrs. I.A. Heath
1967 F.W.G. Church and Mrs. A. Morley
1968 J.F. Cooke and Mrs. T. McMillan
1969 N.H. Russell and Mrs. I.A. Heath
1970 Dr. and Mrs. T.H.P. Dippie
1971 N.H. Russell and Mrs. I.A. Heath
1972 K.N. Cooke and Miss U. Holt
1973 G.E. Fisher and Mrs. T.H.P. Dippie
1974 Mr. and Mrs. R.S. Hill
1975 Mr. and Mrs. D.O. Moseley
1976 Mr. and Mrs. D.O. Moseley
1977 Dr. and Mrs. P.H. Grant

1978 A.A. Johnstone and Miss A. Johnstone
1979 Mr. and Mrs. D.O. Moseley
1980 J.H. Sangster and Mrs. M.J. Walters
1981 Mr. and Mrs. F.W.G. Church
1982 Mr. and Mrs. R.D. James
1983 Mr. and Mrs. P.H.B. Cadman
1984 Mr. and Mrs. V.G. Milne
1985 Mr. and Mrs. P.H.B. Cadman
1986 Mr. and Mrs. B.J. Cooke
1987 T.R. Hampton and Mrs. P.A. Bingham
1988 M.T. Adamson and Mrs. A.M. Holroyde
1989 M.T. Adamson and Mrs. A.M. Holroyde
1990 J.H. Cadman and Mrs. P.H.B. Cadman
1991 J.H. Cadman and Mrs. P.H.B. Cadman
1992 P.H.B. Cadman and Mrs. D.H. Lindop
1993 Mr. and Mrs. M.L. Booth
1994 Mr. and Mrs. I.R. Brander
1995 Mr. and Mrs. C.E.A. Hooper
1996 Mr. and Mrs. B.J. Cooke
1997 Mr. and Mrs. D. McAllister
1998 Mr. and Mrs. C.J. Boak
1999 Mr. and Mrs. F.K. Andrews
2000 J.R. Sambrook and Mrs. B. Brough
2001 A.N. Andrews and Miss J. Andrews
2002 Not known
2003 D.J. Gawthorpe and Mrs. S.J. Gale
2004 M.T. Adamson and Mrs. M.G. Davies
2005 M.J. Ward and Mrs. D.J. Gawthorpe
2006 Mr. and Mrs. H. Picton-Jones
2007 Mr. and Mrs. A.N. Andrews
2008 Mr. and Mrs. M.T. Adamson
2009 M.G. Davies and Mrs. M. Moloney

Competition Winners – Ladies

Heath Coronation Trophy 1953

Silver Cigarette Box presented by Mrs. Marjorie Heath.
A Silver Rose Bowl was presented by her daughter,
Mrs. Gill Hilton, in memory of Mrs Marjorie Heath in 2006

1953 Miss Richards	1972 Mrs. G.E. Fisher	1991 Mrs. J. Hall
1954 Mrs. Whitfield	1973 Mrs. T.R. Gilchrist	1992 Mrs. R. Moseley
1955 Mrs. Richmond	1974 Mrs. T.R. Gilchrist	1993 Mrs. A. Booth
1956 Mrs. Beck	1975 Mrs. A. Booth	1994 Mrs. J. Denham
1957 Mrs. Morley	1976 Mrs. A. Booth	1995 Mrs. C. Hill
1958 Mrs. James	1977 Mrs. J.D. Eddy	1996 Mrs. J. Milne
1959 Mrs. James	1978 Mrs. B. Cooke	1997 Dr. E. Fielding
1960 Mrs. Coslett	1979 Mrs. A. Booth	1998 Mrs. J. Hollis
1961 Mrs. Rayner	1980 Mrs. G.S.C. Trench	1999 Mrs. M. Roxburgh
1962 Mrs. Hearne	1981 Mrs. T.H. Dippie	2000 Mrs. L. Warmington
1963 Mrs. McMillan	1982 Mrs. T.R. Gilchrist	2001 Mrs. A. Saunders
1964 Mrs. Heath	1983 Mrs. H. Lindop	2002 Mrs. J. Hands
1965 Mrs. Hinde	1984 Mrs. R.S. Hill	2003 Mrs. K. Hooper
1966 Mrs. H. Rayner	1985 Mrs. L. Warmington	2004 Mrs. P. Taylor
1967 Mrs. E.L. Dixon-Green	1986 Mrs. J.C. Beharrell	2005 Mrs. J. Hands
1968 Mrs. F.R. Ratcliff	1987 Mrs. R. Moseley	2006 Mrs. D. Milne
1969 Mrs. Rayner	1988 Mrs. J. Cadman	2007 Mrs. M. Davies
1970 Mrs. D. Fisher	1989 Mrs. L. Cooke	2008 Mrs. S. Boak
1971 Mrs. T.R. Gilchrist	1990 Mrs. A. Pickles	2009 Mrs. A. Smith

Jubilee Bowl

Presented by Mrs. F. W. Brooks and Mrs. J. H. Harper in 1935

1935 Enid Pears	1958 Mrs. E.A. Denham	1981 Mrs. J.D. Eddy
1936 Mrs. W.S. Pearman-Smith	1959 Miss B. Jackson	1982 Mrs. J.D. Eddy
1937 Mrs. Betteridge	1960-1968 see minutes	1983 Mrs. A. Booth
1938 Mrs. F.W. Brooks	Competition Book starts 1968	1984 Mrs. D.H. Lindop
1939 Mrs. W.S. Pearman-Smith	1968 Mrs. M. Crosbee	1985 Mrs. P. Dippie
1946 Mrs. R.W. Sheppard	1969 Mrs. Beharrell	1986 Mrs. A. Booth
1947 Mrs. J.H. Bowden	1970 Mrs. James	1987 Mrs. J.V. Hollis
1948 Miss J. Carter	1971 Mrs. L. Rayner	1988 Mrs. L. Warmington
1949 Miss. B.D. Harper	1972 Mrs. T.H.P. Dippie	1989 Mrs. D. Milne
1950 Miss B.D. Harper	1973 Mrs. D.H. Lindop	1990 Mrs. R. Moseley
1951 Mrs. D. Paul	1974 Mrs. R.S. Hill	1991 Mrs. A. Booth
1952 Mrs. P. Crick	1975 Mrs. T.R. Gilchrist	1992 Mrs. C.A. Andrews
1953 Mrs. Wilson	1976 Mrs. T.R. Gilchrist	1993 Mrs. A. Pickles
1954 Mrs. E.A. Denham	1977 Mrs. G.E. Fisher	1994 Mrs. S. Adamson
1955 Mrs. E. Moore	1978 Mrs. B.J. Cooke	1995 Mrs. D. Milne
1956 Mrs. Richmond	1979 Mrs. T.R. Gilchrist	1996 Mrs. S. Adamson
1957 Mrs. Bowen	1980 Mrs. J.C. Beharrell	1997 Dr. E. Fielding

Jubilee Bowl – continued

1998 Mrs. A. Pepper	2002 Mrs. C. Jones	2006 Mrs. M. Roxburgh
1999 Mrs. J. Bigwood	2003 Mrs. D. Milne	2007 Mrs. J. Hands
2000 Mrs. B. Maloney	2004 Mrs. D. Milne	2008 Mrs. J. Carpenter
2001 Mrs. G. Picton-Jones	2005 Mrs. A. Saunders	2009 Mrs. A. Bingham

The Scarf Bowl

Presented by F. Scarf Esq.

1938 Mrs. A.E. Wiley	1968 Mrs. B.C. Kilkenny	1990 Mrs. S. Woolley
1939 Mrs. Beauchamp Brown	1969 Mrs. Heath	1991 Mrs. J. Hall
1948 Mrs. W. Ritchie	1970 Mrs. Dixon-Green	1992 Mrs. B. Brough
1949 Miss B. Harper	1971 Mrs. G.E. Fisher	1993 Mrs. B. Brough
1950 Mrs. I.H. Houston	1972 Mrs. T.H.P. Dippie	1994 Mrs. B. Brough
1951 Mrs. Hooper	1973 Mrs. B.C.B. Pickles	1995 Mrs. S. Adamson
1952 Mrs. Whitfield	1974 Mrs. R.W. James	1996 Mrs. D. Milne
1953 Mrs. White	1975 Mrs. B.J. Cooke	1997 Mrs. A. Pickles
1954 Mrs. Denham	1976 Mrs. V.G. Milne	1998 Mrs. K. Hooper
1955 Mrs. Beharrell	1977 Mrs. T.P. Hawker	1999 Mrs. J. Hill
1956 Mrs. Franks jun	1978 Mrs. V.G. Milne	2000 Mrs. A. Pepper
1957 Mrs. T.C. Pepper	1979 Mrs. A. Booth	2001 Mrs. M. Roxburgh
1958 Mrs. E.F. Kendrick	1980 Mrs. G.E. Fisher	2002 Mrs. L. Ingham
1959 Mrs. Dixon-Green	1981 Mrs. B.J. Cooke	2003 Mrs. J. Bigwood
1960 Mrs. Gilchrist	1982 Mrs. P.J. Denham	2004 Mrs. M. Davies
1961 Mrs. McMillan	1983 Mrs. R. Moseley	2005 Mrs. S. Porter
1962 Mrs. Roberts	1984 Mrs. E. Dixon-Green	2006 Mrs. J. Hands
1963 Mrs. Withington	1985 Mrs. J. Cadman	2007 Mrs. L. Pettit
1964 Mrs. Morley	1986 Mrs. D.A. Warmington	2008 Mrs. J. Denham
1965 Mrs. Wright	1987 Mrs. M.M. Milne	2009 Mrs. L. Wood
1966 Mrs. T.R. Gilchrist	1988 Mrs. R.D. James	
1967 Mrs. T.R. Gilchrist	1989 Mrs. D.O. Moseley	

Bogey Cup

1973 Mrs. R.S. Hill	1986 Mrs. D.A. Warmington	1999 Mrs. J. Hands
1974 Mrs. V.G. Milne	1987 Mrs. T.H.P. Dippie	2000 Mrs. C. Jones
1975 Mrs. D.O. Moseley	1988 Mrs. L. Cooke	2001 Mrs. J. Bigwood
1976 Mrs. T.R. Gilchrist	1989 Mrs. S. Adamson	2002 Mrs. C. Jones
1977 Mrs. G.E. Fisher	1990 Mrs. G. Picton-Jones	2003 Mrs. J. Cadman
1978 Miss J. Stant	1991 Mrs. B. Hawker	2004 Mrs. C. Gale
1979 Mrs. T.R. Gilchrist	1992 Mrs. B. Brough	2005 Mrs. M. Davies
1980 Mrs. A. Booth	1993 Mrs. H. Lindop	2006 Mrs. L. Wood
1981 Mrs. J.D. Eddy	1994 Mrs. S. Adamson	2007 Mrs. J. Denham
1982 Mrs. B. Andrews	1995 Mrs. B. Brough	2008 Ms. A. Saunders
1983 Mrs. L. Cooke	1996 Mrs. S. Adamson	2009 Mrs. L. Wood
1984 Mrs. P. Dippie	1997 Mrs. S. Boak	
1985 Mrs. A. Booth	1998 Dr. E. Fielding	

Mayoress Cups

Presented by the Mayoress of Sutton Coldfield
Mrs. Wilfrid Bigwood 1938

	Silver Division	Bronze Division		Silver Division	Bronze Division
1946		Mrs. Stubbs	1978	Mrs. T.H.P. Dippie	Mrs. V.G. Milne
1947		Mrs. Coslett	1979	Mrs. T.H.P. Dippie	Mrs. G.E. Fisher
1948		Miss Eley	1980	Mrs. E.R.S. Grice	Mrs. R.S. Hill
1949		Mrs. Pepper	1981	Mrs. T.R. Gilchrist	Mrs. L.W. Blundell
1950		Mrs. Pepper	1982	Mrs. W.H. Bagnall	Mrs. B.M. Hawker
1951	Mrs. Heath	Mrs. James	1983	Mrs. A. Booth	Mrs. W. Walters
1952	Miss Eley	Mrs. Heaton	1984	Mrs. B. Andrews	Mrs. N. Brough
1953	Mrs. Coslett	Mrs. White	1985	Mrs. A. Andrews	Mrs. A. Pepper
1954	Mrs. Denham	Mrs. M. Kendrick	1986	Mrs. D.O. Moseley	Mrs. D.A. Warmington
1955	Mrs. Denham	Mrs. Hearne	1987	Mrs. T.R. Gilchrist	Mrs. D.A. Warmington
1956	Mrs. Houston	Mrs. Hearne	1988	Mrs. A. Andrews	Mrs. N. Grice
1957	Mrs. Houston	Mrs. Dixon-Green	1989	Mrs. D.O. Moseley	Mrs. J. Denham
1958	Mrs. Denham	Mrs. Grove	1990	Mrs. H. Jones	Mrs. L. Warmington
1959	Mrs. Boden	Mrs. Gilchrist	1991	Mrs. V. Gilchrist	Mrs. A. Pickles
1960	Mrs. Boden	Mrs. McMillan	1992	Mrs. J. Hollis	Mrs. B. Hawker
1961	Mrs. Withington	Mrs. Hearne	1993	Mrs. R. Moseley	Mrs. D. Milne
1962	No return	Mrs. Heath	1994	Mrs. A. Andrews	Mrs. J. Hall
1963	No return	Mrs. Heath	1995	Mrs. R. Moseley	Mrs. M. Roxburgh
1964	Mrs. Denham	Mrs. Hooper	1996	Mrs. B. Brough	Mrs. A. Pickles
1965	Mrs. Dippie	Mrs. Gregory	1997	Mrs. A. Pepper	Mrs. L. Warmington
1966	Mrs. L. Bramhall	Mrs. R. Hill	1998	Mrs. A. Andrews	Mrs. M. Roxburgh
1967	Mrs. T.R. Gilchrist	Mrs. F. Massey	1999	No entry	Mrs. M. Roxburgh
1968	Mrs. T.R. Gilchrist	Mrs. M. Crosbee	2000	Mrs. D. Power	Mrs. B. Moloney
1969	Mrs. Gilchrist	Mrs. Franks	2001	Mrs. R. Moseley	Mrs. J. Bigwood
1970	Mrs. Dippie	Mrs. Dixon-Green	2002	Miss J. Andrews	Mrs. D. Milne
1971	Mrs. E.R.S. Grice	Mrs. L.W. Blundell	2003	Mrs. M. Roxburgh	Mrs. J. Jones
1972	Mrs. T.H.P. Dippie	Mrs. D.B. Bingham	2004	Mrs. S. Adamson	Mrs. P. Willetts
1973	Mrs. D.B. Bingham	Mrs. I.A. Heath	2005	Mrs. J. Andrews	Mrs. J. Hands
1974	Mrs. T.R. Gilchrist	Mrs. R.W. James	2006	Mrs. R. Moseley	Mrs. J. Denham
1975	Mrs. T.R. Gilchrist	Mrs. R.W. James	2007	Mrs. M. Roxburgh	Mrs. L. Pettit
1976	Mrs. T.H.P. Dippie	Mrs. D.O. Moseley	2008	Mrs. D. Power	Mrs. J. Cadman
1977	Mrs. J. Stant	Mrs. H.J. Hooper	2009	Mrs. L. Warmington	Mrs. L. Pettit

Final Bogey/Stableford

	Silver Division	Bronze Division		Silver Division	Bronze Division
1951	Mrs. Harper	Mrs. James	1981	Mrs. A. Booth	Mrs. V.G. Milne
1952	Mrs. Heath	Mrs. McMillan	1982	Mrs. G.E. Fisher	Mrs. V.G. Milne
1953	Mrs. Denham	Mrs. Aspinall	1983	Mrs. P. Dippie	Mrs. C. Hill
1954	Mrs. Coslett	Mrs. Hardman	1984	Mrs. D.H. Lindop	Mrs. N. Brough
1955	Mrs. Denham	Mrs. Gosnell	1985	Mrs. R. Moseley	Mrs. B. Brough
1956	Mrs. Griffiths	Mrs. Leedham-Green	1986	Mrs. R. Moseley	Mrs. D.I. Pepper
1957	Mrs. Heath	Mrs. Leedham-Green	1987	Mrs. F.K. Andrews	Mrs. E.R. Grice
1958	Mrs. Denham	Mrs. Morley	1988	Mrs. P. Dippie	Mrs. J. James
1959	Mrs. Denham	Mrs. James	1989	Mrs. A. Andrews	Mrs. D. Milne
1960	Mrs. Denham	Mrs. Wright	1990	Mrs. A. Booth	Mrs. G. Holroyde
1961	Mrs. Dippie	Mrs. Hinde	1991	Mrs. A. Booth	Mrs. D. Wyatt
1962	Mrs. Houston	Mrs. Pratt	1992	Mrs. A. Pepper	Mrs. J. Cadman
1963	Mrs. Denham	Mrs. Heath	1993	Mrs. A. Andrews	Mrs. D. Milne
1964	Mrs. Gilchrist	Mrs. Mallett	1994	Mrs. S. Adamson	Mrs. J. Hall
1965	Mrs. Gilchrist	Mrs. Morley	1995	Mrs. R. Moseley	Mrs. J. Hands
1966	Mrs. H. Rayner	Mrs. R. Hill	1996	Mrs. R. Moseley	Mrs. G. Holroyde
1967	Mrs. T.R. Gilchrist	Mrs. Heath	1997	Mrs. A. Booth	Mrs. S. Boak
1968	Mrs. E.A. Denham	Mrs. R.S. Hill	1998	Mrs. A. Pepper	Mrs. J. Hill
1969	Mrs. Beharrell	Mrs. Hinde	1999	Mrs. A. Andrews	Miss J. Andrews
1970	Mrs. Gilchrist	Mrs. H. Lindop	2000	Mrs. S. Adamson	Mrs. J. Jones
1971	Mrs. T.H.P. Dippie	Mrs. I.A. Heath	2001	Mrs. S. Adamson	Mrs. L. Ingham
1972	Mrs. T.H.P. Dippie	Mrs. I.A. Heath	2002	Mrs. R. Moseley	Mrs. K. Hooper
1973	Mrs. T.H.P. Dippie	Mrs. V.G. Milne	2003	Mrs. L. Gawthorpe	Mrs. D. Milne
1974	Mrs. J.C. Beharrell	Mrs. B.C.B. Pickles	2004	Mrs. S. Adamson	Mrs. M. Davies
1975	Mrs. A. Booth	Mrs. B.C.B. Pickles	2005	Mrs. A. Andrews	Mrs. L. Clancy
1976	Mrs. A. Booth	Mrs. P.H. Grant	2006	Mrs. D. Power	Mrs. J. Carpenter
1977	Mrs. T.H.P. Dippie	Mrs. D.O. Moseley	2007	Mrs. S. Adamson	Mrs. D. Milne
1978	Mrs. T.H.P. Dippie	Mrs. D.O. Moseley	2008	Mrs. M. Roxburgh	Mrs. M. Poxon
1979	Mrs. A. Booth	Mrs. B.C.B. Pickles	2009	Mrs. A. Smith	Mrs. G. Holroyde
1980	Mrs. A. Andrews	Mrs. D.O. Moseley			

Ladies Championship

Presented by Mrs. J. Hollis 1998

	Silver Division	Bronze Division		Silver Division	Bronze Division
1998	Mrs. A. Pepper	Mrs. H. Jones	2004	Mrs. D. Power	Mrs. D. Milne
1999	Mrs. A. Booth	Mrs. J. Milne	2005	Mrs. A. Booth	Mrs. J. Cadman
2000	Mrs. D. Power	Mrs. M. Roxburgh	2006	Mrs. L. Warmington	Mrs. J. Cadman
2001	Mrs. S. Adamson	Miss J. Andrews	2007	Ms. A. Saunders	Mrs. J. Drury
2002	Mrs. R. Moseley	Mrs. V. Darby	2008	Mrs. A. Booth	Mrs. J. Drury
2003	Mrs. A. Booth	Mrs. V. Darby	2009	Mrs. A. Booth	Mrs. L. Wood

Final Medal

'Junior' presented by Mr. & Mrs. Greatrex

The Silver Division Trophy was lost in a fire/burglary – engravings start 1966

	Silver Division	Bronze Division		Silver Division	Bronze Division
1927		Miss Horton	1972	Mrs. J.C. Beharrell	Mrs. I.A. Heath
1928		Miss Joyce Foster	1973	Mrs. T.H.P. Dippie	Mrs. P.H. Grant
1929		Mrs. Sydney H. Sherwood	1974	Mrs. T.H.P. Dippie	Mrs. R.S. Hill
1930		Miss K. Tonks	1975	Miss U. Holt	Mrs. E.C. Hinde
1931		Mrs. Betteridge	1976	Mrs. T.H.P. Dippie	Mrs. R.S. Hill
1932		Mrs. Betteridge	1977	Mrs. A. Booth	Mrs. G.S.C. Trench
1933		Mrs. J.S. Ragg	1978	Mrs. A. Booth	Mrs. B.C.B. Pickles
1934		Mrs. G. Hawley	1979	Mrs. A. Booth	Mrs. G.E. Fisher
1935		Mrs. Leyton Greener	1980	Mrs. T.H.P. Dippie	Mrs. R.S. Hill
1936		Mrs. H. Scribbans	1981	Mrs. F.K. Andrews	Mrs. R.S. Hill
1937			1982	Mrs. T.H. Dippie	Mrs. V.G. Milne
1938		Mrs. H. Scribbans	1983	Mrs. D. Fisher	Mrs. L. Cooke
1946		Mrs. B. Fenton	1984	Mrs. T.R. Gilchrist	Mrs. P.H. Cadman
1947		Mrs. A.C. Warmington	1985	Mrs. A. Andrews	Mrs. L. Warmington
1948		Mrs. J.H. Harper	1986	Mrs. J.C. Beharrell	Mrs. N.W. Brough
1949		Miss W.E. Richards	1987	Mrs. J.V. Hollis	Mrs. G.R. Hands
1950		Mrs. I.H. Houston	1988	Mrs. A. Pepper	Mrs. S. Woolley
1951	Mrs. Denham	Mrs. Hooper	1989	Mrs. L. Cooke	Mrs. V.G. Milne
1952	Mrs. Heath	Mrs. Heaton	1990	Mrs. A. Andrews	Mrs. G. Holroyde
1953	Mrs. Denham	Mrs. Hardman	1991	Mrs. A. Pepper	Mrs. G. Holroyde
1954	Mrs. Richmond	Mrs. Hardman	1992	Mrs. A. Booth	Mrs. H. Murray
1955	Mrs. Richmond	Mrs. Hardman	1993	Mrs. R. Moseley	Mrs. K. Hooper
1956	Mrs. Houston	Mrs. Mallett	1994	Mrs. A. Booth	Mrs. E. Fielding
1957	Mrs. Beharrell	Mrs. James	1995	Mrs. A. Andrews	Mrs. G. Picton-Jones
1958	Miss Griffiths	Mrs. McMillan	1996	Mrs. J. Hollis	Mrs. K. Hooper
1959	Mrs. Heath	Mrs. James	1997	Mrs. A. Booth	Mrs. L. Warmington
1960	Mrs. Dippie	Mrs. Gilchrist	1998	Mrs. A. Andrews	Mrs. S. Boak
1961	Mrs. Dippie	Mrs. Hinde	1999	Mrs. A. Booth	Mrs. K. Hooper
1962	Miss Griffiths	Mrs. Hinde	2000	Mrs. S. Adamson	Mrs. J. Drury
1963	Mrs. Denham	Mrs. Church	2001	Mrs. S. Adamson	Miss J. Andrews
1964	Mrs. Gilchrist	Mrs. Hinde	2002	Mrs. S. Adamson	Mrs. L. Gawthorpe
1965	Mrs. Bingham	Mrs. J. Gardener	2003	Miss A. Saunders	Mrs. J. Hands
1966	Mrs. E.L. Lindop	Mrs. I.A. Heath	2004	Mrs. M. Roxburgh	Mrs. A. Pickles
1967	Mrs. T.R. Gilchrist	Mrs. Mrs. F. Massey	2005	Mrs. M. Roxburgh	Mrs. K. Hooper
1968	Mrs. T.H. Dippie	Mrs. J. Hooper	2006	Mrs. P. Taylor	Mrs. C. Jones
1969	Mrs. Beharrell	Mrs. Wright	2007	Mrs. L. Warmington	Mrs. C. Jones
1970	Mrs. Gilchrist	Mrs. Fisher	2008	Mrs. A. Smith	Mrs. L. Pettit
1971	Mrs. J.C. Beharrell	Mrs. R.S. Hill	2009	Mrs. S. Adamson	Mrs. L. Pettit

Bibliography and Acknowledgements

Bibliography

Dickinson, Patrick: *A Round of Golf Courses* 1951
Darwin, Bernard: *The Courses of the British Isles* 1910
Overton, Louise Elizabeth: *Four Oaks Tennis Club Centenary History 1906-2006*
Hiscock, Ted :*Gone are the Days. A History of Little Aston & Surrounding Area*
Pennink, Frank :*Homes of Sport – Golf*
Longhurst, Henry: *My Life and Soft Times* 1971
Pope, Allan (Compiler): *Sandwell Golf Club* Press Cuttings
Fletcher, Robert F.: *Sutton Coldfield Golf Club 1889-1989*
Fletcher, Robert F.: *Sutton Coldfield Golf Club 1889-2003*
Hoskison, Dendra: *Sutton Coldfield Ladies Golf Club 1892-1992*
McMillan, Col. T TD FICE: *The Birth and Death of a Giant – Memories of a Sapper*
Wilson, Mark (Editor): *The Best of Henry Longhurst on Golf and Life* 1979
Vardon, Harry: *The Complete Golfer* 1905

The Golfing Annual: volumes XXI 1908, XXII 1909 and XXIII 1910
Sutton, Martin, F.H. (Editor). *The Book of The Links A Symposium on Golf* 1912
Heath, Peter: *Towards One Hundred Years Edgbaston Golf Club 1896-1986*
Glasson, Michael: *Walsall Leather Industry – The World's Saddlers*

Nisbet's Golf Year 1914
Ladies Golf Union Year Books 1928-1938
Golf Illustrated
The Professional Golfer
Cooke, T.P. (Editor): *The Birmingham Golfer & The Midland Golfer*
The Birmingham Daily Post
The Birmingham Post
The Birmingham Daily Gazette
The Times
Swedish Television Interviewing John Anderson and Norman Russell

Author's Acknowledgements

Book project John Beharrell and David Moseley.

Research David McAllister, Hugh Cave, Janet Denham, Peter Denham, Antony Holroyde and John Owen.

Access to archives, recollections, photographs, film and loan of books
John Andrews, Sue Batten (daughter of M.K. Foster), Peter Bigwood, Andrew Boraston, Diane Bradshaw, Frank Brookhouse, Jeannie Carpenter, Don Davies, Olive Derry (granddaughter of Joseph B. Clarke, Little Aston Hall), Derek Evans, Jane Fleming (Ladies Golf Union), Robert Fletcher (Sutton Coldfield Golf Club), Cicely and David Gale, Arthur Gregory, Sally Harper, Richard Hill, Dendra Hoskison (Sutton Coldfield Ladies Golf Club), Tom Jelves, Sandy Jones, Jeff Knott, Christine Leppington (daughter of Roger Bayliss), Peter Lewis (The Royal and Ancient Golf Club), Heather Lindop, John Matthews, Mearns and Jenny Milne, Patricia Oliver (great granddaughter of A.W. Greatrex), Roger Parker-Jervis (great grandson of Edward Swynfen Parker-Jervis), David Pepper, Fergus Pollock (great grandson of Thomas Pollock snr), Andrew Slater, Jackie Stinchcombe (widow of G. Stinchcombe, Assistant Professional July 1960 to March 1963), David Warmington, David Wright (Professional Golfers' Association).

British Golf Collectors Society's visit to Little Aston for the millennium celebrations

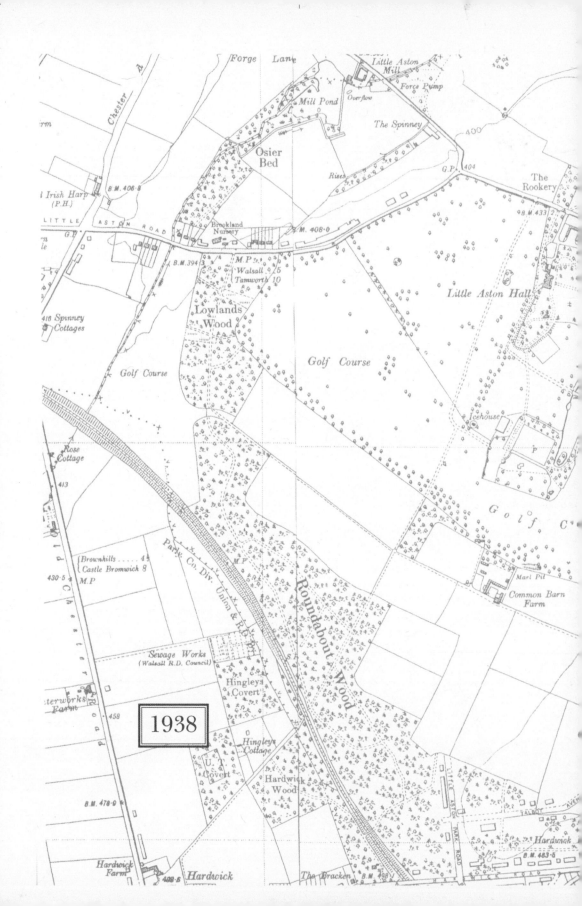

Forge Lane

Little Aston Mill

Force Pump

Mill Pond

The Spinney

Chester

400

Osier Bed

Rises

G.P. 404

The Rookery

B.M. 406·8

I Irish Harp (P.H.)

B.M. 433·2

LITTLE ASTON ROAD

Brookland Nursery

B.M. 408·0

Little Aston Hall

B.M. 394·3

M.P.
Walsall 9·5
Tamworth 10

410 Spinney Cottages

Lowlands Wood

Golf Course

Golf Course

Icehouse

Golf Course

P

Rose Cottage

Golf C⁴

413

Park. Co. Div. Union & R.D. Bdy.

Marl Pit

Brownhills 4½
Castle Bromwich 8
M.P

Common Barn Farm

430·5

M.P

Chester

Roundabout Wood

Sewage Works
(Walsall R.D. Council)

1938

Hingleys Covert

S.P

terworks Farm

458

Hingleys Cottage

U. T. Covert

Hardwick Wood

B.M. 478·0

LITTLE ASTON PARK ROAD

TALBOT

Hardwick

B.M. 483·6

Hardwick Farm

409·6

Hardwick

The Bracken

B.M.